One Wholesome World

Dr. Omkar Nath Wakhlu
Arun Wakhlu

Praise for *One Wholesome World*

"Experiencing violence and conflict all around us, it is quite easy to give in to despair and cynicism. There is also an alternate way – of stepping back to see afresh and begin to understand the big picture. For that, one has to move away from old patterns, our usual habits of looking at events and happenings through the prism of our limited understanding and prejudices. Paradoxically, we may need to look inward first to see the external world with new eyes.

This book, *One Wholesome World*, makes that much-needed attempt. The authors make an honest and heartfelt plea to anchor ourselves in an inner zone of peace and harmony to see the interconnectedness of people and places.

This book is a meditation on what we can do for renewal, how personal transformation can happen to alter the collective state of societies and nations. It is a book that we can use for a deeper understanding of the human instinct that binds us together, that makes us whole in a fragmented world."

— **Anu Aga**, Chairperson, Thermax Foundation and Teach For India; nominated member of the Rajya Sabha (the upper house of the Parliament of India).

"We need new perspectives of who we are, and to understand how we are, deliberately or mindlessly, impacting each other and our one, shared world. Omkar and Arun Wakhlu's book is very timely. It advocates mindfulness, wholeness, interconnectedness. I hope that many people will take time off from the often mindless discourses on social and electronic media that are distracting us from listening to each other deeply and from listening to our own inner selves too, to read their wonderful book and become inspired by it."

— **Arun Maira**, author, Management Advisor, former Member, Planning Commission, India.

"I have been blessed with over 40 years of action-learning experience with innovative approaches to organizational change and leadership development — mostly within and with large corporations based in North America and Europe.

Though most of this design/transformation project work was considered successful from the standpoint of improving culture and business results, none has come close to realizing the potential described in *One Wholesome World*. It's fallen short of what's needed to co-create a truly 'wholesome world — a world we can all celebrate in our lifetime and be proud to hand over to our children.

In *One Wholesome World*, the father/son Wakhlu team have beautifully illuminated key puzzle pieces that have been missing throughout most of the world of traditional organization and leadership development.

I've become totally convinced that it is our destiny as humans to serve as co-evolution-aries — to consciously evolve ourselves and our human systems (e.g., organizations, cities) in ways that best serve the wellbeing of all life, for all time.

I see *One Wholesome World* as a major contribution to accelerating this great turning."

— **Bill Veltrop**, co-founder PathFinders and Monterey Institute for Social Architecture, founder International Centre for Organization Design

"This is not a book but a sermon on life. I am delighted that an entire generation of people who mean well for the planet will have an opportunity to be guided in their thoughts and actions by the wisdom that pops out of every page, every paragraph and sentence. From the part where the authors describe life as an interconnected dance of ideas to all the themes that the authors have delved into, you will be drawn into new thought processes that can enable you to view the present and future through a new lens and make us all rhythmic dancers in the infinite cosmos of the universe."

— **Ganesh Natarajan**, Chairman 5F World and Social Venture Partners Pune.

"*One Wholesome World* offers a transcendent pathway for humankind to shift the way we live with each other and planet Earth. Most of us know that we could be doing better than we are but few have any comprehensive ideas on how. The authors provide us with a map to make a historic shift to a sustainable, just and fulfilling world - what they call a 'wholesome' future. This book is a must read for anyone interested in participating in bringing about this future."

— **John Renesch**, global futurist, prize-winning author, co-founder, FutureShapers LLC

"*One Wholesome World* is a joyful and loving tribute to life. Spiritually infused and practical, it offers an inspiring vision and guidance for thriving in modern times. A gift of ideas and actions for creating a world that works for all from father and son, Omkar and Arun Wakhlu, beautifully illustrated by Arun's daughter, Nitya. If you are seeking hope in the face of fear, uncertainty, and despair, this book provides a pathway. Take a step."

— **Peggy Holman**, author of "*Engaging Emergence: Turning Upheaval into Opportunity*" and co-author of "*The Change Handbook*"

"Our personas, lives and the world around us are divided and fragmented in so many ways. As human beings, we achieve our fullest potential when we are able to be whole, to tap into our higher and child selves, as well as our inner man and inner woman. The wise and brilliant Wakhlus have taken the idea of wholeness and the related notions of wholesomeness and oneness, and delivered to us a brilliant treatise for healing our inner and outer worlds. Evolution has a purpose, and to the extent that leaders can make themselves agents of that which seeks to and needs to emerge, they have access to limitless power. *One Wholesome World* offers an inspiring vision of where we need to go, as well as a practical guide for how we can get there."

— **Raj Sisodia**, professor at Babson College and co-author, "*Conscious Capitalism*" and "*Shakti Leadership*"

"*One Wholesome World* unveils an important dialogue to create a better world through the awakening of Conscious Leadership in all. It beckons unconscious BAU (Business As Usual) living to give way to a more enlightened alignment with the universe to experience oneness and therefore wholesomeness.

Dr Omkar Nath Wakhlu and Arun Wakhlu have through this book set the stage for inviting the readers to travel the distance from human doing to human being".

— **Sujaya Banerjee**, Chief Talent Officer, Essar Group, founder, L&OD Roundtable.

One
Wholesome
World

awakening perspectives and inspiring actions
for a world that benefits all

Dr. Omkar Nath Wakhlu
Arun Wakhlu

www.lightspira.com

Published by: LightSpira, Sweden
www.lightspira.com

ISBN: 978-91-86613-25-9
First edition, 2016

Authors:	*Dr. Omkar Nath Wakhlu, Arun Wakhlu*
Cover design:	*Samarth Kirloskar, Suhasini Kirloskar*
Editing:	*Sangeeta Bhalerao, Sachin Thombare*
Illustrations:	*Nitya Wakhlu*
Graphics:	*Pramod Takle*
Author photographs:	*Arun Wakhlu, Nitya Wakhlu*
Book design:	*Marie Örnesved, LightSpira*

To Life ...

the Magnificent
Wholeness that You are!

Foreword

"*One Wholesome World*", authored by father and son, is an inspiring and interesting book. I congratulate Dr. Omkar Nath Wakhlu and his son Arun, on creating a beautifully written and valuable book.

Dr. Wakhlu is a senior academician and an able administrator. His son has a long experience in the corporate world and a passion for excellence, wholesome leadership and organisational transformation. This book combines the wisdom of an academician and the dynamism of a corporate leader.

The authors have emphasised the value of recognising the intrinsic oneness, interdependence, co-existence, interrelationship and symbiotic wholeness of life. They have brought out the echoes of symbiosis in different facets of life. It is when the natural and fully functioning balance of life is disturbed, that we see the kind of problems (like climate change, violence, disease etc.) that humankind is facing at present. It is only when people wake up to the need to live in harmony with life as a whole ,that we can expect to co-create a world that works for all. The vision of ancient seers, Vasudhaiva Kutumbakam ... the whole world (including all living and non living entities) as one family, is within our reach. This book is a practical manual for inner and outer transformation to take us in the direction of this vision.

I would like to compliment Nitya Wakhlu (Omkar's granddaughter and Arun's daughter) for her brilliant illustrations. They are simple and make things easy to understand.

This book is a must read for all men and women of any age and stature. I am sure it will ignite the minds of all readers irrespective of their age and stage in life. I wish the authors all success in reaching this book to a wide audience. This is the need of the hour.

Padma Bhushan **Prof. (Dr.) Shantaram Balwant Mujumdar,**
(Padma Shri,Punyabhushan, Maharashtra Gaurav),
Founder and President of the Symbiosis Society
Chancellor of the Symbiosis International University

Words of Inspiration

– Rising to universal expansion –

Harih Om Tat Sat. Everyone lives on Mother Earth, a wonderful platform of multifarious life and activities. Yet, seldom does one think of anything like wholesomeness, feeling he is a part of it. It is rarer still to think and strive for a wholesome world, taking whatever steps possible in that direction. But here stand before us Dr. Omkarnath Wakhlu and Arun Wakhlu, a father and son, belonging to Kashmir, the northernmost part of India. They have become a very good pair in authoring their thoughts on individual, family, societal and world life.

Kashmir is known to be a place of beauty and charm. It grows some of the best edible fruits and seeds, relished and cherished by many. The weather and the terrain are alluring to senses, and stimulating to intelligence. Responding to the behest of Nature, Kashmiri thinkers have produced very good thoughts on what constitutes human personality and how it should respond to the surrounding endless nature.

But greed and domination, which always tend to entice and overwhelm human mind, have been casting their stifling shadow upon this beautiful piece of land. This has thrown the people of Kashmir into unimaginable vicissitudes of life, marked by grave challenges to the rule of law. Human mind has listlessly taken to terrorist ways of disrupting peace and peace lovers. The father-author of the book, along with his wife, had been in month-long abduction, a traumatic plight, unpredictable in its course and end.

Yet Kashmiri residents have remained wedded to their geographical and cultural home, the subcontinent surrounded by seas and Himalayas. Their thoughts and writings have permeated India; people living up to Kanyakumari in the south echo their melody and magnificence, proving beyond doubt how unified the identity and aspirations of Indians are.

Life is an experience. But not many are blessed to have the requisite incidences to award the right insight and inspiration to write on life, explaining its complexity and rhythm. The authors, given to an exposure transcending the boundaries of India, have a good measure of experience on the one hand, and international exposure on the other. When life becomes hard and persecuting, human heart craves for a loving communion with the spirit and its transcendental bounties. The intensity can instill the spiritual trio of dispassion, discretion and impulsion.

It is in moments of utter helplessness or forlornness that mind is led to a choice between hope and despair, existence and extinction, confidence and diffidence. Both the father and the son have passed through these trying alternates of life, clinging to their homeland and home thoughts, determined to face whatever such fondness might lead to.

Educated, accomplished, and given to a life of administration and management, the twin authors are quite equipped to think about a world free from constrictions and consternations.

The great Yoga Vaasishtha Ramayana, consisting of 32000 Sanskrit verses, setting forth the eternal cultural philosophy of India, it is said, was composed in Kashmir. The Text records what Sage Vasishtha spoke to Sri Rama, the 16 year-old prince of Ayodhya. The session lasted for 18 days in the palace of Ayodhya, wherein the prince's parents, palace officials and citizenly chiefs were also present. It remains an unsurpassed marvel beckoning the intelligent, curious, scientific as well as religious minds and hearts. Tripura Rahasya, a lofty spiritual narration, and Shaiva Siddhanta also have their origin from the same land.

Whether the world can become full, filled with joy, is a question that puzzles most people. There is no need for diffidence in the matter. Life is an experience and the inner mind is the seat of it all. In Yoga Vaasistha Ramayana, Sage Vasistha presents an inner formula, eternal and practical alike:

पूर्णे मनसि सम्पूर्णं जगत्सर्वं सुधाद्रवैः।
उपानद्गूढपादस्य ननु चर्मास्तृतैव भूः।। योगवासिष्ठः ५.२१.१४

pūrṇe manasi sampūrṇam jagat-sarvam sudhā-dravaiḥ.

upānad-gūḍha-pādasya nanu carmāstṛtaiva bhūḥ.. yōgavāsiṣṭhaḥ 5.21.14

When the mind is full, the entire world is laden with nectar. It is like one wearing leather slippers to make the whole earth laden with leather while walking.

Wholesomeness of the world and blissful fullness are not an imagery, a mere ambition or a contemplation. It is a reality of the human mind. Individuals alone constitute the society, and thus any wholesomeness can and will emerge and pervade only from the individual.

Vasishthadeva sets the path for wholesomeness in terms, clear, concise and unshakeable. It is for the individual to make his world wholesome. By individual effort, originating from his mental plane, alone can wholesome transformation transpire any time. In other words, the effort is spiritual and it rests with each individual. It is in this context that the Wakhlu joint effort becomes relevant.

अयं बन्धुरयं नेति गणना लघुचेतसाम् ।

उदारचरितानां तु वसुधैव कुटुम्बकम् ।।

ayaṃ bandhur-ayaṃ nēti gaṇanā laghu-cētasām .
udāra-caritānāṃ tu vasudhaiva kuṭumbakam - Mahopanishad 6.71-73

This is my relative, this is not; thoughts like this are of the narrow-minded. For those with a lofty behaviour, the entire earth is but one family.

If the individual is a centre, the world is the circle emanating from him. The centre and the circumference are mutual and inseparable. So too, an individual of this world and the world around him are mutual. But how many feel so, and carry the global world or comprehensive consciousness, in whatever they think, speak and do? If only we can be sensitive to the fact of individual-world-mutuality, complementariness, everything on earth will become better, more nourishing and fulfilling for all.

Everyone has the mind with its untold potential. It often remains constricted, but it can also rise up, shed the malady, and bring an expansion anointing oneself as well as the world around with fullness. Every time, significant change and evolution in society have been engendered by individual thinkers and reformers.

Relating life to be an orchestra of ideas, this book speaks about the Supreme Consciousness permeating it throughout. Not recognizing this fact, people foster selfish constricted aspirations and goals, triggering undesirable traits in oneself and others. This vicious circle comes to a stop only when one enquires into himself and arrives at the true expansive identity. The key to wholesome world thus lies in the individual himself.

I wish the authors' effort a rewarding success. May all those who read the book contribute to the benevolent concepts discussed therein, thereby making the world better, sweeter, and more delightful, linking more and more people to the message of Yogavasishtha and Sanatana Dharma.

Harih Om Tat Sat. Love and ashirvaad.

Swami Bhoomanada Tirtha
www.SwamiBhoomananda.org

Contents

Preface

The World is at a cross road. Never before in the history of humankind have we been at such a decisive turning point. As the title of this book suggests, the time has come for us all to join hearts and hands to co-create One Wholesome World. This is a world we can all celebrate in our lifetime and be proud to hand over to our children. It is a world of joy, peace and abundance for all.

Our basic tenet is that the challenges of 'development' that humankind is facing are not purely physical but also social and spiritual. It is difficult to imagine a positive future that does not integrate and balance values and ethics. Adopting a whole systems view of human development includes all these factors and examines how they relate to each other to form a whole.

Sharing the Story

Life is a dynamic tapestry of images, characters, stories and events, all adding up to a forward movement. It is about the progressive unfolding of higher levels of integration and joy in individual and collective lives. This is what the evolutionary philosophers tell us. We want to share with you the story of how this book was born. The seed of the idea initially planted for a monograph, with time, grew into becoming a book. The story of this book is a story of the evolution of the authors, in the context of what has been happening in the world from early 1991 to 2013.

Let's go back in time. Omkar spent most of his childhood in the state of Jammu and Kashmir in Northern India, at a time when it was a picture of harmony between different religious groups, and foraying forward in the field of science and technology. Arun's childhood too was spent growing up in their home in Buchwara, under the Shankracharya Hill in Srinagar, close to the famous and incredibly beautiful Dal Lake. He distinctly remembers the stints of work in the backyard garden, watering the vegetable patches using a *Denkli* (a traditional irrigation system in Kashmir). The fragrance of ripe plums and the taste of organically grown tomatoes and carrots plucked straight out of the garden is vivid in the mind. The images and memories are ones of great beauty, harmony and peace.

As a family, they spent three years in Birmingham, UK (1960 to 1963), and then a year in Karlsruhe, West Germany (1969). The travel brought with it fresh insights and observations. Exposure to these cultures set them thinking. The intermingling of faiths, cultures, nature, science and technology, art and music, mysticism, urban living and semi-rural lifestyles in the lives of the authors has shaped a perspective that is not stuck with this or that. They seem to have been bombarded by all kinds of influences and experiences in a way that this sharing was almost like a natural outcome. Arun has always believed that people who are destined to be 'bridge builders', have to experience both sides of a river. If one is stuck on one side or the other, one cannot be a bridge builder. Both the authors have been blessed to have experienced the east and the west, spirituality and science and technology, rational thinking and art, work in government organizations, business firms and NGOs, as employees and entrepreneurs, as leaders and educators. This wide canvas of roles and experiences has equipped them to share what is in this book. But, there is also a sense of a 'larger hand' in the creation of this book. As you will see later, the authors claim that they could not have written it alone without the hand of Providence. The book is something that we feel 'came through us'.

The Research Adventure

The approach to researching for this book has been both deliberate and aided by serendipity. The authors scanned literature and websites systematically for data and insights. But many times they were lucky to stumble upon ideas which helped the work. They often met people who helped. For example, Arun, while reading a letter from his friend Sushil Bajpai to a Community of Practice on Climate Change, came across the Solution Exchange, an initiative of the United Nations Agencies in India.[1] The site is meant to facilitate Connection, Sharing and Collaboration. Many different communities on issues like AIDS, Climate Change, Disaster Management, Education, Food and Nutrition, Security, Gender, Maternal and Child Health, Microfinance, Water, Employment and others exist on this site. The site is an excellent enabler of integration across fields and also learning and sharing. In a sense this also illustrates what our book is about. While each area of work is important, 'development' is not something that can be boxed into neat compartments. For example, water is connected to health, education, food and nutrition, gender, employment and climate change. Different aspects of development are all interlinked and interdependent. A metaphor will illustrate this: A cake is baked with eggs, flour, sugar, butter, milk and yeast. All are important ingredients, but none is good enough alone! The temperature of the oven and the duration

---

1) www.in.one.un.org/page/un-solution-exchange

of baking have to be perfect to get a good cake. Development is just like this. It requires conscious and interdependent effort.

All books are written over a long period of time. This book has been 20 years in the making! During this time, the book has been incubating like a baby in the mother's womb. As life waited to give birth to the book, the world seemed to be getting worse. The Asian monetary crisis of 1997-98, the rise of the Dot-coms, a series of high profile corporate scandals, the Asian Tsunami of 2004 followed by Hurricane Katrina in 2005, the scary spread of SARS and AIDS, the events of 11th September 2001 in New York and 26th November 2008 in Mumbai, the wars in Afghanistan and Iraq, global warming, the growing divide between the rich and the poor and also between the rural and urban areas on the planet. Meanwhile, Al Gore received the Nobel Prize for his work on alerting people about Global Warming, while Pakistan sunk rapidly into a state of chaos after the assassination of its former Prime Minister Ms. Benazir Bhutto. Dr. Mohammed Yunus saw his work through the Grameen Bank being recognized with the Nobel Prize. The world went into a predicted Food Grains crisis in early 2008. The Global Financial Crisis of 2007–2009 came around the same time. It was considered by many economists the worst financial crisis since the Great Depression of the 1930s. The crisis played a significant role in the failure of key businesses, declines in consumer wealth estimated in trillions of U.S. dollars, and a downturn in economic activity leading to the 2008–2012 global recession and contributing to the European sovereign-debt crisis. Barrack Obama won the Nobel Peace Prize in October 09, barely 9 months into his presidency. This book, through all this, was still waiting to be completed.

During this period, the state of Jammu and Kashmir saw two wars with Pakistan, and the beginnings of a fundamentalist incursion eating into the very fabric of life in the state. 'Development' had also begun to make its impact felt. Over the years, the peaceful and 'whole' fabric of Jammu and Kashmir (J&K) was falling apart. In the late 1980s, terrorism had begun to take its toll in J&K. During the mass migration of the Kashmiri Pandit community in 1990 and the horrible destruction and degradation that came in the wake of militancy, the authors witnessed firsthand what religious fundamentalism does to society. Omkar, and his wife Mrs. Khem Lata Wakhlu (Arun's mother) were abducted by militants of the Hezbullah in September 1991[2]. They were rescued by the Indian Army after 45 days in captivity. This experience left a deep impression on them. Their faith in the larger creative intelligence that runs and supports life grew. The oneness of human experience that they felt during this time touched them deeply.

2) Wakhlu, Khem Lata and Wakhlu, O.N., *"Kidnapped: 45 Days With Militants in Kashmir"*, Konark Publishers: Delhi, 1993

After their rescue on *Dushera* (an Indian Festival celebrating the victory of the good over evil) in 1991, they came to Pune (in Western India). The first seeds of the idea of Wholesome Development were born in conversations in Pragati Foundation and at home in the period of 1991-92. These resulted in a paper being presented at an International Conference on Sustainable Village Based Development, organized by the Colorado State University at Fort Collins, USA. The paper was on the theme "*A New Paradigm of Wholesome Development*" (Wakhlu and Wakhlu, 1993)[3]. The first draft of this book was partially written in 1995. Some chapters that Arun was to complete lay unfinished for several years, as he was caught up (by unconscious choice) in corporate consulting and training. The completion of the book kept going onto the back burner. Despite several attempts by Omkar to push the whole completion through, the book languished and gathered dust. It is now clear to us, in hindsight, why this was to be.

One of the points that we have been constantly aware of is the right timing of things. Looking back, had this book been published a few years ago, we would still have been writing from a 'theoretical' and unproven perspective. The ideas presented here would still have been untested. One of the points cleared up only recently is the way around the ubiquitous 'knowing-doing gap'. When I know something is good, how come I still do not do it? Closer to home, if I know that this book had to be completed, what was holding me back from completing it? While it is easy to 'talk' about Wholesome Development and One Wholesome World, are our lives really walking this talk? Cognitively understanding these things and wholeheartedly living them out are two different things.

The past few years have been deeply transformational for us and our family. We have both moved closer to 'Omkar', the wholeness of existence. For Arun and his partner Anu, the profoundly moving journey through North Queensland, the Great Barrier Reef and Northern New Zealand in 2008, was like a capstone for the experience of writing this book. "What we saw, heard, felt and experienced on this journey reinforced our understanding that what we share here is indeed valuable and relevant." Involvement in sharing the "*Awakening the Dreamer*"(ATD)[4] Symposium of the Pachamama Alliance in India, developing I-Catalysts for catalyzing change and directing courses in "*Ethics and Values in Public Governance*" for senior Indian Civil Servants has further strengthened their understanding, surrender and experience. The global wakeup call on Climate Change (COP21), and the refugee crisis and recent bombings in Europe, was the proverbial 'last straw' that got this process to completion.

---

3) Wakhlu, A. and Wakhlu O.N., "*A New Paradigm of Wholesome Development*" (Proc.) of The International Conference On Sustainable Village Based Development, Colorado State University, Fort Collins, Proc., Vol IV, 1993

4) www.pachamama.org/engage/awakening-the-dreamer

We can state with integrity that we are closer to living life in surrender to the Whole than we were five years ago. The 'Truth' of this book is therefore higher than it would have been if it had been written five years ago. This doesn't mean that our work is over! It simply means that this moment feels 'right' for the release of this work into the world. Our own expertise in unblocking human potential, in developing 'Wholesome Leaders' who can be instrumental in unfolding Wholesome Development, and in catalyzing large scale co-creation and transformational processes is far better today than it was five years ago. That is why we write with the conviction that comes from personal experience.

A book that has guided us during the writing and completion of this book is *"Opening Doors Within"* by Eileen Caddy[5]. It exhorts us to renew and transform our lives based on renewing our mind. Inviting us to hold a clear and inspiring vision of wholeness, of a 'new heaven and a new Earth', it also calls for joyful action.

The above is a lovely reminder to us all, that reading this book is not enough. Ultimately, it will be joyful action now that will lead to the creation of a world which we can all be proud of in handing over to our children and grandchildren.

With humility and gratitude,

Omkar Nath Wakhlu
Arun Wakhlu

24th March, 2016

---

5) Caddy, Eileen; *"Opening Doors Within"*, Soulzone Publications: Mumbai, India, 1986,

Introduction

This book proposes a new paradigm of development. A paradigm is a 'way of looking at things'. The paradigm we propose in this book is that of one wholesome world arising from millions of people reclaiming their wholeness and acting together in the service of the whole. This is like returning home to a space of power, integrity, integration, inspiration, creative intelligence and collaboration. As more people reclaim this, a catalytic transformation of collective human consciousness will occur tipping us all towards one wholesome world.

This is inevitable. This book is part of that global process. This space of wholeness, which is the same as ones essence, was never really lost. It has been and will always be there. However, we have forgotten all about it. To make sure that you dear reader, get the essential message of this book, we will spell it out in advance:

The whole of life is one huge interconnected dance of ideas, information, energy, material, and awareness. It is all one. This whole dance is orchestrated spontaneously by awareness which permeates and is everything in life. This common consciousness is at the root of everything. Our identification with limited notions of who we are and forgetting our oneness is at the roots of the global crisis that humanity is facing today. When people awaken to this intrinsic wholeness and live and work from this space of love, creative intelligence, freedom, and peace; they become instrumental in manifesting joy, peace, and abundance in their individual and collective lives. This astonishingly simple and universally accessible discovery has the power to transform lives both individually and collectively to an extent that can only be called miraculous.

This book is a call for all of us to reclaim this glory and participate in the next evolutionary leap that we are all poised for. The whole book is divided into three broad parts:

- Seeing Anew

- Awakening Capacity

- Love in Action

The first three chapters of the book (under Seeing Anew) look at the assumptions and beliefs that guide our current view of development. We start off by looking at the process of seeing itself. Why is it so important to see the whole picture? How does what we pay attention to, determine our emotional state and consequent actions? This chapter looks at examples of what is working well in the world and how these can be the seeds of co-creating a new world that works for all. Chapter 2 looks at the roots of our current worldview. At how we 'construct' our world through (often unexamined) assumptions. It ends up by showing how our current dominant view of development suffers from three dis-connections. In Chapter 3, we offer a radically new perspective; one which is free of, and inclusive of all viewpoints and perspectives. This is the space of Wholesomeness, based on oneness with the Universal Intelligence that runs all of life. In this, we see how Love can be a foundation for a very different approach to life and development.

Having got a sense of the larger context and foundation, the next two chapters (under Awakening Capacity) explore the process of awakening to Wholesomeness (Chapter 4), and how this personal awakening can take on more collective forms through Wholesome Leadership (Chapter 5). As we heal our connections with our Self, with others and with the environment, individual and collective capacities expand. These will enable us to reboot our capacities through inner transformation, coherent action and new modes of self-organizing. All these will be founded on and guided by Love. We will then begin to allow and catalyze the natural changes that are waiting to happen on our planet at this time in our evolution.

With our capacities awakened and expanded, through a three fold reconnection, we are ready to become instruments of Love in Action. This is the next broad section of the book. Each one of us has a unique role to play in the larger evolutionary play of Life. In chapters 6 to 10 we have focused on a few key areas for Wholesomeness to do its work. Chapter 6 focuses on Peace and Ethics. We see the common root of these apparently different aspects of a wholesome life. Chapter 7 is about Education for a Wholesome World. How does education need to change to bring forth the world we are proud to hand over to our children and grandchildren? Chapter 8 is about Healing - both people and the environment. These two are so inextricably linked that we have combined them into one chapter. Business has the power to transform the world. Can a business become a force of good on Earth? What are the examples of this? How does this work? Chapter 9 examines how businesses can work from abundance and generate even more abundance for all. Chapter 10 addresses the critical aspect of Good Governance, and what Wholesome Governance may look like in practice. The book concludes with Chapter 11 on Reclaiming Our One Wholesome World. It addresses the question of what we can all do to reclaim our One Wholesome World. It focuses on practical actions at different levels and by different agencies to manifest the Vision professed in this book.

Each chapter ends with some actionable points (under the heading Joyful Action Now). These will hopefully inspire and empower you to become one with the wholeness of Life.

What's in it for you?

This book addresses the alarmingly pressing needs of today. We attempt to expand the reader's vision and uncover connections that they may not have seen, or may have seen incompletely. This book is primarily an offering to see things in a simple, clear and complete way. We feel that seeing this wholeness and experiencing new thought forms and patterns will be profoundly liberating and inspiring for the readers.

Finally, we would like to leave the reader with practical tools to make a difference and create an impact in their own spheres of work and life. There will be tools to work at the individual level and also at the organizational and social levels.

The authors are people of action. They therefore believe in making things happen and would like readers to do the same. We only pray that this action is guided and inspired from the purest, most whole and most liberating space of awareness.

Who Might Benefit from Reading This Book?

A book on Wholesome Development to move towards one wholesome world is really a book for everyone. People who are on the journey to wholeness and who feel an inner calling to work for 'something beyond myself' or for 'a larger cause' will find this book useful. It will also resonate with people who have begun to realize that the mind is severely limited as the source of the creative ideas and fresh thinking required to respond to today's challenges. It will attract people who have begun to feel that awareness or the space called 'No Mind' is a better source for action than a conditioned and patterned mind. No Mind is the same as Wholeness.

The common thread and core of the book is relevant to every single person on the planet. However, the capacity to understand its message may be different at different places and amongst different individuals. Perhaps there is a need to translate the core message of this book into the language of different segments.

One can see, however, that the book would benefit the following people:

- **Leaders in Business** who want to understand the larger context within which businesses operate. The book will help them to understand the whole problem/opportunity that business has in front of it. A paradigm shift where we see business as generating true wealth for all, can have huge positive impacts on the planet. The book points towards a new consciousness for business leaders.

- **Students and teachers** in the field of education. A picture of where we are headed as a planet and the larger canvas with its linkages to inner thoughts, forms and patterns is a must for all teachers and students to understand. It is pointless to learn the art of painting and decoration to decorate one cabin of a ship, while the whole ship is sinking! It is time for teachers and students to understand the larger context and purpose for which education exists, viz. the well-being and liberation of all human kind.

- The book will inspire all those people who are serving in the area of **Public Governance**. It will show us how we need to move to create more integrity and integration in public service. It will point the way for wholesome leadership in this very important sphere of life.

- **NGOs and practitioners of development** in the field will benefit from seeing the inner roots of development and the vital need for collaboration and synergy. It will also show us how to infuse the work of development activists and practitioners with the energy and enthusiasm which can come only from the deepest inner resources.

- Finally, this book is for **women and men dedicated to loving action and service**. It is for those who want to make a difference and need guidance and a road map on how to do it. We have found over our years of experience that the larger creative intelligence of life, orchestrates connections in an amazingly appropriate way. To quote mother Teresa, "things happen accordingly". We understand this to mean that life moves according to a larger pattern orchestrated by a loving and kind intelligence. (This morning, on my morning walk the acronym LIFE for 'Loving Intelligence for Everyone', popped into my mind). The fact that you are holding this book in your hands and are reading these words, means that your consciousness has attracted this book into your life.

Wherever you are and whoever you are, know that this is not a coincidence. There is a clear reason why this book is in your hands. If you are still and you listen to the whispers of your Heart, you will know why this book has come to you. The 'work' of the authors is to be instrumental in receiving, expressing and spreading new learnings and insights given by the divine so that humans can reclaim their wholeness. Here is a small hint:

- Will you awaken to your own Wholeness, and allow this clarity to guide your thoughts, words and actions?

- Are you a person who is called to join Hearts and Hands on this unfolding evolution towards one wholesome world?

If the answer is a wholehearted "YES", you now know why this book has come into your life.

What is Different?

This book brings the awareness and insight to reconnect us back to our heart in a way that makes sense to the common man and gives him a path way for action.

Few books show the elephant of development. When we focus on the inner aspect of development the outer ones are missed and vice-a-versa. This books attempts to show an all-encompassing holistic picture of development. We might say it is practically spiritual or spiritually practical. It transcends the common lenses through which development is typically seen: gender, livelihoods, ethics, economics, environment, governance etc. It looks at development from the lens of wholeness and integration with enough attention also paid to the heart of development – which is consciousness or awareness.

The book is bereft of any ideological filters/blinds. We are neither from the left nor the right, not stuck with the right hemisphere or the left hemisphere of the brain. The book comes from an innocent heart and experienced mind attempting to weave together conflicting perceptions, polarities and viewpoints. It offers a new vision of development and also the tools to make it happen.

Join Hearts and Hands for Action

There are many organizations and individuals working hard to solve the challenges we face e.g. the climate crisis. This is great news! It means that we don't really need to build a movement from scratch because it's already bubbling up all over the world, in thousands of ways.

Our hope is that we can all shine the spotlight of awareness on the work of existing organizations, highlighting and appreciating everyone's incredible work and weaving these many efforts together into a tapestry of inspired and powerful unified action—a movement that is global, scientific, and specific. Holding a shared vision of co-creating One Wholesome World, and connecting and sharing on a common platform of awareness with freely available tools, we can help to stitch together a whole that is truly greater than the sum of its parts—a diverse movement that speaks with one collective voice and beats to one universal heart. Guidance will come from being still and listening to the voice of the one Heart of Humanity, our own Self. Manifestation of heaven on the Earth will come from joyful action now.

PART ONE

Seeing Anew

CHAPTER 1

Seeing with New Eyes

"And now here is my secret, a very simple secret; it is only with the heart that one can see rightly; what is essential is invisible to the eye."

— Antoine De Saint-Exupery

"It is in the darkness of their eyes that men get lost."

— Black Elk

Our view of life powerfully affects our way of life. It also deeply affects the way we live and work; on what we spend our limited time and energies. Who we are affects what we are seeing. What we are seeing affects what we spend our energy on. It affects what we manifest in the world. This, in turn, reinforces our notion of who we are being.

Life is interspersed with universal and loving intelligence. Life is happening in all her glorious wholeness in every single moment. I can either see and fully experience life in this moment, or focus on something that is a memory from the past or something imagined from the future. This choice will determine how I feel right now. My feelings determine my action and also the outcomes in this moment. Think about this: The choices of 7 billion people in this moment are making up the world as it is now. Going forward, these choices will also determine the kind of world we will experience in the future. How do we therefore change what we see and what we will focus on? By changing our questions!

How do we see things?

Given this context, and given that the world, as we know it, is going through a metamorphosis of sorts, it is time to ask ourselves some hard questions: How do we see ourselves? How do we see others? How do we see our 'work' in life? How whole and expanded is our vision? Are we running our life based on a narrow and limited view of ourselves and others, seeing only a tiny part? Or do we see the glorious magnificence of life as a whole and allow our life to be governed by this vision? Do we see only the separate waves on the surface of the ocean, or do we see the whole ocean?

There is an urgent need for coherent and concerted change in many spheres. While on the one hand, we have crises and opportunities staring us in the face on many fronts, we also have all the diverse resources needed to meet these challenges creatively and completely. Everything we need to lead a spiritually fulfilling, joyful, healthy, socially harmonious, just and environmentally sustainable presence on Earth exists today. All the money, resources, knowledge and people are available. We have more knowledge, money, technology and networks of people than we would possibly need to solve all our problems.

One might then ask why these desperately needed changes are not happening at all, or are not happening fast enough. Where is the bottleneck? Here is a metaphor I find useful to explain what might be going on:

Imagine a gigantic jigsaw puzzle that has to be solved. The solution will involve putting together all the pieces in a way that forms a coherent picture. Now, if all the pieces are scattered far and wide and the end picture that has to be made is not known, it will be impossible to solve the puzzle. Add to this picture the image of people clinging to their little pieces in distant corners with great protective zeal, and you have a model of what is actually happening on the ground today. All the pieces we need exist, but we do not have peace! Peace will arise when all the pieces come together coherently and smoothly to manifest the picture we all want to see… the picture of a world that works for all. One in which all thrive, and flourish (spiritually and materially), there is social justice and the environment is 'happy'. One where there is joy, peace and abundance for all. This will happen only when each person 'holding a piece' of the puzzle sees the whole picture. Why is it imperative for all to see the whole picture? To hold in our mind's eye, an accurate and complete view of how the world really works? To see all the inter-connections between different things that are happening?

If we do not see right, our thoughts, words and actions will be limited. We will keep co-creating a collective story that we do not want. It will be a story born out of a partial and erroneous view of life. A story of self-deception. It will not be a story of joy, peace and abundance for all.

We have been conditioned to focus on actions and outcomes: do and do more. If the first conference at Rio didn't work, then have one in Kyoto. If that didn't work, have one more in Copenhagen. Now let's hope that COP21, the United Nations Climate Change Conference, in Paris, (in 2015) will yield something different. If we are getting desperate that things are not working, let's have a conference in Rio again (20 years after the first one) to see why nothing is working! We have been taught to believe that if you want different outcomes, simply take different actions. If you have not done enough, do more! It is not enough to keep doing more. We need to see differently...look with new eyes.

To quote Albert Einstein, "We can't solve problems by using the same kind of thinking we used when we created them." John Stuart Mill reflected the same idea when he said in his autobiography: "I am now convinced that no great improvements in the lot of mankind are possible, until a great change takes place in the fundamental constitution of their modes of thought."[1]

The Apparatus of Seeing

Let us look at the apparatus of seeing. Our attention first focuses on something, after which we see it. Attention is governed by the mind. So, if our attention is stuck with something, or in some direction, we miss what lies in other directions. If our attention is caught up in the past or the future, we miss seeing what is right under our noses. If distractions and diversions are eating up our attention and time in the moment, we do not see the obvious. Even if we do, our energy is not sufficient to bring about some impact or change. Before we go further, please read the following lines:

> 350 litres have to be pumped up 60 to 90 metres or more. A cohesive tug helps pumping but no one really know how it works. It is not easy to make one. One can combine two types. Once successful, complications are minimal. All have a memory that speaks in visual forms, when we cut across them laterally. Communication between them is mysterious. Young children can enjoy one. So can adults. Privacy can be significantly boosted by their use. It takes some skill to make, but it is easy to learn. A blessing to travellers, mammalian and avian. Connections occur through an information superhighway that speeds up interactions between a large, diverse population. It hooks up well with others.

1)   John Stuart Mill, "*Autobiography of John Stuart Mill*", Sheba Black Publishing: New York, 2014

The paragraph probably made little or no sense to you. Now just imagine a TREE. Read the same lines once again with the context of a TREE in your mind. Suddenly, the separate ideas now make sense. They connect to each other and to the idea of a tree. This is a simple example of how context provides a mental platform for integration and the generation of meaning. It shapes what we see. It creates the connections in our mind that relate to the whole picture beyond the words. When we miss the context, the big picture, we fail to see. From shaping what we see, the context also determines how what we see occurs to the meaning we give to what we see, the feelings and actions that then emerge from this, and finally our outcomes. When context is missing, content makes little or no sense.

Seeing only a part of the whole picture

In the absence of a clear and shared context, we do not see coherently. Our work is sporadic and disjointed. Fragmented attempts to 'solve the world's problems' will always be incoherent and ineffective.

Closely linked to the problem of not seeing the big picture, is the absence of seeing connections. We do not see how A is related to B. For example, what does our diet have to do with climate change ? Is there a connection between the unprecedented death of bee populations on the planet with the class of pesticides called neonicotinoids? How are bees connected to our very survival on Earth? What are the chain of connections that make this happen? Do we see these connections?

There are also times when we are unaware of the consequences of certain choices and actions because we do not see the connections. Take for example

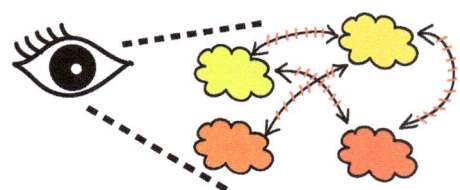

Not seeing connections

the fact that more and more younger children (preschool age and even babies less than a year old) are being diagnosed with vision problems and need glasses. Is this a consequence of watching television? Does it have to do with diet or computer games? Unless we get to the root cause of this situation and understand it fully, we will unconsciously be doing things with our children without understanding the consequences which unfold over time.

Not seeing consequences over time

Another aspect of not seeing clearly is to miss out understanding the feelings, thoughts and beliefs that cause a person's actions. We often interact with others without understanding their 'inner view' of things. Looking 'beneath the surface' requires time and space, and the patience to ask open ended questions and to deeply listen. In situations where we are in a hurry, this is rare.

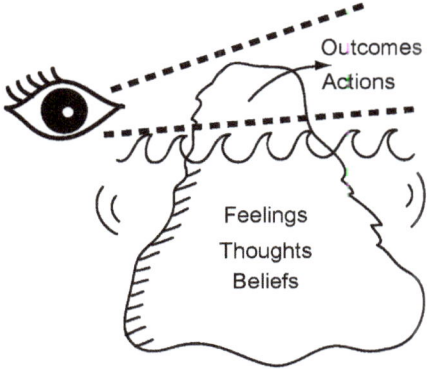

Not seeing "beneath the surface"

Another more basic reason for our attention getting 'stuck' is that in the humdrum of Business As Usual (BAU), we do not look for fresh information or perspectives different from our own. We are locked, as it were, into a perceptual box that keeps us deluded into thinking that what we are seeing is really the world 'out there'. It is a well-known scientific fact that through our five senses our brain receives 400 Billion bits of information every second. Of this we perceive only around 2000 bits of information every second. That is around 0.5 millionth of one % of the data that is available to us from around us![2] It is as if a large part of the population on the planet is going about life semi-asleep, unconsciously. Our attention remains stuck or fixated, and so also our vision.

Choosing not to see

Not seeing correctly also blocks the spending of our energies on things that truly count. I (Arun) have struggled a lot with this problem. As mentioned elsewhere, this book has been almost 20 years in the writing! When I ask myself why this is so, the answer is that I spent my time and energy on other things. Again (using the powerful questioning tool of why?) I ask why I did this. The answer is because I thought that spending my time on other things like consulting and training for my organisation (rather than writing this book) would get me more money. Why did I want this extra

2) The Human Brain/Neuroscience/Cognitive Science: Basic Knowledge 101, www.basicknowledge101.com/subjects/brain.html

money? Because I imagined (erroneously) that this would give me greater happiness! This has mercifully changed now. I am at Peace and focusing on what Life is calling me to do!

Awareness, Perception and Joy

What does seeing have to do with peace, joy and contentment? The mind is ever seeking happiness and peace. When it does not find this anywhere, it goes on searching. It keeps getting restless and fixated on things. When we make efforts to 'calm' or 'quieten' the mind, there is effort, doing and judging. This effort produces more agitation. It's like a man swatting a swarm of flies… in this case the flies of thoughts, feelings and distractions. He is still in the 'I am the doer' mode. Since 'whatever you resist will persist', the endless wheel of doing and searching keeps going on.

In this metaphor, the awareness that witnesses all these thoughts, feelings and distractions is like a bowl of honey. This is where the mind settles down and becomes quiet and spacious. When the mind is quiet, we see clearly. The field of perception opens up and we begin to notice things that were there all along. Our energy is calm and available for action. We are ready to act freely to do what has to be done.

All the things we need to co-create a good life for all are available somewhere on the planet. They are simply lost to our sight. Maybe, it is better to say that we are lost to them. We fell asleep somewhere to the amazing gifts and possibilities that the natural world bestows on us all the time. We forgot the abundance that was possible for all.

What's not Working Well?

The following statistics were first published in 1992 by the retired Peace Corps Volunteers of Madison Wisconsin in a curriculum entitled "*Unheard Voices: Celebrating Cultures from the Developing World*"[3]. Shortly thereafter the statistics appeared as an email that continues to be circulated and viewed by millions of people around the world.[4] They give us an overview of how the Earth would look if it were a community of 100 People.

---

3) The Global Citizen, May 31, 1990, Donella H. Meadows, Hebei University 2001, Zero Population Growth Seattle, "*Unheard Voices: Celebrating Cultures from the Developing World*", Returning Peace Corps Volunteers of Madison Wisconsin, 1992

4) This Data is updated on the website www.100people.org/statistics_100stats.php

If the world had 100 people:

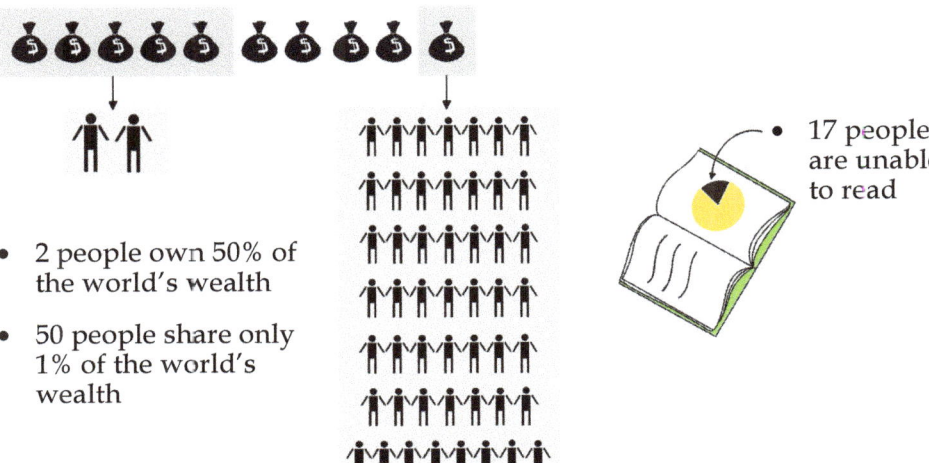

- 2 people own 50% of the world's wealth

- 50 people share only 1% of the world's wealth

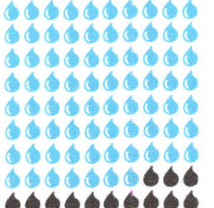

- 17 people are unable to read

- 39 people have no access to basic sanitation

- 13 peope have no access to drinking water

- 1 is dying of starvation

- 15 are hungry and seriously malnourished (that's around a billion people)

- 21 people are overweight

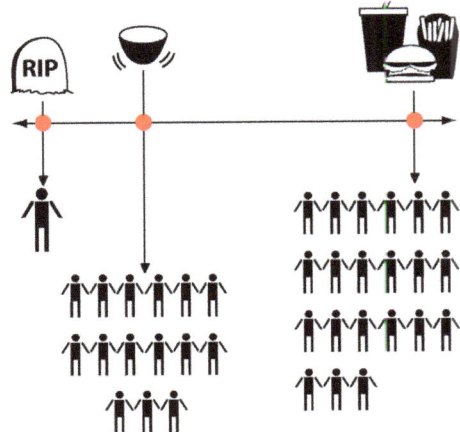

If you have food in your refrigerator, clothes in your closet, a bed to sleep in and a roof over your head, you are better off than 83% people on the planet.

On the environment front, we are all aware of the havoc that our present modes of producing and consuming are wreaking.[5] 75% of the world's original forests have been eliminated. 30% of the world's arable land has been lost in the past 45 years. There are more than 200 oceanic dead zones worldwide. 90% of all large fish have gone from our oceans. The population of elephants is down 90% in the past century. By the mid-eighties, our ecological footprint had overshot 1. We had started to use more that Nature could regenerate. By 2007, we had started to use 30% more than what Nature can renew. Global expenditure, according to 2006 statistics[6], indicates to us where our priorities are.

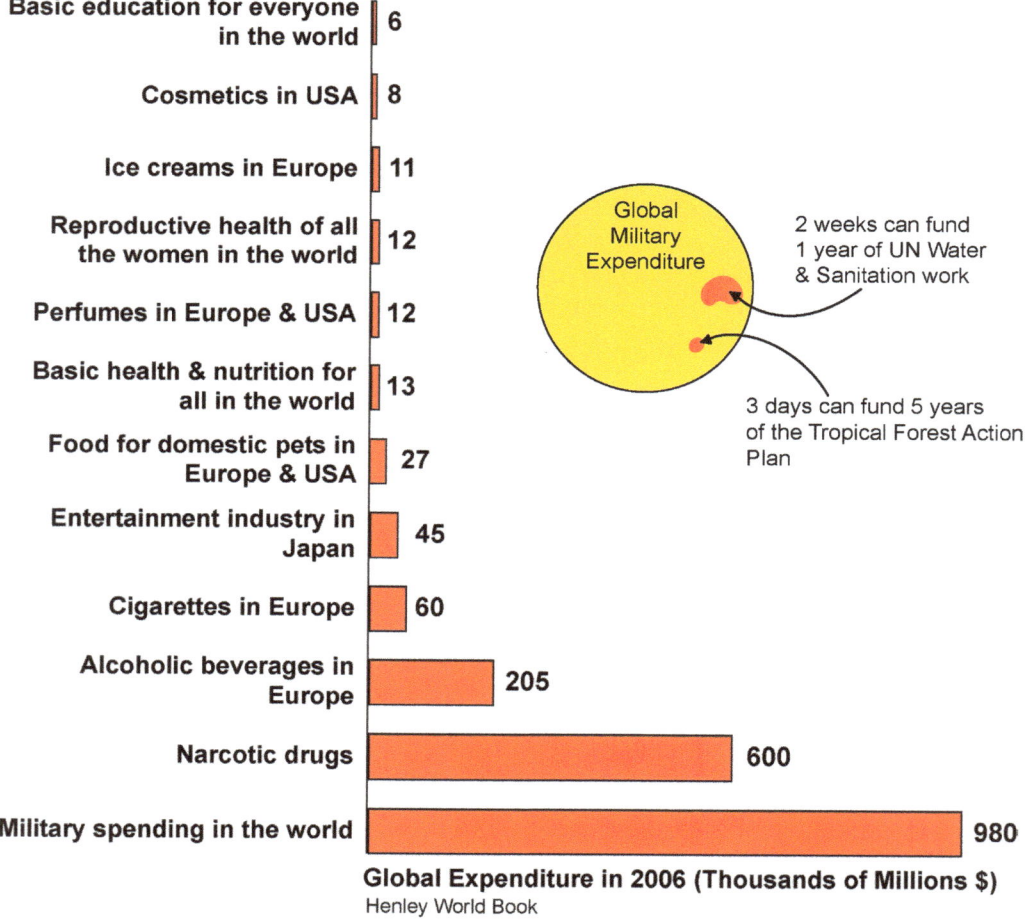

Global Expenditure in 2006 (Thousands of Millions $)
Henley World Book

---

5) Data from the film "*Awakening The Dreamer* ", produced by the Pachamama Alliance www.pachamama.org

6) Adapted from the "*Henley World Study*" as quoted in the book "*Creativity to Reinvent Your Life*" by Miriam Subirana, John Hunt Publishing: London, 2010

But, what's Working Well?

From the foregoing discussion, it is clear that over the decades, enough data and analysis have been generated through detailed studies of parts of the developmental puzzle viz. economy, GNP, education, health, literacy, empowerment, women, people, quality of life, human development and so on. The 'whole', however, is complex. It exhibits characteristics that are not easily related to the detailed studies of the parts. In the context of 'development' studies, what is equally pertinent is the absence of an attempt to co-relate the thinking and psyche of the 'mass-mind' with issues of 'development'. Yet it is a historical fact that the 'whole' system throws up radical surprises. Many unpredicted transformations have occurred through human interventions. Some of these have been more or less self-regulated in a very complex way.

Let's look a little deeper at the process of positive change in the 'whole' from the angle of changes in the individual and collective human mind. It acts like a self-reinforcing cycle: Positive change liberates latent potential for giving of ones talents, living creatively, freedom of expression, strength and wisdom. In a positive mode, each human is his or her natural self: living out one's uniqueness and contributing to the common good. Positive change will come about only when nature is allowed to function in its optimal mode. The 'ego' plays a negative role in blocking nature's optimal flow. This occurs when human thought and actions are restricted by negative mind-sets. Without 'mind-sets' we become free, creative, enhancing love and joyfully expanding. When 'ego' vanishes, nature flowers. That is the eternal law. (Wakhlu, 1990).[7]

It is mental road-blocks and barriers of perception that make development lopsided. These 'mind boundaries' and their impacts on perception, thinking and communication need to be first understood and then eradicated. Among other things, the work involves a deep inner transformation of people leading to their Wholesome Development as individuals. We need to familiarize the collective modern mind with age-old truths and values that have been keystones of civilization for a few thousand years (e.g. please see Box 1.2).

'Development' is essentially a means to achieve peace, harmony, prosperity and happiness for all. In its quest, man has moved in a thousand directions. This waywardness has to be halted. Instead, efforts must be focused on achieving inner transformation leading to all round development of people and eventually resulting in development which is both sustainable and nourishing for all in the long run. Economic growth means increasing a nation's total wealth and enhancing its potential for reducing

---

7) Wakhlu Arun, (1990), *"Back to the Roots - Holistic Thinking for People Development"* Indian Journal of Training and Development, Vol. XX, No. 1, Jan-Feb

poverty, increasing employment, increasing per capita purchasing power and solving other social problems. However, if growth is achieved at the cost of a loss of cultural identity, over-consumption of natural resources and weakened democracy, this growth will be unsustainable growth. Such growth is born of a lack of understanding of the linkages between economic, socio-cultural and environmental factors. It misses the larger purpose of development: All round benefits and the well-being of all in a manner that can be sustained.

A lot of disparity and confusion in human relations - economically, socially and culturally arises from lopsided, unsustainable development. There is a strong undercurrent of insecurity caused by economic imbalance, massive trade upsets, and ecological deterioration. This has led to disturbances in the collective psyche of many nations. A fresh approach is required to meet all these challenges. The need is to understand the common genesis of these apparently diverse problems. Only then can we intervene wisely and continue to progress in ways which will bring total satisfaction and fulfillment to individual lives, arising from economic growth geared to human development.

Considering the prevailing condition, we proceed further with the following assumptions:

- Life, both individual and collective, is one large dynamic whole. Changes in one-part affect, and are affected by, every other part, however imperceptible.

- All spheres of human activity and experience have their origin in the mind of man. Therefore, it is in the human mind that we seek to understand and/or change external manifestations of thought and the nature of choices humans make.

With a clear understanding of subtle inter-linkages and total dynamics within the system as a whole, it should be possible to wisely and beneficially moderate the system and facilitate its evolution towards change and growth leading to peace, wellbeing and happiness for all. Such thinking is of the 'whole' rather than the 'parts'. With several problems, inequalities, imbalance prevailing in our system, we cannot deny the good work which is happening simultaneously.

Humanity's problems are directly a result of the way in which the mind functions; i.e. its linearity, the way it thinks in divisions and aggregation, the way it thinks in opposites, its inability to see the whole beyond the parts. When we transcend from our mind to spiritual consciousness, we break the mind's limitations and thus overcome its problems.

Despite the gathering gloom and darkness as outlined earlier in this chapter, there are many hopeful signs of a slow but steady reversal of things for the better. Many social, spiritual and welfare organizations are working selflessly for human wellbeing without any ulterior motives. As a mystic once remarked to us, "Along with the gathering and strengthening of the darkness, will come an equally strong and powerful gathering of Light". We need to keep this expanding 'light' also firmly in our view. This is more than just an exercise in gaining academic balance. It is also about a conscious fillip to evolution by a strengthening of the positive.

Just as the illustration can be seen as the head of either a duck or a rabbit, we can see the state of the world from two perspectives - the 'bad news' and also the 'good news'. It has been said that whatever we focus on will grow. If we keep our minds tuned to only what is going wrong with the world, we may fall into the trap of not seeing the good trends. A balanced picture would emerge if we look at both sides of the coin. We are inspired by what the celebrated Computer Scientist, Alan Kay, stated memorably some thirty-five years ago: "The best way to predict the future is to invent it"[8]. This inspires us to work wholeheartedly and joyfully towards 'Heaven on Earth'. This book, a labor of love, is a step in that direction.

When we listen to the birds in the morning and get in touch with the power that animates them, makes the plants grow, we rest in peace and hope. There is in the heart a silent knowing that the Universal Intelligence, which has got humankind this far, is alive and well. This Universal Intelligence is known by many names on the planet: God, Brahman, Allah, The Holy Spirit, Jehovah, Ahura Mazda, Buddha Nature, That, I Am etc.. These are all names for the same One. It is the self-organizing principle which we will refer to later on in this book.

The self-organizing processes that make things happen on the planet without human intervention is reason enough for a positive view. Just looking into the processes and changes that happen in one human body evokes a sense of awe and wonder. Let us see some examples of the good things happening around us.

---

8)   http://en.wikiquote.org/wiki/Alan_Kay

Two very successful examples of working Eco Villages which take into account the principles of Sustainability are the Gaviotas village and the Findhorn Foundation Eco Village. There is more about the inspiring example of Gaviotas in Alan Weisman's 1998 book: *"Gaviotas: A Village to Reinvent the World"*[9]. The Findhorn Foundation[10] was the result of Eileen Caddy listening to her 'inner voice' and obeying it. It is today an outstanding example of a spiritual community which lives in a wholesome sustainable way, and also teaches and inspires many others to follow suit. One of their inspired initiatives is the creation of a Global Network of Light. This is a global network of all those who are being guided by a spiritual/holistic view of life.[11]

This is what Eileen Caddy shared on the inauguration of the Global Network: "Blessings on Global Network. May this connection inspire more and more souls to turn within, find that stillness and deep inner peace, and embody these energies… from this center, move and act to bring more love and peace into the world." There are many other collaborative efforts aimed at creating a more sustainable, socially just and ethical approaches to business and development. One example is the European Baha'i Business Forum (EBBF), which believes that "working together across generations, borders, sectors and beliefs brings results"[12]. We believe there exists a field of collective consciousness – often seen and expressed through metaphor – that is real and influential, yet invisible. When we come into alignment with this field, there is a deeper understanding of our connection with others, with life, and with a source of collective wisdom. The work of sensing and aligning is on-going and dynamic. We are calling into awareness this field of collective consciousness, the foundation of life.

A very encouraging trend which one notices is that several groups on the planet have learnt to explore the evolution of consciousness. Ken Wilber and Andrew Cohen have initiated a dialogue on the implication of enlightenment of the evolving universe. They are exploring the spiritual impulse and its realization (the mystical experience) and its links to a radical new understanding of human evolution. Recognizing this need for a dynamic interweaving of different streams of knowledge, groups like the Evolutionary Nexus, to the Storyfield, Radiant Networking and the Collective Wisdom Initiatives are all creating platforms for a new consciousness to unfold. This is aided by tools to harness Collective Intelligence like Open Space Technology, Appreciative Inquiry and The World Café.

Business is also beginning to recognize importance of Philanthropy and

9) Weisman, Alan, *"Gaviotas: A Village to Reinvent the World"* (2nd Edition), Chelsea Green Publishing: White River Junction, VT 05001, United States, 2008. Also see more about Gaviotas on www.friendsofgaviotas.org

10) To read more about the Findhorn Foundation, please visit www.findhorn.info

11) www.findhorn.org/2011/06/the-network-of-light/. Also see a similar network of spirited entrepreneurs: www.pointsoflight.org/global/our-network

12) www.ebbf.org

Corporate Social Responsibility. The donations of people like Bill Gates and Warren Buffet point to a new understanding of the power and importance of business in planetary life. In addition to business, we also have active spiritual organizations who are actually making a difference: The Baha'i Network, Sukyo Mahikari, The Brahma Kumaris, Osho, Sahaj Yoga, The Art of Living, Vipassana International, Transcendental Meditation and United Religions Initiative, to name a few. These organizations have a distinctly holistic and integral approach to life. They all recognize the universal origin of religion and authenticity. All of them are involved in active programs of social transformation and change, beginning with individual transformation. They all have well researched and documented experiences of positive changes in attitudes, health, performance and prosperity in individuals, organizations and communities.

There is ample evidence of NGO's who are working for the down trodden and poor. You find them all over the world. The power of the internet, communication and information technology has truly been a blessing for the evolvement of human kind.

Today it is possible to see what is happening in another part of the world in real time. We can also communicate instantaneously and thereby share insights, ideas, knowledge etc. This will significantly help in both exploring awareness and also mobilizing collective action. All the knowledge required for perfect health, sustainable development, universal education and environmental and social wellbeing is all available. Powerful and proven new techniques like the Emotional Freedom Technique (EFT) and Neuro Linguistic Programming (NLP) and a whole variety of meditative methods are all freely available to us for use.

To summarize, despite the negative facts and trends which have been highlighted earlier in this chapter, we also see clear signs of a global renewal. This renewal is manifesting through the efforts of individual and organizations that have the practical know how and experience to remedy the situation.

Given all that has been shared above, we have ample reasons for hope. It would now be clear that all the building blocks required for creating a different future for human kind are all available. The 'hard' and 'soft' technologies to bring people, processes, money and materials together also exist. Humankind has never been so blessed in terms of the know-how, possibilities, tools and techniques to lead a full life. We are actually like people in an enchanted garden laden with fruit, waiting for us to pluck them.

What is now needed is a grand unifying vision and grand unifying set of processes, which would enable the emergence of a world that works for all. This vision is also emerging slowly, like the sun rising after a dark night. It is our endeavor to contribute our bit in this journey and invite you to do the same. The invitation is open. Despite the growing darkness, there is light at the end of the tunnel.

Environmentalist Paul Hawken (1994), the author of the celebrated book *"The Ecology of Commerce"*[13] holds optimism for the future. He has studied the balance between industry and the environment. "I believe in rain, in odd miracles, in the intelligence that allows terns and swallows to find their way across Earth," he said. In a celebration of restoration, Hawken predicted that civilization was on the brink of creating a new world because the old world is no longer valid. "Self-sufficiency is a human right, we are capable of creating a remarkable future for humankind" he explained. Hawkens sees every negative trend or statistic as a possibility for transformation. In 50 years, with shared global understanding, it would be possible for the world to unite and be "wonderfully messy and deliriously creative."[14]

We intend that this book becomes a catalyst and roadmap for transformation - individual, collective and global. We pray that it becomes instrumental in awakening the many well intentioned people on Earth (of whom there are plenty!) to the power, grace, beauty and joy of Universal Intelligence. May we all dance together as one united and diverse wholeness, to manifest our deepest shared vision of a world that works for all.

Joyful Action Now

1. Start a personal journal to record your thoughts, feelings, observations and insights as you go through this book. Be open to noticing things you may not have noticed before. Let this journal become a space for honest expression and reflection.

2. Be still at times, even if it is just for a few minutes. Just sit quietly and attend to whatever your senses and feelings bring to your attention. As we become calmer, we see more clearly.

3. Listen to the guidance of Life as you sit still. Life speaks to us in the language of feelings. Guidance on what Life wants us to do now is accompanied by feelings of ease, peace, enthusiasm and joy. Keep sensing what Life is calling you to do now. Do it!

---

13) Hawken, Paul *"The Ecology of Commerce: A Declaration of Sustainability"*, (Revised Edn.), Harper Business: New York, 2010

14) Hawken, Paul, *"Reflections on Working Toward Peace"*, http://.scu.edu/ethics/architects-of-peace/Hawken/essay.html

Box 1.1

Words Aptly Spoken[15] by Dr Bob Moorehead

We have taller buildings but shorter tempers; wider freeways but narrower viewpoints; we spend more but have less; we buy more but enjoy it less; we have bigger houses and smaller families; more conveniences, yet less time; we have more degrees but less sense; more knowledge but less judgment; more experts, yet more problems; we have more gadgets but less satisfaction; more medicine, yet less wellness; we take more vitamins but see fewer results. We drink too much; smoke too much; spend too recklessly; laugh too little; drive too fast; get too angry; stay up too late; get up too tired; read too seldom; watch TV too much and pray too seldom. We have multiplied our possessions, but reduced our values; we fly in faster planes to arrive there quicker, to do less and return sooner; we sign more contracts only to realize fewer profits; we talk too much; love too seldom and lie too often. We've learned how to make a living, but not a life; we've added years to life, not life to years. We've been all the way to the moon and back, but have trouble crossing the street to meet the new neighbor. We've conquered outer space, but not inner space; we've done larger things, but not better things; we've cleaned up the air, but polluted the soul; we've split the atom, but not our prejudice; we write more, but learn less; plan more, but accomplish less; we make faster planes, but longer lines; we learned to rush, but not to wait; we have more weapons, but less peace; higher incomes, but lower morals; more parties, but less fun; more food, but less appeasement; more acquaintances, but fewer friends; more effort, but less success. We build more computers to hold more information, to produce more copies than ever, but have less communication; drive smaller cars that have bigger problems; build larger factories that produce less. We've become long on quantity, but short on quality. These are the times of fast foods and slow digestion; tall men, but short character; steep in profits, but shallow relationships. These are the times of world peace, but domestic warfare; more leisure and less fun; higher postage, but slower mail; more kinds of food, but less nutrition. These are the days of two incomes, but more divorces; these quick trips, disposable diapers, cartridge living, throw-away morality, one-night stands, overweight bodies and pills that do everything from cheer, to prevent, quiet or kill. It is a time when there is much in the show window and nothing in the stock room.

---

15) Moorehead, Bob, "*Words Aptly Spoken*", https://en.wikiquote.org/wiki/Bob_Moorehead

Box 1.2

Walk in the Light

This week's weekly guidance, which we received from Eileen Caddy of the Findhorn Foundation[16], seems to sum it all up poetically:

"Let those who have eyes to see with behold my wonders and glories all around them, seeing My hand in everything and giving eternal thanks. Let those who have ears to hear with listen to My still, small voice amidst the noise and clamour of the world and find that inner peace and stillness which comes from being in contact with me. Keep your consciousness raised so that you tune in to the very highest and leave all else behind. Walk in the Light and radiate Light. Fill your heart with love and understanding for each other. Know the truth and the truth shall set you free. Keep your mind on Me and let your eye be single so that your whole being is filled with Light."

---

16)   www.findhorn.org/link/eileen

CHAPTER 2

Examining the Roots: The Prevailing Paradigm of Development

"Examine the assumptions behind your actions. Then examine the assumptions behind your assumptions."

— A Sufi Practice

"Your task as the young is to reinvent the universe, the universe made out of stories – to change the stories, to tell them, to bury them, and to give birth to them."

— Rebecca Solnit, Author of Hope in the Darkness

Seeing That All Development Comes from Thinking/Choices

In the last chapter, we saw how our way of seeing things affects our feelings, decisions and actions. The choices we make individually and collectively are born out of the way we see things. This also applies to the people who make policy decisions. Their ways of looking at 'development' affect what they do.

Many of the earlier approaches towards development have worked on a partial representation of issues affecting development. The very definition of development itself seems to have missed 'seeing' certain aspects. Many of the blocks to seeing completely (as described in Chapter 1) have plagued thinking on 'development' in the past few decades. Some of the intrinsic and important life serving aspects are left out in current approaches to development. The interplay of individual and collective choices is not fully understood. Those who write and teach about it, themselves come with a limited view of the world.

We all have our own mental lenses and conditionings and our own interests and desires. Clifford Goertz (1989)[1] grieves "the tunnel-vision view of the development problem. We still tend to divide things up conceptually in terms of our own particular academic genre and to stay within those artificial confines". Even way back in 1988, Arendonk and Arendonk (1988)[2] raised the question of value based development, pitching 'values' as goals of the development process. They ask about the basic purpose of development. They conclude that the answer lies in the choice that mankind makes today (as we stand at the cross-road of our evolution). We have two alternatives:

1. Modern development for increased anxiety and vulnerability with its culture of the ugly, or

2. Development based on the pattern of values of humility, love, freedom and compassion with all its promise of beauty and joyful work.

Gary Jacobs and Harlan Cleveland (1999)[3] believed that values are central organizing principles or ideas that govern and determine human behavior and are universal in their application. Values can be described as the essence of the knowledge gained by humanity from past experiences, distilled from its local circumstances and specific context to extract the fundamental wisdom of life derived from these experiences. Values give direction to our thought processes, sentiments, emotional energies, preferences and actions.

A very small percentage of the world's population has a grip on the 'mind models, thinking, priorities and images' that drive the spending of billions of dollars and the consequent actions and impacts that affect many others. The four billion or so people on the planet who are still 'poor' and who are still suffering hardly have a voice in this discussion. Much has been written on every aspect of development by academicians, professional experts, technologists, and practitioners. There is some gap in all

---

1) Goertz, Clifford (1989), In Daedalus, "*A World to Make: Development in Perspective*" Jr. Amr. Acd. of Arts & Sciences Winter, 237-241
2) Arendonk, J. Van & Arendonk, S. Van (1988), "*Development for what? Or which culture are we serving?*" Proc. 19th World Conference of Soc. For Intl. Development, New Delhi, March 25-28
3) Jacobs, Garry and Cleveland,Harlan (1999), Social Development Theory, November 1, 1999 www.icpd.org/development_theory/SocialDevTheory.htm

the thinking and viewpoints. We are not trying to develop our self and our society from the core of the heart. There is distancing from the core of development, caused by too much analysis and differentiation. That has created the gross disparities in the global development scenario on many fronts - economic, social and ethical.

Along with the economic and technological development; love, compassion, integration, coordination, values, ethics and the spiritual aspects of human life are equally important for a healthy and happy life. In our review of literature, we have not found even a single definition that has integrated these issues in one place. Both material and spiritual needs are important for happiness and compassion. The need is to integrate physical, social, spiritual and ecological considerations to get a solution to small or big developmental issues. An integration of perspectives from our deepest consciousness to the external reality of our world will provide the 'big picture' for holistic development. There is an immense need to bring perspectives together under one roof and to integrate the diverse issues of culture, education, ethics, values, happiness, health and the environment into a unified understanding.

Perhaps there is a need for a fundamental reorientation of our thinking on development based on the following questions:

- Where are the roots of development?

- How can we think about development without a compassionate and respectful society?

- What are the blocks to development?

- Without integration of individual goals and organizational goals, how can we live in harmony?

- What are the changes required for real development?

Let us look at the deeper roots of the process of development. If we cannot understand and address the issues at the roots, no amount of tinkering with the branches and the leaves will yield any results. We believe that the current rot has to be healed at the roots.

> *"All that we are is the result of what we have thought. The mind is everything. What we think, we become."*
>
> — Lord Buddha

All human development starts with human perception and thinking. It is based on the mind models and cognitive structures we hold within us. Many of these structures are held unconsciously. They are based on unexamined assumptions. These mind models about development shape and filter our perceptions. They get us to direct our attention and energy in the pursuit of certain goals. They carve out and emphasize different aspects of reality. Ways of relating to the world around us that do not fit in with our predominant pattern of thinking are eliminated. We unconsciously delete dimensions which do not fit in with our predominant paradigms. It distorts reality-just as a rope appears like a snake in the dark. As slaves of these unexamined concepts and paradigms, we often generalize and become a victim to seeing things that are not there.

The views that we hold, the underlying beliefs and paradigms from which we operate, the stories we tell ourselves: all affect our thoughts, feelings, words and actions. Our effectiveness is a direct function of the level of consciousness that we hold as individuals. A wise gardener does not expect his garden to thrive by paying fragmented attention to the different parts of his plants - the leaves, roots, bark, or flowers. She rather accomplishes the good of the whole by attending to the roots. We too need to focus our attention on the underlying roots of everything. In order to start the journey of looking afresh at 'development' and inner transformation, we need to first pay attention to 'how we see ourselves and the world around us.'

What are the Mind Models Underlying Development?

Stead (1997)[4] emphasized that achieving sustainability is not about how humans do things; it is about changing how humans view things (Box 2.1). Like the deep part of an iceberg (which is below the surface of the water), these underlying assumptions and perceptions remain hidden and most often unexamined. For example, the current view of what is 'good development' is based on an Eurocentric idea of development. There are beautiful 'gifts' that this view brings in. But when it predominates and swamps out all other dimensions, we have lopsided development and an unbalanced life as a consequence.

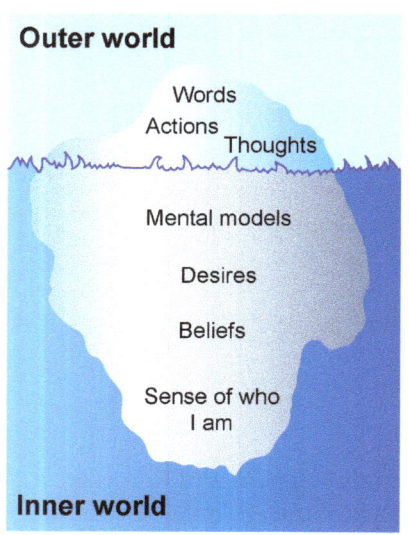

Society is a dynamic, organic and interconnected system. It is like a massive and dynamic web of individuals acting from their own beliefs and paradigms, from their own individual mind models. This web includes all of us - government officials, leaders, students, activists, teachers, homemakers, young people, the elderly, workers, farmers etc. Mind models here

---

4) Stead, W Edward "*Managing on a Small Planet*", From The Economic Times, 22.2.97

refers to our notions of ourselves, the world, and answers to questions like 'Why am I here?', 'What is the larger purpose of my life?' and 'What is my relationship with others?' We build our mind models based on past experiences or on the beliefs and values which have been passed on to us by our parents, priests, teachers, and peers and significant others. It is as if our life is run on 'auto pilot' playing out a narrative made up of many unexamined beliefs and assumptions.

Story-based strategies of change[5] are based on the notion that narratives operate on underlying assumptions. In order to change stories, we need to shift assumptions (worldviews, beliefs, etc.). Underlying assumptions are the unstated parts of the story that you have to believe in order to believe that the story is true. They are the glue that holds the narrative together. When they are exposed and found to be in contradiction with the current experience or values of people, they are vulnerable to being replaced by assumptions that are more authentic and true.

Entire life is a dynamic interplay of matter, information and energy. A deeper look at information and matter also reveals that it is finally all only a vast play of energy. Underlying this whole dance of energy is awareness or spirit. Thoughts shape and mold this energy. Thoughts are the precursors of emotions. Thoughts that stimulate large surges of emotion within us are powerful thoughts because these emotions create, drive and attract the 'outer' realities we see around us. When some predominant beliefs and thoughts are held collectively in the consciousness of many members of a society, they form a coherent belief system. When a sufficiently large number of people come together to form a coherent belief system, then we see the birth of a culture, or a nation or a movement. Each nation, ethnic group, religious grouping, people in any region of the Earth who see themselves as being unique or different, constitute a collective consciousness. What is considered valuable in one part of the world is rubbish in another part. Let us share an example to illustrate this. As a part of the food that is cooked in different parts of India, the head of a fish is valued differently. In Kashmir, it is considered to be something you throw away. Typically, it is fed to the cats. In some parts of the South of India, where people are predominantly vegetarian, the head of a fish will evoke revulsion. In Bengal, the head of a fish is considered to be a delicacy to be served to the most special guests! Each perspective is considered 'normal' in that region.

People so strongly identify with their belief systems, that they almost feel they 'belong' to a particular group holding those beliefs. An attack on their beliefs then becomes an attack on them! Because we feel our beliefs are 'me', and that our belief group is 'us', we have a tendency to vigorously hold on to our beliefs and defend them.

---

5) Easterlin, Richard, Does Economic Growth Improve the Human Lot? Some Empirical Evidence. In Paul A. David and Melvin W. Reder, eds., "*Nations and Households in Economic Growth: Essays in Honor of Moses Abramovitz*", New York: Academic Press, Inc., 1974. Also look up the 'Easterlin Paradox' on https://en.wikipedia.org/wiki/Easterlin_paradox

Becoming aware of these deeply held patterns of belief and becoming conscious of how they affect life individually and collectively, gives us the ability to choose a different perspective. We can consciously choose thoughts, feelings, words and actions that expand human wellbeing or satisfaction. When people are asked what they are ultimately looking for, the invariable answer is joy, peace, health, abundance, freedom from wants, good work, learning, autonomy, safety and security. Being satisfied and happy is about being at ease. Ease with ourselves, ease with others and ease with our environment – a total feeling of peace and completeness. It is about living in a natural, easy, balanced manner and about staying happy, healthy and being truly satisfied. Perhaps this is the key issue in development. What is this state of health and well-being and what blocks it?

A lot has been written about this issue, but what we miss are the blocks. For example, why is it that people spend energy and time on fighting a war rather than on enhancing human well-being? Witness the wars raging in Syria, Yemen and Iraq. At the individual level, why is it that we crave for things we do not have but which we really may not even need? Why do we want to have three cars instead of one? These are some basic questions that the rich elite must answer. They control 80% of the world's resources. No significant changes will happen otherwise. We will only be tinkering around with the problems. The answers to most of these issues lie in the underlying paradigms that we hold and which then mould our life.

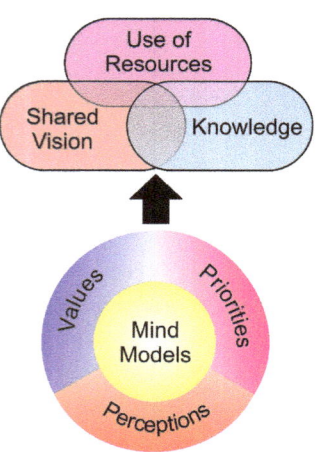

The figure alongside gives us a graphic view of the roots of development. Our mind models and deeply held world view affect our values, priorities and perceptions. These, in turn, affect our shared vision, the way we allocate and share our resources (including time and energy), and also the knowledge we create and use. This is the foundation for many other things in society like the forms of production technology, the nature and quality of work, patterns of consumption and spending, amount/volume consumed per capita, population size and health. They also affect our educational processes, control and use of the media and information, prevalent power structure and peoples' empowerment.

All these factors interact in complex ways. The overall impact is on the condition of human well-being and also on the condition of the global environment. Thanks to the internet, new communication technologies and the globalization of media, the impact of these interactions have become quite powerful. We are now at a cross road in human history where any decisions we take (right or wrong) will be amplified enormously.

Change affecting the life style and the quality of life in one part of the world, through this interconnected system triggers changes all over the world. This is a subtle yet powerful chain reaction, which sometimes proceeds imperceptibly slowly, and often explodes rapidly in quantum jumps, arising from momentous and creative interventions by individuals and institutions. This is a time of both great danger and opportunity.

One of the areas of confusion in thinking about development is confusion about the means and goals of development. The classic assumption is that producing and consuming more things will make us happier. Research has shown overwhelmingly, that an increase in GDP does not correlate with 'happiness'.

In a prophetic speech at the University of Kansas, USA on March 18, 1968, Robert Kennedy remarked, "The gross national product does not allow for the health of our children, the quality of their education or the joy of their play. It does not include the beauty of our poetry or the strength of our marriages, the intelligence of our public debate or the integrity of our public officials. It measures neither our wit nor our courage, neither our wisdom nor our learning, neither our compassion nor our devotion to our country, it measures everything in short, except that which makes life worthwhile "[6]

Echoing the same thought, Bhutan has famously replaced GNP with the Gross National Happiness (GNH) as a measure of progress: "Gross National Happiness (GNH) measures the quality of a country in more holistic way (than GDP) and believes that the beneficial development of human society takes place when material and spiritual development occurs side by side to complement and reinforce each other."[7] This represents a radical shift in how development is seen, designed for and measured; all arising from a different set of underlying beliefs and values. If one  asks the Finance Minister of one of the world's largest democracies what his goals are and he will reply "Growth, Growth, Growth" (meaning economic growth). But the questions that arise are "Growth for what? For whom?"

In a TED talk event, with his inspiring use of statistics, Hans Rosling[8] makes a clear distinction between the means and the goals of development. He looks at a few 'dimensions of development' and indicates their importance as means or goals using '+' marks.

6) Kennedy, Robert F. Remarks at the University of Kansas, March 18, 1968, Robert F. Kennedy Speeches: www.jfklibrary.org/Research/Research-Aids/Ready-Reference/RFK-Speeches/Remarks-of-Robert-F-Kennedy-at-the-University-of-Kansas-March-18-1968.aspx

7) www.grossnationalhappiness.com/wp-content/uploads/2012/04/Short-GNH-Index-edited.pdf

8) Rosling, Hans, "*New insights on poverty*", TED Talk, 2007, June

More '+' marks indicate a higher importance. A '0' against 'Economic Growth' as a goal of development will shock some people, especially our Finance Minister. But when you go deeper into the why of development, you see that money is only a means.

DIMENSIONS OF DEVELOPMENT	MEANS	GOALS
Human Rights	+	+++
Environment	+	++
Governance	++	+
Economic Growth	+++	0
Education	++	+
Health	+	++
Culture	+	+++

What is the use of a large bank balance to me if I am not free to express myself, or if my freedom has been curtailed in other ways? Economic growth needs to serve my health and joy and not detract from it say through toxic food, a ruined environment and mindless work. If I do not have time to play with my children, converse with my neighbors (or even my co-workers) because I am working hard at growing some business and commuting three hours a day through chaotic traffic, some sincere re-thinking on 'development' is called for. Given that the deeper ends of development have to do with intangibles like peace, happiness and freedom, it is surprising how much attention we pay to the accumulation of material goods. While oxygen is vital for life and we would be dead without it, a life spent on accumulating oxygen would be a waste of life.

Our needs are endless. What each person considers to be of value is as varied as the number of people we have. We see people with immense material wealth choosing unhappiness at times. We have seen very rich people fighting with each other for a small fraction of what they already have- wealth which is way beyond what they need. There are people in the world who are blissfully happy with very few worldly possessions.

What is a need?

This is the story of existence. It appears that true lasting happiness has little to do with the accumulation of outer things.

Despite this truth, most 'development activity' has been driven by an occidental world-view. Almost two thirds of the world population is seen by current policy makers as being 'under-developed'. This world-view has led to subordination, subjugation, judgment and an erosion of faith in indigenous cultures. Adherence to the current world-view has led to the manipulation of vast populations by vested interests including those of some people in the media. There are examples of media channels which are more interested in revenues from advertisements, (often beamed through chilling live scenes of terrorist attacks), rather than on telling the whole truth. It is time now to dismantle the current structure of thinking. People's minds and perceptions need to be liberated in a way that will help to generate bold, creative and integrated responses to the grave social and economic, environmental, and ethical challenges that now confront human-kind. Individuals, governments, experts, NGO's, student, leaders, youth, women – all need to awaken to a new paradigm of development which liberates, integrates, inspires and lays the foundation for healing, learning and development. We need to be more respectful of life in all her totality, including nature.

Everything valuable to us as human beings comes from nature and our interaction with nature. The ultimate resource that has made iron ore and aluminum into ships and airplanes, converted grains of sand into tiny silicon chips with brilliant computational power, unleashed energy like that of the sun from hydrogen atoms and modified the genetic codes of plants and animals is the human mind. The real process of development and value creation is a manifestation from the silent depths of thought to solid material outcomes. It is a journey from vision to concrete achievements.

The Seeds of a New Paradigm

Considering the different aspects of development, views of development from different angles, it is very clear that there is a dire need for transformation.

To create a harmonious integrated future, humanity needs a new paradigm. The only way the human family can understand and solve these problems is by shifting to a more expanded and inclusive paradigm that sees the entire Earth as a living system. If everything is closely interconnected, then the quality and truthfulness of all kinds of relationships are supremely important. A natural expression of this paradigm is to bring into balance all key relationships in our lives – inner and outer, masculine and feminine, personal and universal, intuitive and logical and more. This perspective tends to bridge differences, connect people, celebrate diversity, harmonize efforts, and find common ground (Duane Elgin and Coleen

LeDrew, 1997)[9]. The new paradigm would need to frame the concept of 'progress' in a new way. The outcome of a new paradigm would be a world where all enjoy a decent standard of living and a world which is deeply fulfilling for all. The vision of a better life for all will need to also include non-material dimensions of fulfillment – the quality of life, the quality of human solidarity and the quality of the Earth's environment. A shift would be galvanized by the search for a deeper and more lasting basis for human happiness and fulfillment. Sustainability is the imperative that pushes the new agenda. A desire for a rich quality of life, strong human ties and a resonant connection to nature is the lure that pulls us towards the future (Dominguez and Robin, 1992)[10].

Shackles of the past have to be loosened and new thinking needs to be cultivated. In this new dispensation, a pivotal role will be played by a new breed of people whose mind-sets and ways of working are attuned to the conditions of the new environment. Actions and results will be more important than mere planning. In the process leading to development, people will be the most critical and valuable asset, because it will be they who will provide the intellectual capital needed for development.

With transformed consciousness, development becomes a participative endeavor. With transparency, accountability, openness, and complete alignment with well-being of all, using the fullest potential of everyone, we can progress towards development, which is sustainable and wholesome.

Not only will this call for transformation of institutions – schools, universities, and economic and political structures – but also a willingness to be changed ourselves. Considering all the aspects of change, it becomes obvious that the developed as well as developing countries must significantly alter their attitudes in order to meet the challenge and bring about wholesome, balanced, sustainable development. The rich countries have to transform from squandering and mass consumption to thrift and economy thereby saving natural resources and ensuring ecological balance. The poor have to transform and become aware, to control population, improve productivity of land and industry, and invest in human welfare to get rid of want or violence. The critical function before us therefore, is a 'transformation in mind-sets'. This transformation will arise from a holistic understanding of issues. Transformation of mind-sets and raising consciousness will catalyze a harmonious life with material sufficiency and inner spiritual satisfaction. People will then find the ability to enjoy nature, work joyfully with their own hands, express creativity and have peaceful human interactions. Such a situation alone is stable and wholesome. This must be the goal of development.

---

9) Elgin, Duane and LeDrew, Coleen, "*Global Consciousness Change: Indicators of an Emerging Paradigm*", Millennium Project: San Anselmo, CA, 1997. You can access a pdf copy of this report from www.duaneelgin.com/wp-content/uploads/2010/11/global_consciousness.pdf

10) Dominguez, J. and V. Robin, "*Your Money or Your Life*", Viking Penguin: NY, 1992

The question therefore, facing development experts is not one of economic growth alone, but one that will lead to a life for all that is materially sufficient and abundant, spiritually fulfilling, socially just and environmentally sustainable. This would be a life of health and wellbeing and a fearless, free and loving quality of mind for every segment of world population.

Joyful Action Now

1. After a meal, sit down quietly and reflect on what is happening in your body as your body automatically (with no interference from you) goes about the task of digesting the food you have eaten. Reflect on how hundreds of interconnected bio chemical processes are at work, on how the right PH value and temperature are maintained in your stomach to facilitate digestion. How do all the nutrients go to where they need to go? Who is controlling this process?

2. Reflect on what other similar processes are happening within your body with no control from you?

3. What might happen to 'Development' if we interfered less and appreciated more?

CHAPTER 3

A New Paradigm of Development

"What is the mark of every… decadence? That Life no longer resides in the whole. The word becomes sovereign and leaps out of the sentence, the sentence reaches out and obscures the meaning of the page, and the page comes to life at the expense of the whole – the whole is no longer a whole. This… is the symptom of every style of decadence: every time there is anarchy of atoms."

— Friedrich Nietzsche, the Case of Wagner

The larger purpose of people on the Earth is to lead a life of joy, peace and health; to express oneself creatively, to be free, secure and abundant and express their unique talents in the service of others and Life. It is a feeling of deep oneness and harmony with oneself, other 'Earthlings' (creatures of all kinds who inhabit Earth)[1] and the rest of life on our planet. It is about constant growth and change for the better. Finally, it is about lasting happiness.

Building on what we have discussed in Chapters 1 and 2, in this chapter we will look at some of the reasons that this doesn't happen. We will then look at two fundamentally different perspectives that govern how we see things, how we consequently feel and then how we act.

A new paradigm called 'Wholesome Development' is then proposed. Its links to healing the divisions that we are experiencing in Life are explained and the foundation set for 'Inner Transformation', the topic of Chapter 4.

---

1) Read more about the term "Earthling" on http://en.wikipedia.org/wiki/Earthling

The Three Disconnects

In Chapter 2 we saw some of the problems and imbalances arising from the way we see development today. The problems have physical, social and spiritual components. At the root of these developmental challenges is a three-fold loss of connection of:

- people with the source of all of life, their own Infinite Self;

- people with other people; and

- people with the environment.

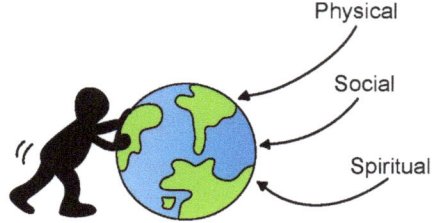

Challenges of Development

We cannot generalize this for all the people who are on the Earth. There are many indigenous people who, even now, live in great harmony with life: with themselves, with others and with the rest of nature. They are truly happy and free. The same is true for most of the healthy children! It is the unaware people amongst us (including us) who unconsciously live in ways which are disconnected. Let us take a closer look at these disconnects.

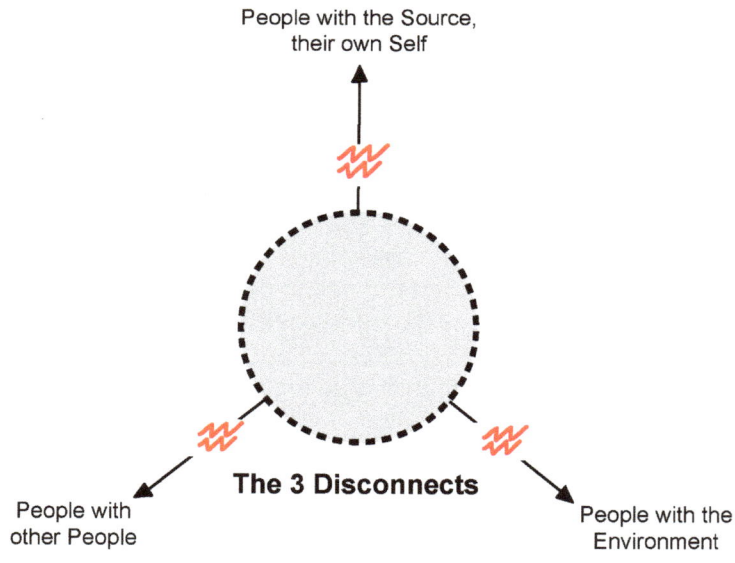

People with the Source, their own Self

The 3 Disconnects

People with other People

People with the Environment

1. **Disconnection with the source of all of life, our own infinite Self:** People are out of touch with the sensations in their bodies, their breathing and their feelings. They are unaware of their intuition as a powerful source of guidance in each moment. Many are out of touch with their unique gifts and the purpose for which they have come to the Earth. Few people are in touch with the truth and reality of who they are: we are unaware (as the Philosopher Pierre Teilhard de Chardin put it so well) that we are 'spiritual beings having a human experience' and not 'human beings having a spiritual experience'.[2]

2. **Disconnection with other people:** Deep empathetic understanding of the feelings of other people is rare. Many of us have lost touch with our neighbors, and the lives of the poor and marginalized people in society. Seeing the stunningly beautiful photographs of lost tribes by Jimmy Nelson[3], one realizes how out of touch we are with indigenous people and those who live in villages (even in our own country). We are out of touch with their heritage, their culture, their world views and also their art. Our lack of empathy for other Earthlings, especially animals from species other than our own, is appalling. And finally,

3. **Disconnection with the Physical Environment:** We have lost touch with the sunshine, the soil, with the plants in our neighborhood, with water, the insects, birds and animals around us.[4]

The root cause of all the problems related to development can be traced to an absence of love, integrity, and integration among human actors. This also encompasses a loss of connection with the spiritual plenum of life along with its social and political ramifications. What is needed is a transformation in human consciousness.

Two Paradigms to work with: Love or Fear

If we think of all of life as one single ocean, separate entities can be seen as waves. They appear to be separate, but are in fact part of the same ocean. They are all made of water. People can see themselves as the whole ocean, or as separate waves. Each way of seeing oneself has implications which we will discuss later.

---

2) De Chardin, Pierre Teilhard quote on www.brainyquote.com/quotes/quotes/p/pierreteil160888.html
3) Nelson, Jimmy, www.beforethey.com. For one of the most beautiful collections of photographs of members of "*Lost Tribes*" from all over the world, visit Jimmy's website.
4) Your Ecological Neighborhood consists of all the birds, insects, trees, plants, microorganisms, animals, which live around you (and so who are your neighbors.) Most of us are unaware of our Ecological Neighbors.

Here is another metaphor to explain the same thing: Imagine a spherical source of light, which is fully uncovered (picture at left). There is light emanating from all parts of the sphere.

Now imagine this sphere is covered up partially (picture at right). The sphere at the right has some dark areas/shadows over it – zones of an absence of light. The sphere at the left represents life as whole. The one at right is symbolic of life limited by and overshadowed by the ego. The ego is simply a false identification of oneself with a limited notion of who I am. It is like a wave imagining falsely that it has a life of its own. Actually, the wave is just some water from the ocean, rising for a short while only to subside back once again!

Based on the foregoing discussion, there are two different views that a person can take of himself/herself and the world. These are two basic Mind Models from which a person can run his or her Life: One based on

- a limited notion of who one is: FEAR, or

- an absence of any bounded or limited notion of who one is: LOVE

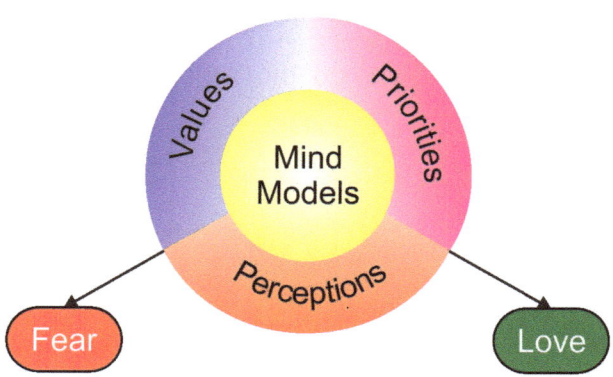

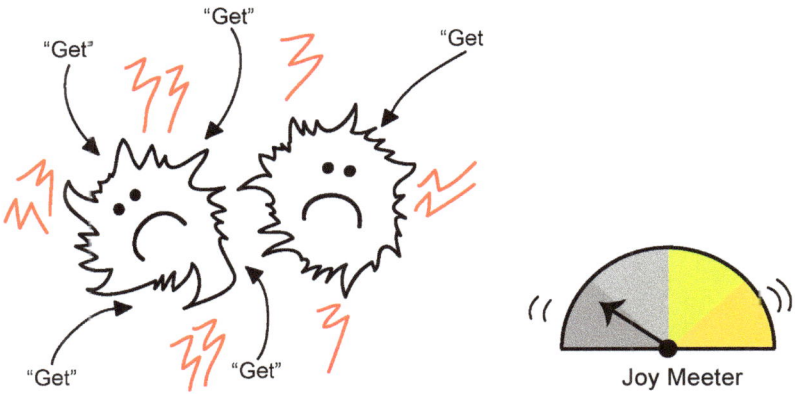

The view of FEAR, by its very nature of limitation, creates rigid boundaries and contraction. It creates an inner sense of being incomplete. A vision of LOVE, on the other hand, leads to flexible boundaries and structures and an easier exchange of resources and information. A system based on LOVE is more integrated.

FEAR is like a scissor that keeps things apart. LOVE is like glue that connects and brings together. FEAR divides and LOVE unites. Fear is connected with getting identified with the Mind. The Mind habitually limits and divides, it labels and defines. It cannot work without doing this. However, beyond the Mind is a space of Awareness or No-Mind. This is a space which transcends all boundaries. This is the space of Love.

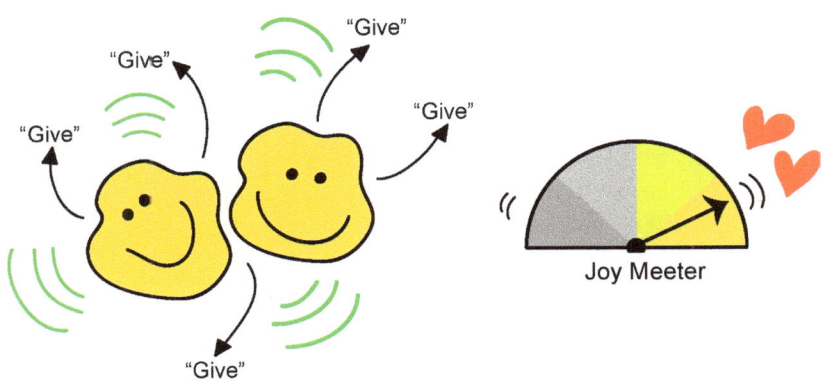

The following picture lists some more consequences of operating from these two different perspectives.

FEAR	LOVE
LIMITED SELF (partial) vs.	REAL SELF (Whole)
Ego, Mind	Mystery, No-Mind
Fear	Love
Stressed and Unbalanced	Healthy and Balanced
Dis-ease	Ease
Rigid	Free
Deficient	Full
Fixed	Flexible
Habitual	Spontaneous
Focused on getting	Focused on giving
Unaware of feelings	Present to feelings
Judging	Accepting
Attached	Detached

There is another interesting connection here. Fear (or identifying with a false notion of who we are) also leads to a sense of deficiency. This leads our actions into all kinds of 'deficiency driven' behaviour which blocks the flow of ideas, energy, resources, appreciation and gratitude. It also leads to other things like comparison, greed, boredom, controlling behaviour, a focus on 'getting', corruption, violence, conflict and a host of other reactions. The focus is on 'what can I get?'

On the other hand, Love (which is being our real and whole Self) leads to a sense of abundance. This generates 'abundance inspired' behavior which liberates and enhances the flow of ideas, energy, resources, appreciation and gratitude. It also leads spontaneously to creative action, compassion, sharing, a focus on 'giving', gratitude and celebrating whatever life brings forth. The focus is on 'what can I give?'

As we live from a space of Love and giving and receiving freely, we experience greater Joy in Life. As boundaries melt away, and the flow of thoughts, words and energy expands, we feel a deep oneness with all of Life. Another name for this oneness is 'Wholesomeness'.

Wholesomeness: Being Love

> *"A human being is a part of the whole, called by us 'Universe,' a part limited in time and space. He experiences himself, his thoughts and feelings as something separated from the rest - a kind of optical delusion of his consciousness. This delusion is a kind of prison for us, restricting us to our personal desires and to affection for a few persons nearest to us. Our task must be to free ourselves from this prison by widening our circle of compassion to embrace all living creatures and the whole of nature in its beauty. Nobody is able to achieve this completely, but the striving for such achievement is in itself a part of the liberation and a foundation for inner security."*

— Albert Einstein

Wholesome, as an adjective, means promoting physical or moral health, producing a good effect; Wholesome food, air, exercise and advice. It also means healthy, sound, salutary, prosperous, auspicious and effective in operation resulting in good. When left in its most natural condition, with little egoistic and fear-based interference from the human mind, Life is naturally and intrinsically wholesome. Life is Love in action, moving us all towards creative expansion and growth, towards balance and health.

Wholesomeness is being one with Life. It is being whole - being one with love which is the heart of Life and its core of ease and freedom. It means responding to Life in a joyous, free, unconditioned, expansive and sustainable manner. It means living in peaceful surrender to Life with a feeling of deep acceptance, gratitude and freedom. (Freedom from fear and ignorance based on a partial understanding of life.) Wholesomeness is liberation from the narrow confines of prejudice, religiosity and sophistry. It is transcending the fragmenting and limited theories, intellectualizations and arguments put forth by the mind. In fact, it is letting go of the mind (with love in the heart) while remembering that the mind too has its own useful role in the whole scheme of things.

Wholesomeness understands that Life is abundant right now. There are infinite possibilities and resources all around. Seeing all as 'Perfection in Progress' and a huge opportunity to develop our capacities, there is no aversion or running away from anything. Neither is there a craving for anything. The inner and outer aspects of life are held in a unified harmony.

There is perfect oneness between the spiritual aspect of life and the temporal. The dynamics of the material aspects of Life (matter and energy) are seen as being supportive of inner growth. All is seen as serving evolution and the expansion of joy, peace and well-being for all.

Wholesome Development

Having got a sense of what 'Wholesome' means, let us now take a closer look at the word 'development'. The word 'development' has its genesis in the Latin word 'vellum' which means a 'veil'. The word 'envelop' means to cover. 'Develop' means to remove veils or to uncover. If the veils in our mind which separate human beings from the environment and other humans are slowly dissolved, everyone would begin to respond in ways which are more constructive and positive.

The artificial boundaries drawn between the individual and the whole create the basic shift away from wholeness to partiality. The environment is viewed as separate from humankind. One human being is seen as being separate from another. These separations and compartmentalizations are the root cause of the dysfunctional aspects of development as we see it today. For example, one can produce in a factory whatever suits the limited goal of making profits, and in the process pollute a river which kills cows, trees and crops in a village downstream. Unawareness and separateness from the whole leads to a plethora of problems: conflict, violence, chaos, dissatisfaction, disease and much discord.

The central issue in development is therefore this: can we remove these man-made boundaries which keep us from seeing each other and the whole as one inseparable and totally interdependent entity?

Wholesome Development is an antidote to this. It is the development of the whole and not just a part of a system. Specifically, it refers to the following:

- The well-being of all the people, from all strata of society, all over the world;

- The sustained well-being of all living creatures and all dimensions of the environment;

- The well-being in all spheres of life, the inner and the outer; the physical, socio-emotional and spiritual aspects of all people.

In short, it means that all people lead a healthy, full and productive life in balanced and harmonious inter-dependence with each other.

Flowing in alignment with the movement of nature is Wholesome Development. The question arises as to how we can know that the process is truly flowing with nature and not stagnating under the cloud of some griping illusion. How do we know that the system is operating in this optimal state? This is readily known when there is no stress, disease, or unbalanced pressure in any part of the system. At the individual level one would experience feelings of freedom, enthusiasm, joy and lightness - a sense of deep ease, peace and effortless and harmonious action. At the collective level the process would be evident by an absence of strife and violence; prevalence of peace and harmony, joyful work for all, a sense of community, and a stable and healthy eco-system.

Wholesome Development then is the movement away from the unnatural conditions of inequity, violence, disharmony, injustice, disease, and hunger towards the most natural optimal conditions of creativity, freedom from hunger, joyful occupation and full living. It is moving from 'Ego Systems' to 'Eco Systems' (as Otto Scharmer and Katrin Kaufer put it)[5], from pieces to peace and from competing with each other to completing each other. It is a movement towards joy, love and freedom in action: a free-for-all by all!

Wholesome Development, in this context is therefore, to be regarded as the sum of events and activities that arise when the most natural, unblocked, undistorted flow of nature's processes are allowed to take their own course. This happens all the time, naturally and on its own. When we get in the way with our egos and create roadblocks with our unwholesome ideas of what we should or should not be doing, problems arise. Development is life as it is! What development is not is the outcome of deficiency driven ego-based interventions based on partial views and understanding: the plethora of models of experts, the managing of the managers, the activities of ego-centers of all kinds, the patterned superstitions of 'oughts' and 'shoulds' including the prescription of do's and don'ts. The figure below captures these ideas:

Wholesome development is a movement	
From	**To**
Divided	Integrated
Diseased	Easy
Imbalanced	Balanced
Unaware	Aware

$\longrightarrow$

5) Scharmer, Otto and Kaufer, Katrin, "*Leading from the Emerging Future: From Ego-System to Eco-System Economies*", Berrett-Koehler Publishers: San Francisco, 2013

Here are a few implications of this model:

- The ultimate unity of wholeness arises when the veil overshadowing our vision is removed. This is a seeing of that which is, interfering less, and being as we are. There arises then, a unity of 'being' and 'doing' that is 'wholesome'. It is doing out of being and being out of doing.

- The foremost task of development is to inspire people to understand the boundaries we discussed earlier, and to see that they are not real. The very absence of such boundaries is the peace and wholesomeness that we are all seeking.

- Being 'natural' or 'whole' does not imply being caught up in strong desires or cravings and aversions. It is living out of a pure and creative mind. When people operate from an inner okayness, they will spontaneously live ethically honoring the rights and freedom of other people. They will not let others' actions interfere with their rights. Such a system will be self-balancing and self-rectifying.

- Wholesome Development is to be viewed therefore, not as a static end state but as a dynamic, unfolding process – continuous in the sense that even when the whole world is developed, nothing will stop. Activities will go on but all these will arise from a different 'inner state' of no-mind/fullness/totality.

- From this standpoint, Wholesome Development does not imply any fixed standards uniformly applicable to people everywhere. Each one has to develop in his or her own unique way because everyone has a specific role in the overall scheme of the totality of existence. People have to be true to their own selves, live out their nature and that is the limit of natural development for the individuals. In doing so, there is no room for judging each other's contributions to totality. Squirrels, oaks, chestnuts, fish are what they are and play their own role in the totality. If an individual is doing something which militates against his or her true nature, then there is no development for that person. Similarly, if a social system or any of its subsystems is operating in a way which goes against the natural order or state of nature, that system is not developed.

Wholesome Development and the Threefold Integration

Earlier on in this chapter, we read about the three disconnects that plague modern industrial societies on our planet today. Wholesome Development, as defined above, provides the glue to heal these three disconnects. By its very nature of being respectful of nature, it is also sustainable.

The definition of sustainable development (used in the 1987 Brundtland Report)[6] is the most widely accepted one: "Meeting the needs of the present generation without compromising the ability of future generations to meet their needs. Finding ways for people to be healthier, safe, freer and richer that do not exceed the planet's carrying capacity or sacrifice the happiness of our children's children…". Gro Harlem Brundtland (1987, The World Commission on Environment & Development). Wholesome Development can then be seen as a threefold integration as shown in this diagram:

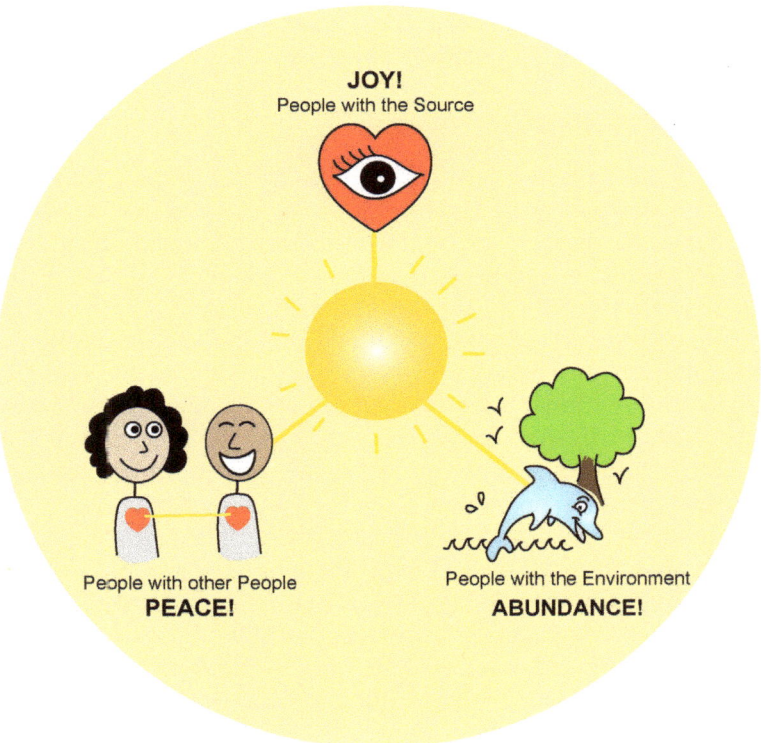

The emphasis here is on balance, equilateral harmony, integration and equilibrium within these interactions. These connections are between people in their relationships with one another in the social setting; between people and their physical environment which they must use and yet conserve in a sustainable manner; and of people with their own selves to ensure joyful ethical action in consonance with the larger design of nature.

---

6) *"Our Common Future"*, also known as the Brundtland Report, from the United Nations World Commission on Environment and Development (WCED) was published by Oxford University Press in 1987. Read more about it here: https://en.wikipedia.org/wiki/Our_Common_Future

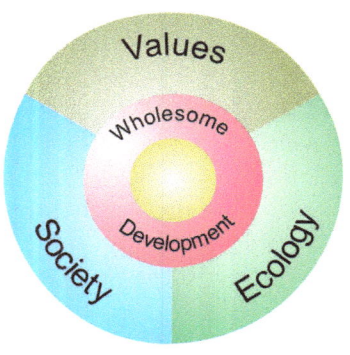

Another view of the threefold integration is shown in the diagram here. It represents balanced positive attention flowing to Values (based on Joy within); to Society (based on Peace with other people), and to Ecology (based on a mutually thriving relationship with the environment).

The three aspects of integration are really three strands of the same rope: the rope of Wholeness. This is what people need to cultivate if we want to see a shift in the direction of Wholesome Development at a manifest level.

Wholesome Development of People

Society is like a honeycomb of interconnected individuals and organizations. It resembles a massive cellular organism made up of 7.2 billion individual cells all with their unique genetic blueprints operating in a complex dynamic continuous mode: living, ageing, dying and creating variegated sub-systems. In a system of such complexity, if we think of the individual as the system, then the development paradigm of 'wholesomeness' is consistent and complete. In this state, individuals operate in relation to their external connectedness to the whole. Therefore, wholesomeness must not only be limited to the individual but be the characteristic of the whole society. So, unless the 'whole' is developed in that sense, development would not be wholesome.

In the final analysis, therefore, the challenge of transforming the thinking on development boils down to the problem of developed and undeveloped people (being different actors) in the whole system. Dysfunctional human behavior, which knows no geographical or political boundaries, arises from conditioning and mind models of deficiency and limitation. These are also at the root of corruption, immoral and unethical behavior, and the resulting social imbalances caused by these.

The primary task of Wholesome Development of People is the transcending and removal of mind boundaries. As a Canadian friend, Devon Reid[7] says, "For this we will need to begin seeing things as 'wholes'. How can we look at people, projects and the planet in 'wholes'? How do we look through a looking glass that does not 'analyse', 'fragment', 'deconstruct', 'differentiate' but sees the 'connection', 'association', 'similarity'… the wholeness of things? How does seeing things in their entirety create a different 'meaning' than seeing it in parts? What are the advantages, disadvantages and how can we 'relearn' to see ourselves, each other and our environment in this way?"

---

7)   Reid, Devon in an e-mail to the Authors, 2005

This will require bringing back into the collective modern mind, all those basic truths and values which have been the cornerstone of human civilization for over 5000 years. Reclaiming this wisdom will lead to ideas and actions which will alter human perception, feelings, behaviors and lead to a new way of life. In this age of Information Technology and the communications revolution, it will be relatively easy to achieve this rapid change in our perceptions. A creative flowering of homo sapiens would be the ultimate objective of social change leading to wholesome sustainable development. This would be true development arising from the Wholesome Development of People (WDP) for whom, in the final analysis, development is meant. The pathway to this is Inner Transformation.

Joyful Action Now

1. Sit silently seeking the guidance of your innermost Self - your Heart. Ask the question: 'What do I need to be whole?' Write down your answers using speedy and non-stop writing for a few minutes. Do not stop to read what is emerging till it is over. Reflect on what has emerged. What single action does it inspire? Plan to do that now.

2. Sit silently for a few moments and look all around you. Remember that everyone and everything that you see have all come from the same mass of hot gaseous material that was once a part of the Sun. See all as one dynamic whole. How does this perspective alter your feelings?

3. Make a list of your 'Ecological Neighbors'. Here is a small activity guide www.converge.org.nz/nbio/part2.html.

4. Take a decision to accept life just as it is as 'Perfection in Progress', and to start enjoying it here and now. What are some of the things you can start or stop doing? List them down and set up some time to make that happen.

Box 3.1

Love is the Law of Life

"Love is the law of God. You live that you may learn to love. You love that you may learn to live. No other lesson is required of Man. You are the tree of Life. Beware of fractionating yourselves. Set not a fruit against a fruit, a leaf against a leaf, a bough against a bough; nor set the stem against the roots; nor set the tree against the mother-soil."

— Mikhail Naimy[8]

8) Naimy, Mikhail, *"The Book of Mirdad: The strange story of a monastery which was once called The Ark"*, Watkins Publishing: London, 2011

Box 3.2

Are We Gone?

When this body dies, we appear to have gone! All the atoms and molecules that made up this body simply re-mingle back into the totality of all that makes up the Earth.

There are between 10^{49}-10^{50} atoms that make up everything on Earth. All these atoms, at some point in time, were a part of the Sun. Look around you and remember that all that you see, including all your friends and foes, all were a part of the Sun at some point.

And as atoms mingle and intermingle, as they constantly do, bodies are formed and dissolved.

Consider your own body. Where were these molecules and atoms before they came together to make this body you call yourself?

Assuming that the weight of your body is around 70Kgs, where was the approximately 42 litres of water ($\sim$ 60% of Body Weight) that make up the body now? Which river, lake or well was it a part of? Could it have been a part of other bodies, or even animals?

It is pretty much the same with our breathing.

According to Harlow Shapely[9], "There are about 3×10^{19} argon atoms in each breath we take…. Your next breath will contain more than 400,000 argon atoms breathed by Gandhi".

We can extend this thought to say that your next breath also includes argon atoms breathed in by Buddha, Jesus, Genghis Khan, Martin Luther King, Rabia and Rumi during their lifetimes. All the breaths you breathe in your lifetime will have argon atoms in it that will be breathed in and out by millions of other people.

How interconnected we all are! And how much we forget our intrinsic oneness with all of life.

---

9) Shapley, Harlow, *"Beyond the Observatory"*, Charles Scribner's Sons: New York, 1967

PART TWO

Awakening Capacity

CHAPTER 4

The Peculiar Journey of Awakening to Wholesomeness

The Peculiar Nature of the Journey

One of the famous stories of the legendary Mullah Nasr Uddin is about him fretting over the loss of his one and only donkey. Alas, even a frantic search for his donkey bore no fruit. After a long time, he realized that the donkey that he had been searching for everywhere was actually always with him: he was riding it! Another similar story is of the man who looked everywhere for his spectacles not realizing that they were actually propped up on his head the entire while. Have you heard of the musk deer? The musk deer looks for the source of this beautiful, mindboggling scent all over. He travels far and wide, wandering crazily over difficult terrain and suffering the torment of thorny bushes in search of the scent. But, alas, no luck. Little does the musk deer know that the incredible scent is actually emanating from his own musk gland on his belly!

Do we notice the peculiar similarity in all these stories? Peculiar because the common thread in all of them is that someone was looking for something they already had. It was never lost. Exactly the same is the case for Wholeness. It is never different from 'you'. The problem arises because we forget who we are. While we try to find ourselves in all external situations, we miss the profound beauty and grace of the infinite treasure of who we really are. Why do we forget? Why do we become so out of touch? So disconnected? Because we are mostly active and usually seeking outwards. We are always on the run, thinking that something 'more' will give us the lasting happiness we still have to find. If only we took a few moments and just quietly settled down, we would find peace and silence within us. This is the source of the everlasting peace that we are looking for. It is a space that holds all viewpoints but is not held by anything. It is in this space that everything is born and nourished. It is this space into which everything finally dissolves and rests. Everything is in the embrace of this unbounded, limitless space.

Everything that humans do is a search for this space. Ironic as it may seem, this is both funny and sad. All the effort, the slaving and fatigue that people suffer is in order to find the essence of this very space. We look for peace and joy outside us. We run around like headless chickens. If only we could just be still for a few minutes and realize how magnificent we already are: how beautiful, powerful and creative !

Why are we like this? Because we ourselves are the creators. There is no difference between the creator and 'I'. We are already home! The discerning reader may then ask what this so called 'journey' is all about? This peculiar journey is from Now – Here to Nowhere! It is a process of reclaiming what is – of waking up to what is already here and now. That is it!

Human beings are intrinsically whole and abundant. You just have to watch children to understand this. They are one with their feelings and with the abundance and wholeness of life. A sense of wholeness and abundance is the foundation for a joyous, creative and ethical life. This implies that in their most natural and pure state people will automatically be joyous, creative and ethical. However, this doesn't happen. The reason for this is that people have forgotten their real and whole Self. While they are the ocean, they wrongly imagine that they are a limited wave. This is an illusory state of limitation and separation leading to unethical behavior. The antidote to this is to awaken people to their intrinsic wholeness. When one is whole, one will spontaneously be creative and ethical in one's actions.

"When I let go of what I am, I become what I might be."

— Lao Tzu

"As long as I am this or that, I am not all things."

— Meister Eckhart

Our understanding of 'Wholesome Development' is based on an integrated, total and holistic view. This view, the foundation of Wholesome Development, is not only about ourselves and our experiences, but also of everything that happens around us. Only when we are wholesome ourselves, can we be active instruments of unfolding wholesomeness in our life.

There is, however, an important distinction between the direct, *intuitive* recognition of wholesomeness (where one *is* whole) and a similar understanding that is based on an intellectual understanding of the concept. It is like the difference between a picture of a glass of water and a real glass of water. The former cannot ever quench thirst.

Many people who "talk" about spirituality, of holding an integral worldview, of sustainable development do not necessarily follow these in their own lives. We have all seen "gurus" who preach one thing but have huge gaps in their personal integrity. A mere intellectual understanding of Wholesome Development is simply not wholesomeness. It is only when the emotions have been purified, and the body-mind has been gently brought into a relaxed alignment with the flow of life as a whole, that one begins to feel wholesomeness in one's life. Cognitive development is certainly necessary, but it is not sufficient for being wholesome. An intellectual understanding of this book can be of some minor help. However, it doesn't guarantee anything. You cannot think your way to wholesomeness. A book about fire can do little for a man shivering in the cold. I cannot roast a potato on a power point presentation of a blazing fire! Likewise, this book is just like a map of Wholesome Development. While a map is very helpful, it is not the same as the territory. We all need to clearly see that merely learning this road map, talking about it at conferences and having endless conversations on it is not the same as awakening to wholeness, and being a shining example of wholesome living.

The walk and the talk need to go hand in hand. While going through this chapter, it will be important to remember that the impact of what has been shared can come alive for the reader only through regular practice and diligent cultivation of this understanding. After some time, as the process of inner transformation and understanding ripens, these practices may not be necessary.

Change vs. Transformation

We often use the words "change" and "transformation" interchangeably. There is however a vast difference in the two. Change refers to a shift in the same form. When we say we want to change our organizational structure, we shift roles and move people around. In a similar process, we can change our physical surroundings and perhaps even our behavior. We could, for example, be more polite, more tactful or more creative. Such changes can be made without any fundamental transformation occuring.

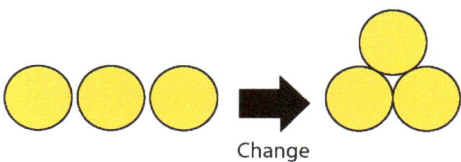

Change

Transformation, on the other hand, means a transcending of form to create a new form. The word transformation therefore implies a movement from one form to the other. Transformation automatically and necessarily involves change. An analogy to describe the process of transformation is that of the journey of a caterpillar to a butterfly.

Transformation

When we get sincere about our journey on the path of wholesomeness, we are not talking about a mere change here and there. We are talking about a huge shift in our paradigm of seeing ourselves and our relationship with life. We are talking about inner transformation which is the foundation of both sustainability and wholesomeness.

What is Inner Transformation?

Inner transformation refers to a deep shift in the way a person sees himself and his relationship with the world. It is distinctly different from a mere change of perspective. This is because it implies a radical restructuring of one's paradigms and mental models. The word 'inner' here refers to the roots of our mind including our deepest beliefs, values and assumptions. This is the place where radical transformations happen. A person may be totally oblivious of the fact that his life is being run on 'auto-pilot' by his beliefs, values and assumptions.

He may, for example, have an intensely acquisitive attitude towards money which he is unaware of. He may also not be aware that he can examine and change his assumptions about money. As his awareness grows, he may begin to observe his craving for money. He may notice that he sees money as an end in itself.

Probing deeper into his beliefs, values and assumptions, he may recognise that money is only a means to peace and well-being, and not an end in itself. His relationship with money is then transformed. This is how inner transformation occurs.

Working with the roots of a tree changes the quality and life of the tree. Deep surgery at the level of our beliefs, desires, motives, sense of who we are and notions of purpose leads to changes in the 'tree' of our own life. Most of these inter-related elements are hidden beneath the surface. Like an iceberg, we only see the outer manifestation of these deeply held structures. Lasting transformation, therefore, can only happen when we plunge deep into our minds and reach the inner most point of pure awareness. The outer world of our thoughts, words and actions (and all that these create in the world) is thus slowly transformed. As the inner roots are transformed, the outer tree and fruits also undergo radical change.

Another way of looking at what is happening at the roots is to use the analogy of a bright light (our unbounded awareness) getting slowly covered by soot. As long as the soot is covering the bulb, it will not be able to give light. To give light, the soot has to be wiped off.

This is exactly what happens to human experience. The infinite creative and positive power that is naturally present in each and every one of us (by virtue of our own consciousness) can be rendered ineffective if not tended to properly. The stress of our lifestyle, the pollution of our environment, and the collective stress of our world keeps us from functioning to our full potential.

Building on the above, we can think of ourselves as "bright bulbs" which have temporarily been covered with soot. When we are covered with soot, we operate in a limited way. When we are open and unblocked, and functioning freely, we operate with a creative force for positive change. Inner transformation is simply the process of shedding our illusions, limiting beliefs, negative thoughts and ideas of lack, which block the glory and abundance of the real Self. It is awakening to our essence - our essence which is always there, but of which we are not fully conscious. The process of inner transformation or unfolding spirit is one of:

- Removing blocks

- Restoring the natural balance and flow

- Purifying

- Uncovering

As we have seen earlier, Wholesome Development is really the sum of the outcomes of individual choices. Each individual makes their choices according to their prevailing perceptions and mental models. Bringing about Wholesome Development will necessarily have to come about through the inner transformation of people, one person at a time. The starting point for this process is within oneself. Just as a sleeping person cannot wake up another sleeping person, all of us who aspire to be instruments of Wholesome Development need to start the process of inner transformation within ourselves. As Mahatma Gandhi had said "We need to be the change we want to see in the world."

Awakening to our Self: Window of Awareness

In a parable about awakening, Lord Buddha spoke of how we can use a thorn to take out another thorn embedded under our skin and then throw away both the thorns. In the same way, certain mental exercises can take us along the path of inner transformation to the point where we can jump out of our limitations and then revel in the "wholeness" of life, our own Self. We then need to constantly remind ourselves of this wholeness in our lives and to stay connected with this oneness. A set of daily practices have been shared later on in this chapter to enable us to do this.

It is said that there are as many windows to wholeness (or life) as there are people. Each person's window is unique. In what follows, nine such windows (leading onto the sky of wholeness) have been shared. You can choose the one which "calls you" i.e. the one most suited to your body-mind and which feels most comfortable for you to play with. Stay focused on the sky of wholeness to which the window leads. Do not get stuck at the window.

Window 1: I am Nothing

We have been conditioned to believe that we are somebody or something. We think we are this body. We are identified with the mind, with our roles, cultures, religions, nationalities and a hundred other things (For example "I am introvert" or "I am a disorganized person").

The truth is, you are nothing. No-thing. You are pure emptiness; silent, peaceful, and unbounded nothingness. This is an infinitely spacious and powerful 'nothingness' because the whole Universe moves in it. To use a phrase popularized by Maharishi Mahesh Yogi, you are pure creative intelligence.

Window 2: I include and am everything

Expand the boundaries of who you are to include everything. This body is in me. This chair I see is in me. The mountain over there is in me. The clouds and trees and birds are in me. Saturn, Jupiter and the Sun are in me. The galaxies and stars and the entire Milky Way are in me. In the infinite sweep of my own Self, I hold all. I am an infinite hold–all which holds the past, the present, and the future. I hold all that wasn't, all that was, and all that will be. All is none other than my own Self, my own Body. I am everything and everything is in me. I am All.

Window 3: I am Love

My essence is love – the mystery that holds the whole universe together. Through this essence, I am the stuff that underlies everything, connects everything and joins us all in one mysterious dance. I am seeing that the same energy which gives life to the trees and the birds is my own. I am connected and attached to everything that exists. I am a space of under-standing and courageous action. I am the source of deep caring because I am connected. I deeply and completely love, accept and forgive myself. I deeply and completely love, accept and forgive others. All that is happening in my life is part of the creative plan of the whole. Everything is a blessing. I take everything as a dance of love in action and with a spirit of deep gratitude. My life is love in loving action.

Window 4: Being in the Now

Whatever is present here and now is my window. Wherever my foot falls, is the way. This, here now, is my way to wholeness. All is perfect as it is. All is whole, now. The rustle of leaves outside my window, the distant crowing of the crow, people talking below on the road, the thud of a plastic bucket being put down on the floor, the tinkle of bangles, the sniffle of the nose, creaking sound of the opening door, the sound of the airplane passing by overhead. All this is the whole, and it is sacred. This paper, this pen, this nib moving on paper, the sound of the chime, splash of water. All this is the whole of life at play; life working and life dancing, here and now. I am totally present to and one with this moment.

Window 5: I am Eternal Awareness

Everything that changes is not I. Everything that moves is not I. I am the screen on which all these changing images dance, onto which they are projected. I am the underlying awareness, which sees all change, all movement, and all transition in the realm of space and time. I am that, which existed before this body–mind was born, and which will remain ever after this body-mind has fallen back into the elements. I will remain long after the water that makes up this body has returned to the biosphere, much after these thoughts and memories have merged again into the noosphere. I am that eternal, unchanging witness which watches all changes, but cannot be seen. I see all and remain as I am – pure, eternal, unbounded and changeless awareness.

Window 6: Working Wholeheartedly

Working wholeheartedly is working from a space of joy and love. It is doing things here and now for the sheer joy of it. It is working from an inner awareness that understands that I am not the "doer", but that the work is "happening" through the movements of the whole. It means working with total energetic presence in this moment, doing things which are aligned with our own joyful expression that within us seeks expression. Working wholeheartedly is working with an integration between what I love doing and what needs to be done in this moment. It is a sharing of our gifts in the service of the whole.

As we share our gifts from this space of love, and connect with others in compassionate service, we become whole. We lose a sense of the past and the future and are in a state of **FLOW** – **F**ullness and **L**oving **O**verflowing in **W**ork. This FLOW is wholeness at work!

Window 7: Letting Go

Let go and let life do its work through you. This is complete inward surrender to life, while still acting with enthusiasm and energy in whatever life brings up to be done. This letting go is born of a deep understanding that through the interconnected movements of life, all things get done. That the ways of the whole are ultimately loving and evolutionary, always, and in all ways. Remember that all that happens will strengthen what has to be strengthened, and destroy what has to be destroyed. Letting go is remembering that all that happens is a part of a large interconnected web of events and processes, all designed to unfold love, unity and understanding. Surrendering does not mean surrendering action. It means surrendering a sense of 'doer-ship'. It is surrendering the limited 'I'. It is realizing that everything depends upon where we choose to draw this arbitrary boundary called 'I', and that I can choose to let-go of this whole process of definition, and just surrender to the mystery of being whole.

Letting go is also a letting go of judgment, of comparisons with past memories and with future dreams. It means just being with what is, and doing whatever needs to be done now. It is trusting Mother Gaia with **FAITH** - **F**orsaking **A**ll, **I** **T**rust **H**er, trusting that all rivers will take me to the ocean. Joyously letting go into the flow and knowing that the whole is love, and love will never let love down.

Window 8: I am Whole

There is nothing in this existence which is not me. Everything is contained in and is me. The totality of life is me. I am whole. Nothing is outside me. All is inside. In fact, there is no inside or outside, because all is one. I am that one. There is no other. All is my Self, all is whole. This dance, called life, this marvelous unfolding called existence, is all "I" in its totality. I am beyond all opposites, beyond all judgments, beyond all duality, for I am whole. I am the day and the night, happiness and sadness, the calm and the storm, turbulence and peace, moral and immoral. I am all. In me is contained everything. I am full. I am abundant and infinitely resourceful, for all is contained in the whole, which is the source.

Window 9: I am

Just remember 'I am'. While eating, remember 'I am' which is witnessing your body–mind eating. While reading this, remember the 'I am' which is witnessing your body-mind reading this piece. No matter what you are doing, remember the 'I am' which cannot be seen, or touched or felt or heard or imagined, but which witnesses all this and remains the same always. When the mind is sad, remain as the 'I am', which is like the sky watching a cloud of sadness that goes by. When the body–mind is joyful, remember the 'I am', which watches this happiness rise and fall. Remember the intrinsic freedom of 'I am', it's vast, limitless and unconditional peace. This is who you are.

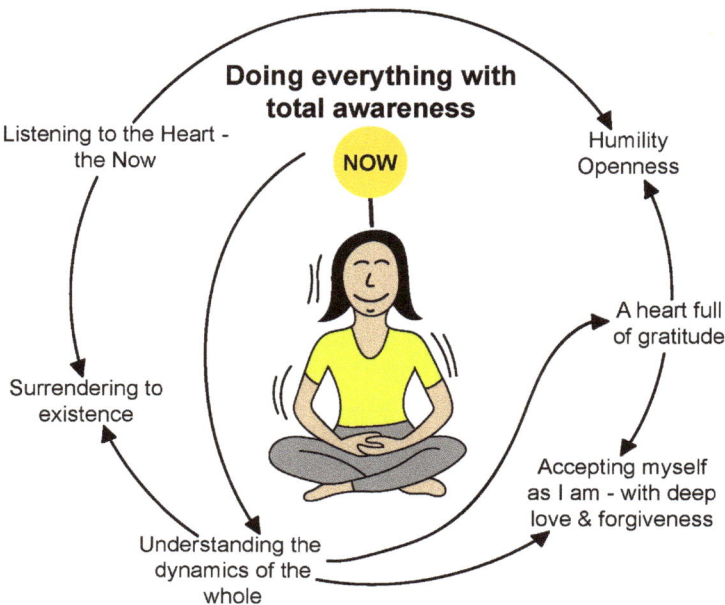

The diagram can serve as a reminder of the kind of life one can expect to lead after we have started on the journey of inner transformation. A deep understanding of the intelligent ways of the whole and a surrender to this flow leads to a heart full of gratitude. As we grow in gratitude, and understand how we are part of a beautiful, dynamic interplay of processes and their interactions, we grow in humility. This, in turn, strengthens our understanding and oneness with the whole.

Intuition and Trust, doing while being

When you are settled or when you are at home in wholeness, there is no separate 'doer' doing anything. All your thoughts, words and actions emerge spontaneously from an inner space of total freedom. There are no barriers, there is no resistance, and there is nothing to be achieved. There is only a spontaneous and natural flow of events which are born out of peace, joy, freedom and infinite resourcefulness. Action happens by itself.

The Chinese called this 'Wei-wu-wei', doing through non-doing.[1] In the *"Bhagvad Gita"*, Shloka number 18 in the fourth chapter refers to the same paradoxical truth (doing through ending action and knowledge), "He who recognizes inaction in action and action in inaction is wise among men, and he is a Yogi and a true performer of all actions".[2]

There is a basic difference between working in this way and the way we are normally used to. There is a limited and bounded 'doer' who is doing something in the latter and no doer in the former. In one there is a sense of separation from other people and from nature and in the other there is a complete oneness with life.

Benefits of this Journey

The journey of transformation helps us to reclaim our inner balance, making us free of the destructive patterns that we have formed through the course of our lives.

- Through the journey, our observer Self becomes more and more prominent. We are able to watch the sea of consciousness, without having to dive into it. We begin to become aware of the small patterns that we have formed; we realize their insignificance and are then, slowly, able to shed them.

- As our observer Self becomes stronger, we can 'see' our thoughts without aggravating them or fighting them. In inciting situations, if we practice paying attention to our bodily sensations and breath, we are being mindful. Our attention is taken up by this and hence, we become less likely to react. We see our thoughts as just thinking and our experiences as just experiences, without reacting to them.

- Sogyal Rinpoche (1992) states "the practice of mindfulness defuses our negativity, aggression and turbulent emotions... Rather than suppressing emotions or indulging in them, here it is important to view them, and your thoughts, and whatever arises with an acceptance and generosity that are as open and spacious as possible."[3]

- We will see a little later, how this technique can be practiced for short durations and how it becomes so much a part of you, that it can even be practiced in stressful situations, while being fully alert and responsive. Normally in such a situation, without the benefit of this practice, we would become reactive and unskillful, letting our momentary discomforts take over.

---

1) Loy, David, Wei-wu-wei: Nondual action, in *"Philosophy East and West, Vol. 35, No.1"* (January 1985) pp. 73-87. Accessed on http://enlight.lib.ntu.edu.tw/FULLTEXT/JR-PHIL/loy3.htm

2) Gandhi, Mohandas K and Desai, Mahadev (Translator), *"The Bhagavad Gita According to Gandhi"*, Wilder Publications: Radford, USA, 2011

3) Rinpoche, Sogyal, *"The Tibetan Book of Living and Dying"*, Random House: Sydney, 1992

- Creativity unfolds as we let go of the mind. We continue to use the mind, but more like a useful slave. It is no longer a master. Originality, flexibility and fluency of ideas, unfold. Ability to focus and comprehend improves. There is more laughter.

- As we become more used to this practice, as stated above, we start understanding the transient nature of our feelings and thoughts.

- As our mind relaxes and becomes less conditioned to our automatic reactiveness, we are able to act more skillfully. For example, in a stressful situation, where your most likely response is to be angry, you make a joke about the feeling.

- Life becomes more interesting and fulfilling. One is more 'in the moment'.

- For people suffering from physical or emotional pain, this pain becomes the central theme of their thoughts. In this state of mind, if mindfulness is practiced, one's awareness is heightened, and the pain becomes a nourishing not diminishing practice.

- Regular practice of mindfulness has a positive effect on one's physical health. Research has shown that it can improve physiological processes like metabolism, blood circulation and resting. Chronic illnesses like asthma and high blood pressure have been known to be cured with regular mindfulness practice.

- One's own sense of self-worth and self-respect improve significantly. One experiences deep 'sense of being okay' which is not dependent on any external condition. The understanding that one is pure and the unbounded awareness melts any limitation or fear. Discovering one's true Self leads to a dramatic shift in the paradigm we hold in life. Life thus becomes playful and less serious. This contributes further to our effectiveness. Stress is significantly reduced.

- Unpleasant feelings and notions are not dwelled upon. They are just observed and allowed to flow by. Neither are they encouraged, or resisted.

- With this alignment secured, you also become more aware of the importance of your physical well-being. The natural response of looking after your health arises from the understanding that my body is a part of the magnificence of life. This makes exercising a natural outcome. Laziness disappears, and regular exercising takes a stronger and more permanent place in your life.

- Job satisfaction, productivity and performance have all been found to increase through regular practice of being present. This is the outcome of all the above factors, as well as increased energy and vitality, decreased anxiety and hostility, and significantly better team work.

People who are awake to their own wholeness spontaneously provide the leadership for social transformation to occur. They attract social coherence and collective action. Through the liberation for their own capacity, they become instrumental for the liberation of the collective capacity for good.

Joyful Action Now

At this point, the practical reader of this article would be wondering how we can get people to make this inner transformation a reality in their lives? What could be practical ways to cultivate and remind us of wholeness in our lives? There are as many pathways to wholeness as there are people. Each person has their own unique way of being with life. For one it could be jogging, for another dancing, for yet another cooking the most delicous food and serving people in the neighbourhood. There are no fixed prescriptions here.

Some of the practices described below when implemented regularly will help us progress on the journey of inner transformation. The list below comes more like a 'menu of possibilities' rather than a fixed prescription. Feel and sense into what calls you and works for you. As you come closer to wholeness, you will experiencece feelings of joy, peace, freedom and ease.

1. Do one or two things every day that touch your heart. Things that you really love or care about. If you love listening to music, ensure that it is part of your everyday time table.

2. While speaking and listening to people, ensure that you look at them deep in the eyes. Remember that when you make eye contact, you connect with the essence in people.

3. While greeting people and saying "*Namaste*", keep in mind its true meaning; "When my wholeness meets you (the same wholeness), I salute this sacred wholeness that is one". This will ensure that one will never feel either superior or inferior to the other because the same wholeness that is you is also present in the other.

4. Before eating, remember in gratitude the food prepared lovingly for you. Thank existence for it. Say to yourself, "I am feeding the source". You will consequently rarely eat too much or too little.

5. When you walk, walk in mindfulness. Every day, slow down your pace for a few minutes and be conscious of how you walk.

6. While having a bath, be grateful for your body and body parts. They enable us to do the will of the whole.

7. Make music, dance and exercise a part of your daily ritual.

8. Explore a date with yourself – two hours per week solely and wholly for what you love doing, by yourself.

9. Regularly take up practices to clear away the roots of negative emotions in the body-mind. There are many ways to clear these up. One is keeping a journal in which you can regularly pen down your feelings, thoughts and experiences. You can also use the Emotional Freedom Technique (EFT) and Optimal EFT to clear up emotional blocks.[4]

10. Meditate. Practice meditation at fixed points of reference every day, sunrise, sunset, full moon, and new moon. Half an hour of meditation in the morning and about half an hour in the evening is recommended. Choose a separate place in your house for meditation and spiritual practice. The space gets identified with meditation and simply entering it, calms the mind.

11. Listen to your inner voice regularly. It is the voice of the whole in your heart. Whenever you have a problem or are confused, rather than consulting the outer guide, refer to this inner guide.

12. Discern between pleasure and happiness vs. joy and bliss. Pleasure is eating a bar of chocolate or buying a new dress. It is short-term and short-lived. Bliss and joy is a continuous state and is not affected by events/people. This unbroken bliss is who you really are.

13. Have a set of regular affirmations that will help you to remain aware and conscious of the Self.

14. Laugh a lot. Laughter releases beta endorphins that help our immune system and give us a feeling of wellness.

15. Remember that life is like a cinema. "I am the screen of awareness" – different images are played on it – bomb blasts, love scenes. I am *nitya* (eternal). All that happens is a stream of impermanent images (*anitya*). Nothing happens to our intrinsic wholeness, which is who we are.

16. Be aware of what you eat, and what you use - both on yourself, and in your environment. Choose natural, organic products.

---

4) See www.emofree.com and http://optimal-eft.emofree.com/ for more information on these powerful processes of healing

17. Live a life of kindness, compassion, and charity - it keeps you connected to your center, your source, that infinite reservoir within you that is your powerhouse.

18. Don't judge people, or situations - approach each moment with the knowledge that it contains within it the potential for any number of possibilities.

19. Simplify and slow down your life - don't clutter it. When you feel yourself beginning to speed up, repeat your mantra to slow down. Don't confuse slowness with sloth. In slowing down, we attend meticulously to details, giving our very best to even the smallest undertaking that we take up. Do one thing at a time - attempting to do too many things may seem to be more efficient. In reality it fragments us. Whatever you choose to do, give it your full focus and attention.

20. Every day consciously do something for others even though they may not have asked for it. Merely focusing on what you want to do, your own goals, needs, wants, plans, and ideas makes one feel lonely, insecure and disconnected from others. Listen to your heart and the needs of others. Serve them joyfully and with ease and grace. This also helps to build the feeling of oneness and interconnectedness.

21. Choose your friends and company well. The right association will enable faster movement on the journey to inner transformation. The people you meet often and exchange friendship with, need to be people on the same evolutionary journey as yourself.

22. Read books that uplift your spirit and mind. Choose your books/TV programs/magazines as carefully as you choose your friends. Be selective. It is useful to start and end the day with reading what spiritual masters have written.

23. Try to bring more mindfulness in your daily actions. This can be done by consciously slowing down the pace of things you normally do, such as eating your food, writing a letter, walking down the stairs. Do them at half the speed that you normally do!

All these practices make you aware of your essence. This enables you to create a joyful and unshakeable foundation for wholesome living.

Box 4.1

The Pause Diet for Joy and Peace

The Pause Diet is elegantly simple. Not only is it highly relevant to mindful eating, but its use can easily be extended to bring checks and balances into other areas of our life. In our hectic, distracted routine, food is often given extreme treatment. That is, we either over-indulge or pay scant attention to what is going into our system. Mindful eating is a practice with many obvious and subtle benefits. The Pause Diet suggests that we give our self the time to notice and register what we are eating and if we really need to have any more. So a simple way to be more mindful is to:

Pause before you eat: Make it a habit to stop a brief moment, before you buy or order food, or before you take a serving.

1. Pause before your next bite or spoonful: Place the fork or spoon down between mouthfuls. You will begin to truly appreciate the meal.

2. Pause halfway through what you are eating: Give yourself a moment to relish the taste, feel grateful for the nourishment and to sense when you are actually full.

These steps seem rather obvious in hindsight, isn't it? But actually practicing them takes a great deal of awareness. Here's how we can extend the use of the Pause Diet to enhance our overall wellbeing:

For Thoughts

1. Pause the thought and ask yourself the classic Byron Katie question: 'Is this true?' This may end the stream of thought right in its tracks, before it creates any further worry or strife.

2. Pause the thought stream as it rises, and step out into observer mode. Notice how the thoughts rise and fall away. Without resisting them or energizing them, the simple act of 'moving out of the story' for a fraction of time can ease them away.

3. Pause as the cascading thoughts gather momentum and gently remind yourself of the observer mode. This forms the basis of many meditation and chanting practices.

For Emotions

1. Pause to remind yourself – 'I am experiencing this emotion'. For example, instead of thinking 'I am angry', remind yourself that 'I am experiencing anger.' This helps to acknowledge the emotion while not identifying yourself with it. It is a reminder that the emotion is transient and will pass.

2. Pause to question the cause of this emotion – Very often, the true cause of the emotion is far different from the apparent reason on hand. Understanding what is really bothering will help you to resolve the emotion as also notice any underlying behavior patterns.

3. Pause to breathe – Acknowledgement, acceptance and peace come more easily when you simply return your attention to your breath. In heightened emotional states, we are setting off a cascade of physiological changes. These can be moderated by conscious breathing, especially in your heart area.

For Actions

1. Pause before making any commitments or taking any action – Check to see if the action is in keeping with your values and priorities. Check to see if it makes you feel more like who you really are.

2. Pause as you begin the task – Focus your attention to the here and now, so that you can do full justice to whatever it is that you are doing.

3. Pause during the task to re-evaluate. Once you have begun a task or project, new information will begin to flow. You may need to make changes that incorporate this experience and knowledge.

Wishing you a lighter and brighter life!

Sangeeta Bhagwat[5]

5) Bhagwat, Sangeeta, *"The Pause Diet for Joy and Peace"*,
www.serenereflection.wordpress.com/2010/12/25/the-pause-diet-for-joy-and-peace.

BOX 4.2

THE NOW EXERCISE

This note is about being present to whatever is happening in the moment with full awareness and with relaxed acceptance. It is about being in a space of joy, creativity and peaceful enthusiasm, ready to respond appropriately to whatever challenges life may bring moment to moment.

The Benefits

Being present to whatever is happening in the moment has many benefits. Some of these are:

- The body-mind is deeply relaxed, joyful and at peace; one is more receptive and so notices accurately what is happening within and outside;

- One has more access to the creative intelligence that runs all the life. This enhances one's bandwidth of possibilities. The creativity of one's response is higher.

- All the above points lead to more appropriate, creative and speedier responses to situations.

- One feels more in touch with one's inner guidance, with other people and with nature.

A Few Practices

Being in the moment is more of a "knack" than a practice. It's more like something that grows on you and becomes an approach to life. However, it helps to cultivate this "knack" with these few practices. These are given below:

- Attend to the senses and what they are bringing in, in this moment. Attend to what you are hearing, seeing, touching, smelling, feeling and tasting right now. Tell yourself "Pure awareness is receiving all these". You are that pure awareness

- Slow down your movements. Eat slowly, walk slowly and move your body slowly. Consciously slowing down brings you into the moment.

- Stop everything once in a while ("STOP") and just be a witness to whatever is going on. Witness the inflow and outflow of breathing.

- Sometimes affirm to yourself slowly: "My holiness blesses the world"; "Unbounded love and wholeness am I"; "Creative intelligence and peace am I"; "All is well and all is perfect now".

"Managing from the Heart" by Arun Wakhlu[6]

---

6) Wakhlu, Arun, *"Managing from the Heart"*, Response Books: New Delhi, 1999

CHAPTER 5

Awakening Wholesome Leadership and Collective Action

"If you want to build a ship, don't drum up the people to gather wood, divide the work, and give orders. Instead, teach them to yearn for the vast and endless sea."

— Antoine De Saint-Exupery

How do we manifest and co-create One Wholesome World? To start with, we envision it together and hold this vision collectively in our intentions. We then water the seeds of these intentions by loving and collective action in the service of the whole. We celebrate each moment as bringing us a beautiful opportunity to act from love in tune with the wholeness of life. Good leaders, who are one with life, can catalyze this process.

The future of our planet will depend upon the quality of leadership at all levels. No matter where you look, you see that some of the most life-affirming and valuable things that humankind has experienced have arisen from people who were "on fire": by leaders who held a powerful vision and passionately worked with others to manifest it. By realizing their fullest potential and by inspiring others to do the same, and also by acting as integrators, such leaders generated new capacities for action. They became instrumental for the liberation of the collective capacity for good.

In this chapter we will look at a possible Vision for One Wholesome World; how life is already working (through spirited people) for such a world to evolve; and how Wholesome Leaders can be instrumental in awakening collective action towards realizing this vision. The Vision for One Wholesome World draws from many voices:

- The thoughts of participants in a global gathering for One Wholesome World, which met in Caux, Switzerland from 17 to 23 July 2012[1]

- The Vision Alignment Project[2], which shares many positive visions for a world that works for all

- The Vision of Orin and Da Ben[3]

- *"The Age of Empowerment"*[4] by Matthew Webb

Bold, vivid and specific
vision of what you want

THOUGHTS BECOME THINGS

If you picture something in your head,
and feel the joy of creation in your heart,
you can hold it in your hands

1) Read more about this gathering organized by the Authors at
www.onewholesomeworld.wordpress.com/2012/07/29/global-gathering-on-one-wholesome-world

2) *"The Vision Alignment Project":* www.visionalignmentproject.com

3) Orin and Daben, www.orindaben.com

4) Webb, Matthew, *"The Age of Empowerment"*: www.infinityaffinity.org/age_of_empowerment.htm

Vision for One Wholesome World

A Vision that is aligned to wholeness, to our innermost space of joy and peace, is a powerful starting point for something to materialise. When we imagine something so clearly that almost all the cells in our body feel the joy of creation, we can know that our Vision is aligned with the whole. The term 'Vision' then refers to the picture of a tangible outcome that we hold in our mind and also to the energising feelings that go with it.

Holding a clear Vision is the starting point for manifesting something. When disturbing world events occur, use your imagination to picture the eventual positive outcome. Rather than focus on how bad things are, hold a vision of the possibilities of transformation that exist in every area of life. Refuse to live in fear or to pay attention to negative scenarios – do not think of them, imagine them, or worry about them. Every time a negative picture comes into your mind, do not pay attention to it. Replace it with a positive vision for humanity. The Vision for One Wholesome World is given in three parts: One Life, One Family and One Earth. It has been written in the present tense, as if it has already happened! This will hasten its manifestation.

We are all One Life

Enlightened people have realized that at our deepest core, we are all one. We have the same source of energy inside us. Awake to the magnificent wholeness of life, there is hope, optimism, and positive actions for a brighter future for all.

Awake to their real and whole Self, and understanding the larger context of life as a whole, people are mentally clear, emotionally calm, and spiritually aware. Everyone is in touch with their creativity, strength, courage, and wisdom. People everywhere make life affirming decisions. Energetically inspired by the higher Self, they carry out actions skillfully. All serve from their natural gifts and talents. Humanity experiences an outpouring of love, new ideas, and deep compassionate connections.

Every leader is a radiating point of light, hope, inspiration, and courage.
Humanity is in alignment with the evolutionary flow of Life.

The innocence and pure minds of our children are respected. Being a parent is a joyous and holy process. Parents work in harmony and joy to let children explore nature and as they absorb respect, love of self and caring in their lives, so that they can use their talents to their maximum, and find happiness in themselves. Every single child has access to receiving the education that he or she deserves, so that each child can nourish his or her gifts to the maximum – an education where the child is respected and parents and teachers realize and guide the child to follow his or her real Self. An education that engages, integrates, encourages and supports, builds togetherness and love as it resonates with the Wholeness of Life and the unfolding of the higher good.

We are all One Family

Having awakened to the understanding that all of humankind is one, people treat one another with love and respect. People are responsible in their actions and thoughts as they understand that the best way to serve themselves is to serve others. In the co-creation of a world that benefits all, lies our benefit. Criticism and judgment have been replaced with understanding, love, and cooperation. There is an unprecedented level of cooperation, teamwork, and sharing. Boundaries between peoples, gender, nations, and races have dissolved. We have a world in which conscious communities of all kinds exist. People live and work in many small rural and urban communities which are green, sustainable, thriving and joyously healthy. People freely share their gifts. Each person and group helps another to realize their dreams in service of the whole. People are supportive of those in need, and are generous with their assistance and sharing.

Business has become ethical and life affirming. Profits are made based on win-win-win partnerships taking care of the needs of all stakeholders including nature! Business is led by Wholesome Leaders who are one with the wholeness of life and people are treated with courtesy and love. Innovation, collaboration and creative recreation flourish.

People are trusting as they know that business is an honorable and safe process: every deed done is beneficial and strengthening of people, community and our Mother Earth.

We are all One Earth

People realize that the life in the mountains, rivers, pebbles, flowers, and all animals is the same life that runs in their own body. People know their deep oneness with each other and with the plant, animal, and mineral kingdoms. They treat nature the way they would like to be treated themselves. People know that the universe is friendly and always working for them. They know that nature is the best guide and friend one could ever have! People all over the world walk hand in hand with the intelligence and energy of life as a whole.[5]

5) Putting together this Vision of One Wholesome World was completed on the Christmas Day of 2013

Many people on the planet wholeheartedly resonate with this Vision of One Wholesome World. Spirited and inspired people all over the world today are focusing their collective love, energy and spirit to unitedly create a better tomorrow through a sustainable world. However, a big challenge still remains unresolved and this is 'the challenge of learning to work well with others'! The world is becoming increasingly complex with multiple power centers, different actors in the global system, Non-Governmental Organizations (NGOs), interest groups, warring factions (both state and non-state actors), different departments in the same government, neighboring nations like India and Pakistan, and pockets and islands of innovations failing to come together as one for the wellbeing of the whole.

The lack of coherence and cooperation amongst Non-Governmental Organizations (NGOs) for example is legendary. Competition among NGOs for what is seen as limited funds sometimes leads not only to a lack of integration between different projects, but also to the wasteful duplication of activities. In a recent conference on Social Innovation, people talked of an 'Ego System' instead of an 'Eco System' of NGOs![6]

We find all the pieces of the jigsaw puzzle around us but no grand picture. From our own experience, we have seen this happening in the Government of India where related departments like Education, Environment, Health and Rural Development rarely talk to each other. In such an environment, innovative partnerships, dialogue and coalitions are required if we would like to co-create the big picture.

The Need for Resonant People to Join up and Create Bigger Capacities

The time has now come to work together in larger 'wholes' at the ground level. This means that people do not compete with each other, but complete each other. Each one of us brings unique gifts, talents, connections and resources to life. What I have, no one else has. I am unique. What you have or can do, no one else can. Your family history, connections, friends and experiences are non-replicable. We are all like unique pieces of a gigantic jigsaw puzzle, each piece having its unique shape and color. As we join these unique jigsaw pieces together, within the context of a common shared Vision, newer capacities begin to unfold, in ourselves and also collectively.

> *"When you are inspired by some great purpose, some extraordinary project, all of your thoughts break their bonds. Your mind transcends limitations; your consciousness expands in every direction; and you find yourself in a new, great and wonderful world. Dormant forces, faculties and talents become alive and you discover yourself to be a greater person than you ever dreamed yourself to be."*
>
> — Patanjali

---

6) Scharmer, Dr. C. Otto and Kaufer, Dr. Katrin, *"Leading from the Emerging Future; From Ego-System to Eco-System Economies"*, Berrett-Koehler Publishers: San Francisco, 2013

As we dissolve boundaries and open our hearts for more fluency and movement, there will be empowerment and abundance. We can all use each other's resources. Both affluence and influence will increase, expanding our collective capacities greatly. This will enable us to surpass the limitations and do things we would have never thought possible before. Not only the big corporations, but even small players need to be activated and we will see the magnanimity of our collective capacity.

Like a chain reaction, one conscious mind will create and connect with another. This collective action and intent will bless us with easy going relations, knowledge sharing and enhanced community living.

Robust and proven processes of conversation and dialogue are available to co-create the solutions that the world needs today. Bringing together apparently incompatible groups and forces, (for example those working on Environment and Business, Indigenous Cultures and Globalization) may well be the heart of the process of creating a more wholesome civilization on Earth.

Perhaps nothing captures the essence of collective action for Wholesome Development as the African word *Ubuntu*. *Ubuntu*[7] (also referred to as *hunhu* in its *Shona* equivalent) is a *Nguni Bantu* term which roughly translates to 'human-ness', or 'humanity towards others'. In a more spiritual sense, it refers to 'the belief in a universal bond of sharing that connects all humanity'. We are all bound by a shared humanity or humanness. *Ubuntu* in the *Xhosa* culture means: 'I am because we are'. It is almost like saying that emotions cannot exist (for long) as islands. I cannot remain happy while all around me (including animals and forests) are unhappy. The joy and wellbeing of others is my joy and well-being. The idea of *Ubuntu* is best illustrated through a well-known parable:

> A professor suggested that the children in an African tribe play a game. He placed a basket full of fruit and sweets near a tree and told the children that whoever got to the basket first would win all the treats. When he gave the shout for them to run, they all took each other's hands and ran together. On reaching the basket by the tree, they all sat down together to enjoy the fruit and sweets. When the professor asked them why they had all run together, when one could easily have had all the treats for himself they said: "*Ubuntu*! How can one of us be happy if all the other ones are sad?"

---

7) Read more about Ubuntu on https://en.wikipedia.org/wiki/Ubuntu_(philosophy)

Speaking of Nelson Mandela's deep understanding of the spirit of *Ubuntu* (at his memorial service in December 2013), Barack Obama, explained that Mandela deeply understood the ties that bind the human spirit. Also that he recognized that we are all bound together in ways that can be invisible to the eye; that there is a oneness to humanity; that we fulfil ourselves by sharing ourselves with others, and caring for those around us.[8] These acts of sharing ourselves with others, and caring for those around us are also the very means of our own evolution.

Co-creating a world we can all be proud of handing over to our children and grandchildren will require us to work with a spirit of *'Ubuntu'*. In many indigenous societies, like the villages of Africa and India, even today, whenever people need to think and act collectively, they sit in circles. The circle is a beautiful symbol of unity and wholeness. It has no beginning and no end. It is balanced and has no hierarchy. The space inside the circumference is symbolic of the common space of Spirit. It invites us to share from the heart. The circle is the form we need for connection, conversation and co-creation.

How can there be an explosion of circles in the world? Of people who are doing their individual work and are also teaming up with other people to do the work of the whole? How can we create circles of connection, conversation and co-creation among:

- All positive forces in a local geographical area – neighborhoods, villages, clusters, cities etc.?

- People in different domains of knowledge – economics and environment; who, in turn, will also need to talk to people in education and health etc.?

- People within the same domain – the best leaders and practitioners in Water Harvesting, Organic Agriculture, Holistic Education from all over the world?

- People from different faiths, religions, belief systems and cultures: to bring about integration with Spirit – the source of all values, our core of humanity and inspiration within?

Luckily, there are already many people on the planet who are acting as the 'Weavers of Life'. As servants of the Whole, they see the big picture and connect people accordingly. They are like the imaginal cells in a caterpillar which eventually gather to form a butterfly!

---

8) Obama,Barack speaking at the memorial service for Nelson Mandela in December 2013
www.youtube.com/watch?v=4vUB363cRqE

The metaphor of the Imaginal Cells[9]

A powerful metaphor which has been used often to envision the metamorphosis that will now happen on Earth, is the metaphor of the imaginal cells. These are the cells of the butterfly that course around in the body of the caterpillar.

These butterfly cells (few in number) are very different from the more widespread caterpillar cells. In fact, the immune system of the caterpillar thinks that these imaginal cells are alien to the body, and so destroys them. Meanwhile, new imaginal cells continue to proliferate. The caterpillar's immune system now finds it difficult to destroy them fast enough. More and more of the imaginal cells survive.

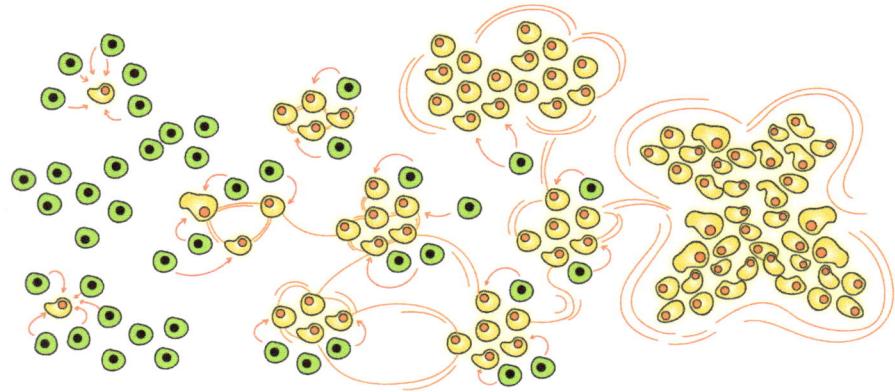

And then something amazing begins to happen: isolated and disconnected imaginal cells begin to cluster together into small cohorts. The small cohorts of imaginal cells then begin to cluster into even larger groupings. All imaginal cells in the cluster vibrate at the same frequency and begin to exchange molecules and form symbiotic relationships. Then, within the chrysalis, where this whole drama of metamorphosis is unfolding, the whole string of imaginal cells starts behaving differently from the caterpillar cells. This is the birth of the organism we call a butterfly!

9)   The Collective Intelligence of the Imaginal Cells:
      www.blogofcollectiveintelligence.com/2004/05/27/the_collective_intelligence_of
      Also see Imaginal Cells in Butterfly Mysteries: www.butterflymysteries.com/imaginal-cells.html

The cells in a fertilized human embryo slowly begin to take on different forms and roles as they grow in the mother's womb. Similarly, the integrated imaginal cells in the chrysalis (which are now collectively a butterfly), begin to take on different forms and roles to form the complete butterfly. The remaining cells of the caterpillar now serve as food for the imaginal cells. A new butterfly is eventually born.

When we reflect on this process of metamorphosis, we are in awe of the intelligence and beauty that characterizes this transformation. What might happen if leaders who resonate to the vision of one wholesome world, started connecting, conversing and co-creating? What might happen in a neighborhood if people who share the same passions and cared for the same things started clustering together? What new forms of human endeavor and celebration would emerge?

How does this Work in Practice?

When we link up wisely in an exchange of gifts, we evolve towards wholeness. We move from 'competing' to 'completing' and from 'working' to 'playing'. We all feel blessed to be able to serve from the greatest gifts we have. As this process deepens, our rigid boundaries slowly begin to dissolve opening up more flow. Affluence, health, balance and joy are natural outcomes. Our life becomes a joyful and a relaxed dance with the whole.

We all need to listen to inner guidance and take responsibility for acting on the calling. The larger orchestration of events and forces will happen spontaneously if we trust the evolutionary flow of life. It seems that all the positive spiritual forces on the planet need to form a network now. The time for this has come. This joining of hearts will create the magic of group resonance. Renee (2003)[10] defines collective resonance as "a felt sense of energy, rhythm, or intuitive knowing that occurs in a group of human beings and positively affects the way they interact toward a common purpose." It is associated with high energy and high creativity. As we walk hand in hand with life's energy and with each other, our work becomes easier and resourceful. Amazing coincidences provide support thereby creating the multiplier effect.

How does this actually happen on the ground, in the real world? How do I link up with other people who are like the Imaginal Cells around me and on the planet? We will not go into how to use Facebook, LinkedIn and Twitter. We are assuming that you dear reader would already be good at this. Here are some tips and tools for you to play with:

- See what has joy, juice, energy and meaning for you. What feels natural, easy, peaceful and enthusiastic? Stay focused on these gifts alone. This is the universe telling you what piece you need to bring forward to contribute to the one dance called life.

---

10) Levi, Dr. Renee A., *"Group Magic: An Inquiry into Experiences of Collective Resonance"* www.resonanceprcject.org/research1.cfm?pt=2&id=76

- Look for others whom you can serve with your gifts. See how your gifts and offerings can complete them, make them happier, relaxed, peaceful, healthy, and prosperous. Actively offer to be of service to those who may benefit.

- See others who can serve your needs. Request them clearly for what you need. It is okay to ask so that you can bask in the warmth of their giving. By receiving graciously, you are giving others a chance to share/give. You are serving them too!

- Make simple and crystal clear agreements based on the principles of abundance, balance, giving, gratitude and transparency.

- Take joyful action now. Finish things off enthusiastically.

When we connect with others like this around a shared Vision or interest, more people will enlist them. Let people know the benefits of participating (in these circles), such as:

- Developing community: They will have the opportunity to be part of a creative, thoughtful group exploring meaningful issues together.

- Creating a new future: They will help bring new conversation into the world, and be at the core of those who are creating the future.

- Becoming informed: they will learn about the direction our civilization is taking and choices we have for living in the twenty-first century.

- Having fun! They will meet people who are interested in the profound changes occurring in our time, and explore problems and possibilities in a hopeful and creative way.

The circle has only one center. It is a symbol of gathering in wholeness. There is no higher or lower in a circle. In an organization where we were providing consulting services, just an act of seating people together in a circle, forgetting hierarchy, age, background etc. created a powerful feeling of oneness which was touching and palpable. Sitting in a circle reminds us of one common spirit.

Cristina Baldwin (1998) in her book *"Calling the Circle: The First and Future Culture"*[11] says that there are three principles of peer-spirit circling:

- Rotating leadership

- Sharing responsibility

- Relying on spirit

11) Baldwin, Christina, *"Calling the Circle: The First and Future Culture"*, Bantam: New York, 1998

All people of the circle help their fellow members by taking responsibility. Leadership is all about passion and responsibility. The responsibility is shared. Each person pays attention to what needs to be done or said, or does what has to be done. Moments of silence and intense observation guide action. Actions emerge as we trust the source and as we trust each other. Listening and silence are symbolic of the inner space of spirit and also of the space within the circle. Powerful tools like *"Appreciative Inquiry"*[12] and *"Open Space Technology"*[13] exist to bring out collective intelligence and collective action. (See Boxes 5.4 and 5.5 for more information). Following a few simple guidelines for group dialogue can ensure that the deliberations in a circle can lead to expanding insights and creative action.[14] An outstanding book by Peggy Holman, *"Engaging Emergence: Turning Upheaval into Opportunity"*[15], is a bible for anyone wanting to learn more about this process.

The process of awakening will be like one candle lighting another. The planet is ripe for such a movement at this point in time (2016). It is wholesome leaders, led by love, who will set an example and inspire others. This will make the much needed transformation happen by supporting and catalyzing these processes. They will be like "Hosts" rather than "Heroes" as Margaret Wheatley puts it beautifully in her article.[16]

Wholesome leaders will be the harbingers of heaven on Earth. By simply being one with the wholeness of life, which is Love, (and working actively in the moment from that space of joy, freedom and awareness) such leaders will awaken the latent wholeness in others. Pragati Leadership Institute[17] has already been doing this for several years.

What is Wholesome Leadership?

Wholesome leadership is defined as the leadership that arises when one is being one's whole self. It is standing up and acting for what has meaning and heart for oneself in a way that inspires others to follow. It is leadership by love for the unfolding of peoples' fullest potential. It is leadership that is guided by love and executes actions with consummate skill. It marries the head, heart and hands.

---

12) For More Information on Appreciative Inquiry (AI), please visit the "*Appreciative Inquiry Commons*": http://appreciativeinquiry.cwru.edu

13) For more information on Open Space Technology (OST) please see www.openspaceworld.org

14) There are more valuable insights on the processes and tools required to evolve collective wisdom on Tom Atlee's website www.co-intelligence.org/CIcontents.html

15) Holman, Peggy, "*Engaging Emergence: Turning Upheaval into Opportunity*", Berrett-Koehler Publishers: San Francisco, 2010. Also see www.peggyholman.com/papers/engaging-emergence

16) Wheatley, Margaret and Frieze, Debbie, "*Leadership in the Age of Complexity: From Hero to Host*", www.margaretwheatley.com/articles/Leadership-in-Age-of-Complexity.pdf, 2010

17) Learn more about what Pragati Leadership Institute (P) Ltd, an organization based in Pune, India does at www.pragatileadership.com

The role of a wholesome leader requires constant balancing between opposing polarities. His or her attention has to be on both ends in order to move forward. Some examples of the polarities that leaders have to struggle with are between:

- Working in the work-place/professional contribution vs. spending time with family/personal life

- Physical activity vs. rest and renewal

- Mental activity vs. pause and reflection

- Focussing on doing work and contributing vs. building capacity for the future

- Focus on task vs. focus on caring for people and their development

- Following the rules with a strong focus on process compliance vs. changing the rules and challenging the process

- Making sure routine work gets done vs. unleashing the creative talent and creativity of people

- Focusing on material growth (outer abundance) vs. inner development and evolution (inner abundance)

- Defining one's roles clearly and distinctly (differentiation) and harmonising across roles to work for the whole (integration)

- Hard and tough management styles focusing on the healthy bottom-line vs. kind/soft management aimed at keeping people happy

- Having a culture of change, innovation and continuous improvement vs. maintaining a sense of stability, security and order

- Getting people to follow their heart (and do what has meaning and passion for them) and still get the collective work done

- Having standard processes and norms in a system and yet valuing diversity and dissent without which there would be no progress

- Giving people freedom and autonomy which they need for fulfilment in their work and at the same time maintaining a basic modicum of control so that the system does not collapse from stupid mistakes

Going by these contradictory pulls and pressures that a leader has to deal with, one might say that their lives would be a constant struggle and a constant nightmare trying to balance between these! However, we can draw relief from the fact that all of nature is a wonderful showcase of the dance and balancing of polarities. The changing seasons, night and day, being born and dying, stiffness and flexibility, breathing in and breathing out; all demonstrate a beautiful harmony which has been working very well for millions of years. It is man's mind that creates the problem with 'either-or' thinking. Nature simply flows on as one unified whole where there is a cyclic and intimate relationship between the pairs of opposites. We find the principles of order, openness to possibility and minimum waste constantly at work in nature.

As leaders, can we learn to be one with nature? This will call for recognizing that any imbalance between two polarities (which is the same as getting stuck with one end or the other) will lead to stress and disease. In fact, disease is nothing but a system out of balance needing to restore itself back to health or wholeness.

How does a leader balance between polarities?

The body-mind is a beautiful signalling mechanism in which our feelings indicate the state we are in. Feelings of peace, freedom, joy and ease indicate that we are operating in balance. Feelings of expansion, growth flourishing and celebration indicate that we are one with the flow of life. Our most natural condition is precisely this. We are meant to live in this way.

When we are out of balance and the flow of creative intelligence is blocked, we experience feelings of stagnation, tiredness, dullness, lack of joy and contraction. A note of caution; be careful not to get stuck with one description of wholeness vs. the other. It is about acceptance and being choicelessly aware of what is happening and trusting the awareness to guide us in restoring balance.

The key to living in balance is to remain centred in this space of no-mind or awareness which is beyond all polarities (See Chapter 4 on Inner Transformation). It is to flow hand in hand with the power of life. When we are fully present in the moment, totally open to what the senses are bringing into awareness and also conscious of all the thoughts and sensations in the body-mind, we are one with life. This oneness has a built in creative intelligence which literally shows us what we need to do in each moment. In other words, the wholeness of life is both a source and a guide. It is the playful purpose for which we are here – to be one, to be healthy, to be at peace, to serve and contribute and to celebrate the fullness of life.

The Application and Benefits of Wholesome Leadership

Wholesomeness as a way of being (and seeing!) is intensely practical. It is a way of living which has implications for every aspect of our life. This is not surprising, considering that it is about the oneness of everything. As wholesome leaders living out non-duality in practice, the following are some benefits for us, our teams and organizations and the larger context in which we live and work:

Sense of Peace and Equanimity — In the midst of intense external activity, there is a sense of eternal and unshakeable calmness within. This inner zone of peace is an unchanging reference and anchor for the busy leader. While intense external activity goes on, the mind remains equanimous and undisturbed. No strong cravings and aversions disturb the Wholesome Leader. The consequence is that work that needs to be done gets done speedily without any distractions. The calmer we are the more is the amount of work we can do. As we stop reacting to things and situations, the quality and output of our work improves.

Energy and Health — Health is the free and unhindered play of life's energy. Wholesomeness is the same as health. The free play of energy naturally leads to balance and harmony. This translates into an experience of joy and peace. Being wholesome therefore is being naturally energetic and healthy. Even when the body-mind occasionally goes into states of imbalance, the clear understanding of the intrinsic spirit (which is always whole/healthy) and the ephemeral nature of the imbalance, quickly leads to a correction of the imbalance.

Enhanced Integrity — We experience an increase in integrity as we become more inner-directed and guided by our inner voice. When we clearly see the distinction between what is true and not true, it is easier to choose that which makes for wholeness and the truth. Joy, love, oneness and peace are the hallmarks of Wholesomeness. This is the supreme reference for ethical behavior. The wholesome leader spontaneously chooses all that expands these qualities.

Being Inspired and Inspiring Others — Work done from an inner space of fullness and abundance, where there is a deep sense of playfulness and joy, is intrinsically rewarding. The wholesome leader does not work for rewards in the future; he/she is not driven by any sense of deficiency or greed. He/she works for the sheer joy of it!

While such leaders do have goals and ambitions, these are actually the goals and ambitions of life as a whole. They are not driven by the need for individual benefits, glory or personal gains. When one is everything, there is no need to work for something!

Wholesome leaders see work as a means to help people grow. When we remember the unbounded potential of people and the infinite capacity that goes with it, we enable people to give their very best and grow to their fullest. When people are given the space to express what they deeply care about and feel respected and listened to, it creates a space for healing and inspired action. When we turn to each other in honest and respectful conversation, we are both healed and become instrumental in healing others. We begin to flow more in harmony with the whole.

People are infinitely creative. We have invariably been amazed and awestruck by the sheer brilliance of what people come up with after they have been given a few simple tools and the space to play with these. After many years in this field, we still feel like small children, full of wonder, when we see these emerging displays of inspired human energy.

Harmonious Relating — Wholesome leadership leads to trusting, warm and harmonious relationships with others. This leads to better learning and better team work. When one knows that the essence of everyone else is the same as one's own (since there is only one) you spontaneously treat others with respect and care. This, in turn, creates a field in which people are encouraged to be themselves. When a person is seen as a wave on the ocean of divine wholeness, one is naturally respectful and reverent. Integration across boundaries, geographies, cultures, religions, departments and roles becomes easier. Wholesomeness does not recognize any sin. The essence of human beings is eternally pure. It only recognizes error and consequences. When life is seen as a process of movement towards wholeness – infinite purity, freedom, love and power, how can we ever condemn anyone? The only difference between people is in their degree of unfoldment, not in their intrinsic nature. With this in our heart, we look on all human beings with compassion. We are easy and quick to forgive. This perspective is both healing and liberating.

Increased Creativity and Innovation — Being whole frees us from the traps of limited perceptions and paradigms. This enhances our capacity for creative living and innovation. Our creative core of awareness is unbounded. As Swami Vivekananda says "All the powers in the universe are already ours. It is we who have put our hands before our eyes and cry that it is dark. Know that there is no darkness around us."[18]

---

18) Vivekananda, Swami, *"Practical Vedanta (Part 1)"*, Lecture delivered in London, 10th November 1896, www.ramakrishnavivekananda.info/vivekananda/volume_2/practical_vedanta_and_other_lectures/practical_vedanta_part_i.htm

When one is peacefully identified with this creative space, there is an intense feeling of confidence and faith. When I see that all is transient and illusory and is made up of awareness, and that I am the source, it is easy to manifest and ordain seemingly impossible things. Intense focus, faith and persistent application of attention can manifest anything. Whatever we focus on and hold intensely in our thoughts is attracted into our lives. However, the wholesome leader has no desire to manifest anything which is not aligned with the natural flow of life.

Alignment with one's True Calling — Being true to yourself is the natural outcome of living a wholesome life. As we recognize and serve the truth, and make it our guiding principle in life, we are drawn to do the things that come naturally to us. Such work is a joy to do because it is born out of alignment with our gifts and talents. It leads to a higher quality of service and intrinsic motivation.

Living with Opposites — The ability to flex between different roles and polarities come easily to a wholesome leader. Since s/he is not identified in any way, and is also not bound by strong likes and aversions or the limitations of the role, s/he can bring the whole power of her/his being to a role. All roles are played freely and without any inhibitions. Because one is free to choose any appropriate response to situations as they arise, there is minimum waste and the highest level of productivity. Energy is constantly available from the whole and is not wasted in anything negativity connected with the past or the future. This makes the leader supremely productive and effective. Such leaders are known to produce unimaginable results from the power of aligning with the wholeness of life. They become a force of good with the mysterious and spontaneous orchestration of people and resources to their work. Their work, in any case, is the work of life itself.

Care for the Environment — More loving and compassionate behavior towards the environment emerges naturally. When we see that there is only one life that animates all creatures, plants and people on the planet, a natural affinity fills the mind. We see all aspects of creation as the different transient manifestations in a dream. When we see the same silent witnessing awareness behind all, we spontaneously treat all of creation with great respect and love. When we know the truth that the same One is manifesting as many, we feel deeply liberated. We are therefore naturally compassionate and caring towards animals, plants, the environment and the ecosphere because we see the interconnections.

Catalyzing Collective Evolution — Wholesome leaders become natural catalysts for integration of people and organizations around higher purpose and bigger goals. As people who are living their full potential, begin to connect other such people and organizations, there is an increase in the collective capacity to make a difference. This is a form of collective evolution. (Evolution is the progressive unfolding of higher capacities. It is a gradual process in which something changes into a different and usually more complex and better form.)

In conclusion, we could say that wholesomeness provides an excellent foundation for a new kind of leadership that would help us to meet the current and future challenges of business and society as a whole. As more and more people start living a wholesome or full life and start connecting, conversing and co-creating with each other, new capacities for action are born. New fields of possibility open up for manifestation. All these happen spontaneously, with little human interference. As Howard Zinn[19] has remarked, small acts of responsibility and service to the whole, when multiplied by millions of people, can transform the world.

We are fascinated by the collective potential of millions of people all doing simple things. For example, if each person planted two trees and ensured that two other people planted two trees each and in turn, followed exactly the same process, we would have over 549 Billion (549,755,813,888 to be precise) trees in just 39 moves of this process! (There were approximately 400 Billion trees on Earth in 2005, based on NASA Pictures and estimates).[20]

> *"Simple, clear purpose and principles give rise to complex intelligent behavior. Complex rules and regulations give rise to simple stupid behavior."[21]*
>
> — Dee W. Hock, Founder of VISA

To see how this dance-like self-organizing process works in nature, do a video search (on YouTube) for the *"Murmuration of Starlings"* and take a look at any of the videos. You will see a beautiful ballet performed by birds. Notice that there is no leader or orchestrator doing anything. Just a flock of birds, each one joyfully sensing and obeying the call of each moment. The result is a collective dance that emerges spontaneously from their simple intelligent individual actions.

---

19) Zinn, H. 'The optimism of uncertainty'. In Loeb, P.R.(Ed.), *"The impossible will take a little while: a citizen's guide to hope in a time of fear"*, Basic Books: New York, 2004.

20) Pennisi, Elizabeth, *"Earth home to 3 trillion trees, half as many as when human civilization arose"*, www.sciencemag.org/news/2015/09/earth-home-3-trillion-trees-half-many-when-human-civilization-arose, 2nd September 2015

21) Hock, Dee W. *"Birth of the Chaordic Age"*, Berrett-Koehler Publishers: San Francisco, 2000

Thanks to the internet and especially social media, the world will see a lot of the magic of self-organizing and emergence unfolding in the coming years.

Leaders of the future will understand this. They will recognise that a tiny seed of clear intention, sown in the fertile soil of faith and joyful action, and nourished with much appreciation and gratitude, will bear positive fruits. They will work closely with universal intelligence, responding from an inner space of humility, gratitude and acceptance. The inspired actions of many wholesome leaders all over our planet, will collectively serve the evolution of humankind. This will usher in an era of prosperity and peace for all.

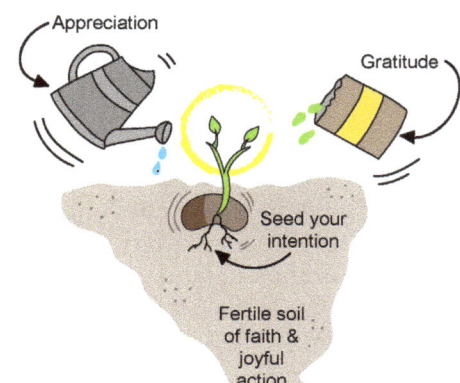

Joyful Action Now

1. On matters of values and basic principles, be honest and tough. Remember a good leader has to balance qualities of nurturance and challenge. Are there any areas you need to 'get honest' on? List them down and take the risk to do it.

2. Challenge and stretch people out of their 'rest houses' and request them to challenge yours. This implies being open to giving and receiving feedback. Challenge the assumptions and processes and always ask people "what are we doing today which will show us that our tomorrows will be better than our todays?" Set up a meeting to do this with your team.

3. The mystic poet Kabir[22] always reminds us of how close and uncertain death is. The bell can toll for us any moment! He uses this as a reminder to do what we have to do now, to not delay or postpone. For death can come any time. Carefully read these two lines by Kabir:

   "If you don't break your ropes while you're alive, do you think ghosts will do it after?"

---

22) For more on Kabir, please see https://en.wikipedia.org/wiki/Kabir

"Friend, hope for the Guest while you are alive. Jump into experience while you are alive! Think...and think... while you are alive."

4. As a person, what are the few important things in your life that you need to commit yourself to? What would you be doing today if this was the last day of your life? List these important things down. Now take a few action steps to complete the most important of the tasks you listed.

5. Read this beautiful Zen story (which I saw on Page 23, of the book *"The Corporate Mystic"* by Gay Hendricks and Kate Ludeman)[23]:

   "Master", said the student, "where do you get your spiritual power?"

   "From being connected to the source" said the Master.

   "You are connected to the source of Zen?"

   "Beyond that", said the Master, "I am Zen. The connection is complete".

   "But isn't it arrogant to claim connection with the source?" asked the student.

   "Far from it", said the Master, "It's arrogant not to claim connection with the source. Everything is connected. If you think you are not connected to the source you are thumbing your nose at the universe itself."

6. Now write non-stop for five minutes whatever comes in response to the starting sentence 'My connection to the source...'. Do not censor. Whatever comes in your mind is okay. Let go and enjoy yourself. What insights does your sharing reveal?

7. About connecting with other people in the service of life, scan around and list down who are the people/organizations 'calling you' to connect, converse and co-create? See where you experience an inner signal of 'resonance': Feelings of Lightness, Inspiration, Freedom and Enthusiasm (LIFE). Listen to your heart and follow its guidance. It speaks for the Whole in the language of feelings!

---

23) Hendricks, Gay and Ludeman, Kate, *"The Corporate Mystic: A Guidebook for Visionaries with Their Feet on the Ground"*, Bantam Boks: New York, 1996

Box 5.1

MEDITATION IS THE WAY

"Meditation is the way, which can bring a sudden flare-up in your being. And not only that, it can start a chain reaction. One flares up and suddenly people of the same type, who have not even tried meditation, who are not even seekers, who have never thought about anything spiritual, catch the infection - it is contagious.

So a few people around the Earth get the quantum leap and then thousand more will become part of a world-wide fire. And that is the only way to save whatever millions of years of evolution has brought to us."

Osho: The Transmission of the Lamp Talks in Uruguay[24]

---

24)   Osho, Rajneesh, The Transmission of the Lamp Talks in Uruguay, *"Laughter is the highest spiritual quality"*

BOX 5.2

We are the New Civilization

Flemming Funch[25], with the thought of making the whole planet better, founded the New Civilization Network. He believes in the power of weaving together the diversity of human experiences. The following is his vision:

We are here.

We are waking up now, out of the past, to dream a bigger dream.

We are friends and equals, we are diverse and unique, and we're united for something bigger than our differences.

We believe in freedom and cooperation, abundance and harmony.

We are a culture emerging, a renaissance of the essence of humanity.

We find our own guidance, and we discern our own truth.

We go in many directions, and yet we refuse to disperse.

We have many names, we speak many languages.

We are local, we are global.

We are in all regions of the world, we're everywhere in the air.

We are universe being aware of itself, we are the wave of evolution.

We are in every child's eyes; we face the unknown with wonder and excitement.

We are messengers from the future, living in the present.

We come from silence, and we speak our truth.

We cannot be quieted, because our voice is within everyone.

We have no enemies, no boundaries can hold us.

We respect the cycles and expressions of nature, because we are nature.

We don't play to win, we play to live and learn.

We act out of inspiration, love and integrity.

We explore, we discover, we feel, and we laugh.

We are building a world that works for everyone.

We endeavor to live our lives to their fullest potential.

We are independent, self-sufficient and responsible.

We relate to each other in peace, with compassion and respect, we unite in community.

We celebrate the wholeness within and around us all.

We dance to the rhythm of creation.

We weave the threads of the new times.

We are the new civilization.

---

25) Read this interesting interview with Flemming Funch at www.newciv.org/c4c/funch.html

BOX 5.3

OPEN SPACE TECHNOLOGY (OST): AN OVERVIEW[26]

What Is Open Space?

It is a self-organizing practice of inner discipline and collective activity which releases the inherent creativity and leadership in people. By inviting people to take responsibility for what they care about, Open Space establishes a marketplace of inquiry, reflection and learning, bringing out the best in both individuals and the whole.

When To Use It:

*   Where conflict is holding back the ability to change
*   Where the situation is complex
*   Where there is a high degree of diversity
*   Where there is an urgent need to make speedy decisions
*   Where all stakeholders are needed for good decisions to be made
*   Where you have no preconceived notion of what the outcomes should be

Action plans and recommendations emerge from discussions as appropriate. You create a record of the entire proceedings as you go along.

Four principles apply to how you navigate in open space:

*   Whoever comes is the right person: Whoever is attracted to the same conversation are the people who can contribute most to that conversation – because they care. So they are exactly the ones – for the whole group – who are capable of initiating action.

*   Whatever happens is the only thing that could've: We are all limited by our own pasts and expectations. This principle acknowledges we'll all do our best to focus on NOW-the present time and place – and not get bogged down in what could've or should've happened.

*   When it starts is the right time: The creative spirit has its own time, and our task is to make our best contribution and enter the flow of creativity when it starts.

*   When it's over, it's over: Creativity has its own rhythm. So do groups. Just a reminder to pay attention to the flow of creativity – not the clock. When you think it is over, ask: Is it over? And if it is, go on to the next thing you have passion for. If it's not, make plans for continuing the conversation.

---

26) For more information on *"Open Space Technology (OST)"* please see www.openspaceworld.org

BOX 5.4

APPRECIATIVE INQUIRY (AI): AN OVERVIEW[27]

What Is It?

A powerful approach that invites people to learn through their personal stories of accomplishment and aspirations. Used by individuals, organizations and communities, it begins with an affirmative interview to identify the best of "what is" in order to pursue dreams and possibilities of "what could be."

Probable Outcomes

Fundamental shift toward cooperation, equality of voice, high participation, inquiry and improvisational learning as daily practices.

Group Size

20 – 2000 involved in interviews, large scale meetings and collaborative actions.

Typical Duration

3 hours to 4 days. The longer it runs the more embedded into daily practice it becomes.

The Steps In Brief

- Select a focus area or topic(s) of interest.
- Design an interview to discover strengths, passions, unique attributes.
- Example questions:
- Describe a peak experience or "high point" in your work. What was happening? Who was involved? What made it such a powerful experience?
- What do you most value about... yourself? Your work? Your organization/school?
- What core factors give life to your organization/school?
- What three wishes do you have to enhance the health and vitality of your organization/school?
- Identify patterns, themes and/or intriguing possibilities in the interviews.
- Create bold statements of ideal possibilities ("Provocative Propositions").
- Co-determine 'what should be' (consensus re: principles & priorities).
- Take action.

---

27) For More Informat on on Appreciative Inquiry (AI), please visit the "*Appreciative Inquiry Commons*": http://appreciativeinquiry.cwru.edu

PART 3

Love in Action

CHAPTER 6

Seeing and Being Whole: Unfolding an Era of Ethics and Peace

"World peace must develop from inner peace. Peace is not just mere absence of violence. Peace is, I think, the manifestation of human compassion."

— Dalai Lama XIV

"Life is one whole. Existence is a dance of millions of interdependent processes working in harmony and guided by the Great Unifier (you can call Awareness and Creative Intelligence by whatever name you like) When we are one with its flow and are collaborating with this dance of unity, we are at peace. There is joy in our hearts. When we are out of touch with this dance, we are not at ease. There is no peace in us. Remembering our Wholeness is the foundation for restoration of values"

— Arun Wakhlu

A world that we will be proud to hand over to our children and grand-children will be a world of ethical behavior and peace. It will be a world in which people act caringly towards themselves, other people and our environment. It will be a world governed by love and deep compassion.

Ethics, peace and wholeness are all a part of a unified triad. As with many things in this book, we have attempted to show the connections between these apparently disparate dimensions. An integrating model is shared. With real life examples and stories, we would share how one can contribute to a more peaceful and ethical world.

The Common Core of Ethics and Peace

Ethics can be defined as value-based standards of right and wrong that prescribe what humans ought to do, usually in terms of rights, obligations, and specific virtues.

It is about a code of moral standards of conduct for what is 'good' and 'right' as opposed to what is 'bad' or 'wrong'. Ethical behavior is that which is 'right' or 'good' in the context of a governing moral code. Ethics and ethical behavior are driven by values.

If there was no one else on Earth, we would not need any codes of ethics. This is because ethics is about the quality of relationships that we have. When we are in touch with and caring towards ourselves, others and the environment, we are behaving ethically.

Peace is a state of dynamic balance and ease. While many of us think of it as an absence of conflict, disorder, confusion and disease, a more positive definition of peace is that which encompasses and goes beyond all pairs of opposites. Dr. Harrison Owen, the originator of Open Space Technology (see Box 5.3 at the end of Chapter 5), defines peace this way: "Peace is the dynamic interrelationship of complex forces productive of wholeness, health and harmony. The practice of peace is the intentional creation of the requisite conditions under which peace may occur."[1]

There can never be any conflict or confusion if there is unity or wholeness. When we are in touch with the joyous and peaceful wholeness of life, we are naturally peaceful. Not only do we feel peaceful, we are also one with the resourcefulness and creativity of life. When our thoughts, words and actions arise from this space of peace, they will be pure and unselfish. This inner feeling of peace and wholeness generates ethical actions.

Let's take an example: If we say that the factual truth about something is X, and I say it is X, I am telling the truth…I am congruent and whole. When I say that it is Y, when actually it is X, there is a split. The false thing (Y) that I say and the truth in my mind (X) are different. I am no longer whole and so not at peace!

Swami Vivekananda[2] says that "Ethics is anything that makes for oneness and what makes for separation is unethical". If I attack someone (an

---

1) Owen, Harrison, *"The Practice of Peace"*, Human System Dynamics Institute: Circle Pines, Minnesota, 2004. You can also read this book at www.openspaceworld.com/final%20pop%20hdsi.pdf

2) Vedatitananda, Swami, *"Morality & Ethics - according to Swami Vivekananda"*, www.academia.edu/11196613/Morality_and_Ethics_-_according_to_Swami_Vivekananda

"other" person), and cause him pain, I am not whole. There is "Me" and there is the "other". I am the cause of suffering for both, the other and me. If I realize this, then I stop causing suffering to others.

Our actions will be ethical if we are in touch with the 'Wholeness of Life'. This means being present in the now, and obeying the promptings of Life's natural flow of joy, peace and abundance.

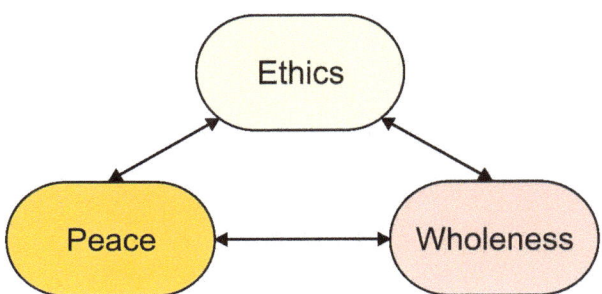

All unethical behavior in human beings emerges from unawareness: A loss of connection with life. Ethical action, as we see it, is the action which is good for all (including the environment) both in the short and the long run. 'Good' is that which is conducive to health, happiness, peace, abundance, equity and balance for all people and all aspects of the environment.

For people who are not aware, acting ethically is fraught with inherent challenges.

- The connections between causes and consequences of actions are not always clear; they are often separated in space

- Sometimes a cause may have a delayed consequence. This also makes it hard to link up due to the separation in time

- We are sometimes out of touch with our feelings. Feelings act like internal physical and emotional indicators of whether an action is ethical or not.

All three difficulties stem from a lack of awareness and integration – a lack of being 'in touch' with the whole picture now. Incidentally, the word 'integration' comes from the Latin root *in tangere*, which means 'to be in touch'. The words *integer* and *integrity* both have the same root. When we are disconnected from things, and are not 'seeing' correctly, truthfully or completely, unethical actions arise. This lack of 'seeing' things wholesomely comes from having a partial notion of who I am. A sense of deficiency and lack of abundance also originates from being identified with a partial or limited notion of who I am.

Swami Vivekananda alluded to this when he wrote: "Our Upanishads say that the cause of all misery is ignorance; and that is perfectly true when applied to every state of life, either social or spiritual. It is ignorance that makes us hate each other, it is through ignorance that we do not know and do not love each other. As soon as we come to know each other, love comes, must come, for are we not one?"[3]

This illusion or ignorance of our true self is the root cause. We are whole and complete beyond all limitations. An infinite creative intelligence orchestrates entire life in a most magnificent and glorious fashion. This happens without the slightest human intervention, whatsoever.

The Source of Peace in all areas is the Peace within

"Nothing can bring you lasting peace… You have it already, if you stop disturbing it you will see that it is there always."

— Swami Sachitananda

This body-mind called "Omkar Wakhlu" is not who I am. This body-mind consists of water and food, some memories and dreams. It is made up of atoms, protons, electrons and neutrons. These owe their existence to mysterious entities called Quarks, held together by Gluons. All these dance together in a vast sea of open space, gorgeously peaceful, free and empty open space. This mysterious essence is who I am. It is the most open space there is. People have called it by different names: Spirit, *Allah*, *Brahman*, the Mystery, *Tao*, Being, *Sat-Chit-Ananda*, Buddha Nature, Awareness, Suchness and the Peace that Passes Understanding. This I am is one. It is none other than your own essence, now. For there is only one center, only one silence, only one peace, one energetic field called life.

So who is writing all this? In the light of the above, can we say that it is life who is writing all this? Through the movement of all these particles (which are really quanta of vibrating energy), it is life which dances forth expressing itself spontaneously.

As one witnesses this unfolding drama, from this empty (and incredibly full) space of awareness and peace, all seems like a playful dance – a creative play of learning. Forms and actions emerge from and dissolve back into this peaceful ocean of life.

If I am totally at peace within, I am at peace with my fellow human beings and the natural environment. I am whole. I am complete. I am integrated. When there is peace and silence in body-mind, relationships,

---

3) Vivekananda, Swami, *"The Complete Works of Swami Vivekananda, Vol 3"*, Advaita Ashrama 12th Edition: Kolkata, 2014

animals, plants, I am in a space of wholeness. I am I. There is no other.

When we understand that we are the peace that passes understanding and that we are a mystery that integrates and holds the opposites in life, then we 'become peace.'

This means that any notion of a separate and changing 'self' is witnessed by a silent emptiness we call 'peace'. In this mysterious space, there is no doer. You watch your body and mind go around walking, talking, and eating. You know that this is not who you really are. In this field of silence and peace, there is an intimate connection to everyone and everything. There is immense love and compassion. This is not directed at 'someone' and not for 'something'. It is what your unbounded essence is. You are love. You are wholeness.

Thoughts, words and actions that emerge from this mysterious space inspire others to return home to wholeness as well. They are catalytic, medicinal, and facilitative in bringing people to remember that they too are whole. These words don't do anything miraculous. They simply remind people of who they are. Waves of ethical and peaceful behavior thus ripple outwards. We need now, more than at any other time, to spread these ripples of ethical behavior.

> If there has to be peace on the Earth, it has to start with me. How can an expansion of peace and ethical behavior begin with me?

In a global gathering for One Wholesome World (held in Caux, Switzerland from 17 to 23 July 2012)[4], one thing that became crystal clear to many of us in the gathering was that change has to begin with me. Even when we are initiating collective action of any kind, our own purity of intent and integrity are important in ensuring success.

While writing this book, the thought did occur sometimes that this book may be more about our own purification and learning rather than about changing the world. In any case, there is no such thing as a 'world out there'. Each person's objective experience of the world is different. As we write these words peacefully in the comfort of our homes in Pune and Srinagar, Kashmir, there are zones on the Earth like Ukraine, Nigeria, Iraq and Syria where people are experiencing unimaginable suffering due to divisive strife and war. All this is happening simultaneously in this now.

Our own inner state projects a 'reality' outside that perfectly matches this inner state. This is like a radio receiver which, when tuned to the frequency of BBC, will attract only BBC and not Radio Moscow. A friend named Marilyn Overcast[5] shared the following with me a few months before the gathering in Switzerland: "When you are healed, Wholeness

---

4) Read more about this gathering organized by the Authors at
   www.onewholesomeworld.wordpress.com/2012/07/29/global-gathering-on-one-wholesome-world/
5) To know more about the work of Marilyn Overcast, please visit www.fluentsource.org

will be revealed". We do not need to 'do' anything really. Just see with new eyes and with pure awareness.

If you look around at life at her pristine and most natural best, you cannot help but marvel at her innate intelligence and wisdom. Wellbeing abounds! The Earth and all her creatures are already wholesome, ethical and peaceful. Life is magnificent, miraculous and perfect as it is. It is our own vision, perception, feelings and actions that are disconnected from the peaceful and ethical flow of life. It is these that need healing.

One person at the gathering in Switzerland who kept emphasizing this point was Sister Ajahn Bodhipala, a Buddhist Nun from the Amravati Forest Sangha in Hertfordshire, England[6]. She said that we all need to work on purifying the mind, thereby, bringing out more compassion in our actions before we co-create One Wholesome World.

When we closed our gathering with our commitments for action on Post-Its, Sister Ajahn Bodhipala held up a blank Post-It before the group. She said, she was committing herself to 'No Commitment', to the pure and sublime freedom and peace of the Buddha within all of us. She asked, whether by committing herself to cultivating the wholeness/love and compassion that is at the heart of all life, would she not be making a difference to the world?

Her example touched many of us, who had gathered. I later came across this quote from Jaluluddin Rumi[7]: "Yesterday I was clever; I wanted to change the world. Today I am wise and I want to change myself".

Another sage, Lao Tzu[8], said in the same vein: "Would you like to liberate yourself from the lower realms of life? Would you like to save the world from the degradation and destruction it seems destined for? Then step away from shallow mass movements and quietly go to work on your own self-awareness. If you want to awaken all of humanity, then awaken all of yourself. If you want to eliminate the suffering in the world, then eliminate all that is dark and negative in yourself. Truly, the greatest gift you have to give is that of your own self-transformation."

Reclaiming our oneness with the peace and compassion within has a profoundly positive impact on how we relate with other people. We become the source of more joy and harmony in our interactions.

---

6) Learn more about the Amravati Forest Sangha in England at www.amaravati.org
7) Rumi, Jallauddin, *"Quotes About Cleverness"*, www.goodreads.com/quotes/tag/cleverness
8) Walker, Brain Browne (Translator), Hua Hu Ching, www.brianbrownewalker.com/hua-hu-ching. This quote is based on the teachings of Lao Tzu. It is Verse No. 75 from the above book which was actually written some 500 years after Lao Tzu lived by Taoist Wang Fou, ca. 300 CE.

Peace with others and in a Community ... the Importance of Listening

"Only the development of compassion and understanding for others can bring us the tranquility and happiness we all seek."

— Dalai Lama XIV

War and strife are not initiated by a large part of the population. In India and Pakistan, less than 4 percent of the population is indulging in war. The reason why they outnumber the rest of the 96 percent – the mothers, children, youth, sane and conscious people, is that the rest of the population is passive. They are not doing anything about it. It is most harmful to know and yet be indifferent to action. Our inner voice and feelings of joy can guide our actions.

Life speaks to us in the language of feelings. To understand our emotions and see that we are the creators of these emotions is one aspect of Emotional Intelligence(EI)[9]. How to sense and appropriately respond to other peoples' feelings is the other aspect of Emotional Intelligence.

Now here is a big idea to bridge the connection. If our feelings of ease, grace and joy tell us that we are in touch with life in this very moment and that we are ethical (i.e. one with the wholeness of life), then Emotional Intelligence becomes the main skill needed to steer through things ethically, moment to moment, and to keep our responses aligned with life. To summarize:

- Our sense of wholeness is based on being present in this moment

- Being present is accompanied by feelings of ease, joy, peace and energy

- Ethical responses are born out of wholeness

- Emotional Intelligence is a tool that can be used to see our own and others' feelings and do what it takes to be aligned/whole; The foundation of this is awareness.

---

9) Goleman, Daniel, "*Emotional Intelligence*", Bantam Books: New York, 1995

Nonviolent Communication (NVC)[10]

> *When our communication supports compassionate giving and receiving, happiness replaces violence and grieving!*
>
> — CNVC founder, Marshall B. Rosenberg, PhD

The purity of heart, in the sense that you are in your natural state of compassion, is nonviolence. Nonviolent Communication is based on this principle. We have seen earlier also, that we are all made from the same energy and hence share the same needs. All our actions are born out of the desire to satiate these needs and our behavior is shaped as we try to fulfill these needs. Each person's natural state of wholeness is peaceful and quiet. The violence that is acquired is because of nurture, not because of nature. While this is not new, people need to be reminded to practice it in their lives. You feel so good when you connect to another person and are able to share some things with them. Each relationship becomes a unique bond and is cherished and treasured deeply. It always makes a person happy to make a new friend. In fact, many problems of judgments and ego dissolve when we make more friends and get over our loneliness.

By active listening we can develop empathy for others and discover our own compassion and grace. This reveals the awareness that all human beings are only trying to honor universal values and needs, every minute, every day. NVC can be seen as:

- a spiritual practice that helps us see our common humanity using our power in a way that honors everyone's needs, and

- a concrete set of skills which helps us create life-serving families and communities.

This form of communication is simple, yet powerfully transformative. We can empathetically listen and honestly express our observations, feelings, needs and requests. The underlying concept is that the approach to communication should emphasize compassion as the motivation for action rather than fear, guilt, shame, blame, coercion, threat or justification for punishment. In other words, it is about getting what you want for reasons you will not regret later. NVC is not about getting people to do what we want. It is about creating a quality of connection that gets everyone's needs fulfilled through compassionate giving.

When being in touch with our wholeness, our thoughts, actions and words are joyful and sensitive. We can understand others better and explain ourselves easily, without having to raise our voice. Our intimate personal

---

10) Read about Nonviolent Communication (NVC), also known as Compassionate Communication or Collaborative Communication at: https://en.wikipedia.org/wiki/Nonviolent_Communication

relations become stronger and even our other relations – to the county, rulers, priests, groups and institutions become clearer. There is utmost joy when communication is smooth and correctly interpreted.

At the center of Nonviolent Communication[11] is an initiative that aims to see a world in which everyone values everyone's basic human needs and lives from a consciousness that connects with the universal life energy and natural oneness of life.

We can have communities of compassion where each one helps the other to resolve conflict and meet the unmet needs. The method for this process is peaceful and accommodating. One does not need to have high level of communication skills or any other form of education as such. This kind of communication based on compassion and genuine respect and love for one another might take time to happen and might even happen irregularly. But, if we continue to work from this inner space, we will be able to master it, and spread it to other people as well. An outstanding example of deep empathy in action and also authentic self-expression was the life of Peace Pilgrim[12].

Peace Circles/Peace Pilgrims actions for Peace in the world

Peace Pilgrim (1908-1981), as she called herself, walked 25000 miles to spread her message of peace which was: 'Overcome evil with good, falsehood with truth and hatred with love'. The belief is that the message of peace can be spread to one and all, through mere word of mouth. The peace in our lives is a reflection of our own maturity or immaturity. It is we who can make this world harmonious and loving. There are several steps that one needs to take in order to achieve the balance between inner and outer peace. A person may go through these in any order, at varying points in their lives, until they realize that their life is in giving. Once a person reaches that step, and feels oneness with all life, there is no looking back. For this, we need to have the right attitude towards life, find our place in the life pattern, live with good beliefs and simplify life to harmonize inner and outer well-being. By being honest and embracing the reality, even if it is rife with problems and situations that seem difficult to face, we can be happier and more balanced. While many people may believe in ideal practices and have the right approaches, like we have seen above, the kind of people who know and yet who don't act are the most harmful of the lot. It is absolutely essential, that we practice what we believe in and what we know is right. In the deep silence of our beings, we can understand where we fit in the larger scheme of things.

---

11) You can also visit the website of the Center for Nonviolent Communication at www.cnvc.org

12) Peace Pilgrims Home Page is www.peacepilgrim.org. The Authors have been deeply touched by her message and also the Story of Her life: *"Peace Pilgrim: Her Life and Work in Her Own Words"*. You can download a free copy in pdf format here: www.peacepilgrim.org/book/ppbook.pdf

On days when you feel lost about your purpose in life, take time to listen to your inner voice. Sit quietly for some time. In the inner space of peace and joy, your place in the larger pattern of life will be revealed. How many of us burden ourselves because we try so hard to fit into a particular clan of people? We have innumerable, useless possessions and we clutter our minds, as well as our homes, with rubbish. When we are in touch with our wholeness, our wants and needs become the same. We will be surprised to see how little we need as opposed to how much we are always yearning for. This harmony between our needs and wants will make us peaceful and content people. Even collectively, we will be impactful and resources will be more optimally utilized and universally spread.

But all this cannot happen without purifying the toxins that are in your body (because of ill habits) or in your mind (because of polluting thoughts).

Our actions are a reflection of our thoughts. Sometimes, though we do the right thing, our minds are plagued with negative thoughts and motives. We think of our own benefit in everything and sometimes think unkindly of others. The imbalance that this causes reflects on our bodies physically as well as mentally. By changing their business motive to earnest service of their customers, many people have seen success in businesses.

Peace Pilgrim tells us to relinquish self-will, feelings of separateness, attachments and negativity. At the base of it all, we are all made from the same energy and hence must let go of any feelings of separation that we feel with one another. The attraction and dependence on materialistic things should dissolve. Not only objects, even the wanting to possess people and run their lives, should be relinquished. Only then can harmony be maintained and inner peace established.

Peace and Ethics towards the Environment

"The most violent weapon on Earth is the table fork."

— Mahatma Gandhi

"Because we all share this planet Earth, we have to learn to live in harmony and peace with each other and with nature. This is not just a dream, but a necessity."

— Dalai Lama XIV

"Spiritual progress," said Gandhi, "demands from us at a certain point that we stop killing our fellow living beings"[13]. Schweitzer, St. Francis, Jesus, Einstein, Tolstoy, Rachel Carson, and many others have taught us that nonviolence toward all sacred life must be our aim. The universal spiritual ideal to 'love one another' requires us to embrace all beings, not just people, in our circle of compassion. As our faith grows, so does our desire to live by our highest ideals. When we stop eating animal products, we are no longer eating violence, and our hearts and souls can at last be at peace.

It is not enough to talk about peace. We have to eat peace. Food has to come out of eating mindfully and peacefully. We describe health as peace with the body and environment and peace as the health of the body and environment. Peace is health and health is peace. Environmental ethics will be important to identify, clarify and emphasize the moral values that need to be promoted in relationships with the environment.

Our attitudes, beliefs and behavior are affected greatly by the food we eat. In fact, the food of the community can reflect its culture as the food that we consume will shape our physical, social, spiritual and psychological environment. Will Tuttle has written about the World Peace Diet[14], a diet for spiritual health and social harmony. He says that the food we consume is the most intimate connection between the natural order and with our living cultural heritage. The very obvious source of the stress, complications and dilemmas that we face in our life today is the food we eat. The violence that we commit for our plates to satisfy our palates comes out in our behavior in various ways. When we kill animals for food, we are going away from the natural compassion that we as people of Earth have. This results into wars, materialism and disconnectedness, taking away our inner and outer peace.

Our food becomes us. What we consume becomes our body. Which other relation is more intimate and sacred than that? And each thing that we consume comes from so many more overwhelming processes of nature. The clouds, the trees, the rain, the soil and the breaths of animals – they have all gone into making the food that we eat. Thus, it is food that is the most sacred connection we share with the infinite. It is a manifestation of the entire web of life. It is a form of love that our environment feels for us.

Animals have a nervous system to protect them from predators and also from self-damaging behaviors. When we eat them, we eat the actual organs of the animals. As Dr. Will Tuttle says in his book "Our meals require us to eat like predators and thus to see ourselves as such, cultivating and justifying predatory behaviors and institutions that are the antithesis of the inclusiveness and kindness that accompany spiritual growth."

---

13) Gandhi, Mohandas Karamchand, quoted in "*The Hidden Love of Jesus For The Animals*", www.donoteatus.crg/Hidden_Love_of_Jesus_For_The_Animals_Layout.htm
14) Tuttle, Will, "*World Peace Diet: Eating for Spiritual Health and Social Harmony*", Lantern Books, US: New York, 2005. Also see www.worldpeacediet.org

Besides the ethical and aesthetic aspects of a plant based diet, there is also a strong connection between dietary patterns and global warming.

In an article of the UNEP Global Environmental Alert Service (GEAS)[15] dated October 2012, growing greenhouse gases were attributed partly to increases in the production of meat. Quoting a study by Steinfeld et al. (2006)[16] it states that "The true costs of industrial agriculture, and specifically 'cheap meat', have become more and more evident. Today, 'the livestock sector' emerges as one of the top two or three most significant contributors to the most serious environmental problems".

Animal agriculture causes many stressors to the Earth – desertification, deforestation, pollution, overuse of water, using grain to feed animals instead of hungry people and greenhouse gas emissions.

The good news is that creative mitigating efforts like Meatless Monday[17] and an interest in Vegan diets is on the rise. As people expand their understanding of cause and effect, as empathy and compassion for all living beings grow, outer patterns of behavior (including what we eat) will change. Collective action makes this change easier.

Peace Circles

"World peace must develop from inner peace. Peace is not just mere absence of violence. Peace is, I think, the manifestation of human compassion."

— Dalai Lama XIV

We need to come together and help each other to understand and reflect upon the message and method of peace. By sitting and reading paragraphs, discussing what they mean, taking the essence of their meaning and developing an action plan through action oriented goals, can be the aim of small peace groups. This will not only get like-minded people together in one area but it will get people together globally. These peace groups will also be able to share their learnings and action plans of their respective areas with others. We will be able to share best practices.

Instead of depending on the government and other official bodies for maintaining peace and order in society, we ourselves need to be harbingers of peace. We can understand how to resolve internal conflict, avoid physical violence, and reduce fear and hatred. Initiatives like a Peace Week or a

---

15) UNEP Global Environmental Alert Service (GEAS), "*Growing Greenhouse Gas Emissions due to Meat Production*", October 2012. http://na.unep.net/geas/getuneppagewitharticleidscript.php?article_id=92

16) Steinfeld, H., Gerber, P., Wassenaar, T., Castel, V., Rosales, M. and de Haan, C., "*Livestock's long shadow: Environmental issues and options*", Food and Agriculture Organization of the United Nations (FAO): Rome, Italy, 2006

17) www.meatlessmonday.com

Peace Day, even a Peace Fair can be organized to spread the message, so more willing people come together and create a silent, determined movement to change the ways of the world.

Joyful Action Now

1. Coming Home to Peace as your Self:

   Come home to the simple understanding that you are an infinite space of love, awareness and peace. From this sky like standpoint of awareness, look at all the things that the limited 'you' would have done in the past that you hold on to (either with positive or negative feelings associated with them). One by one say for each of these 'events':

   - "From the space of infinite love, awareness and peace that I am, I deeply and completely forgive all these things that I have held on to. I completely and totally love, accept and forgive whatever has happened. I am at home now. I am free."

   - Whenever you look up at the sky, remind yourself "I Am the infinite sky of peace. Everything is like a cloud. This too shall pass."

   - Listen to your body. Pay loving attention to each part. Feel into what needs to be done to bring back balance and peace to different parts of your body. Listen with an open and receptive presence. The body--mind will know what is needed. Let it unfold naturally and peacefully.

2. Peace with Others:

   - Sit still and listen to the peace that you are. Scan all your relationships and see if there are some that need to be restored to peace, harmony and balance. Look beyond the changing cloud like forms of the 'other' and recognize that the same sky of peace that you are is the essence of the 'other' too. Listening to the heart will guide you on what you need to do to bring the relationship back to harmony and balance. It may take the form of an apology, forgiveness, listening to the other and sharing ones perspectives in a peaceful and truthful way. For every conflict, make peace your aim. Remember that you both ARE already peace at your core!

- See if you want to start a Peace Circle[18] in your neighborhood, family or at work.

- Find some cause to donate money, knowledge or effort to. There is nothing like heartfelt giving to bring you back home to balance and peace.

3. Peace with All Animals and also the Environment:

   - The co-creation of One Wholesome World begins with me. Food is an important aspect of our lives. Check out where your food comes from:[19] the more local, and seasonal, the better!

   - See what choices you can make to buy and eat local food.

   - Choosing vegetarian or vegan food can further add to your health and also to the well-being of the planet.

18) You can download a simple guide from: www.peacepower.info/modules/PeaceCircles.pdf
19) www.foodmiles.com

Box 6.1

A Sufi Story "Peace Begins With Me"

An old man sat motionless on his death bed. He knew that his "time" had come. He wanted to share a few words of wisdom with his son. Gathering his last bit of strength, he slowly whispered to his son "Son when I was a young man, I set out on a mission to change the world. As time passed I found that the world with all of its problems was too big for one man to change. So I decided to change our country. As time passed I could not change our country with all of its problems. I changed my focus again and decided to change our city, but the problems of our city were too much for one man to handle. So I decided to just try and change my family and home. Son, as you know there are too many problems in our family and home for me to solve!

Now as I lie on my death bed, I have come to realize that if I would have just set out to change myself that would have changed our family, which would have had an effect on our neighborhood. The change in our neighborhood would have had an effect on our city. This would have had an effect on our country. Changing our country would have brought forth a change in the world."

With these final words, the old man took his final breath, closed his eyes, never to open them again. In the Holy Quran Allah has said "Allah does not change the condition of people until they first change that which is within them."

Box 6.2

Love all God's creation[20]

"Love all God's creation, both the whole and every grain of sand. Love every leaf, every ray of light. Love the animals, love the plants, and love each separate thing. If thou love each thing thou wilt perceive the mystery of God in all; and when once thou perceive this, thou wilt thenceforward grow every day to a fuller understanding of it: until thou come at last to love the whole world with a love that will then be all-embracing and universal."

— Fyodor Dostoyevsky

20) Dostoyevsky, Fyodor, Pevear, Richard (Translator), Volokhonsky, Larissa (Translator), "*The Brothers Karamazov*", Farrar, Straus and Giroux:New York, 2002

BOX 6.3

BRIEF REPORT ON THE USE OF OPEN SPACE TECHNOLOGY FOR TWO PEACE CONFERENCES

"Every time Space opens; Peace seems to break out. And the application is not only in the global arena of conflicted people, but also in the multiple arenas of human life were Peace appears in jeopardy, including families, community organizations, and businesses."

Dr. Harrison Owen[21]

This brief note describes the use of Open Space Technology(OST) for two related conferences held at Asia Plateau, Panchgani (the international conference centre of Initiatives of Change in Western India). The two conferences were:

1. Indo - Pakistan People to People Dialogue for Peace and Prosperity, Date: 5th – 8th August 2001 | No. of Participants: 70

2. All J&K People to People Dialogue for Peace and Prosperity, Date: 12th - 15th February 2002 | No. of Participants: 62

Indo – Pakistan People to People Dialogue for Peace and Prosperity

A group of people, led by the Pragati Foundation[22] in Pune, India, and the Foundation for Human and Economic Development[23], USA, had a very inspiring and energizing Indo-Pak Dialogue at Panchgani in the summer of 2001 (8th -11th August 2001). One of the resolutions adopted at Panchgani was that another dialogue should be held, in which the people of undivided J & K could share their authentic heritage and voice their true collective aspirations. The next conference was aimed at accomplishing the above objective.

All J&K People to People Dialogue for Peace and Prosperity

This dialogue and reconnection, gave the participants a chance to reconnect with the underlying values that forge the spirit of Jammu and Kashmir. These draw from the human principles of love, brotherhood and the oneness of all humankind. It was also felt that a solution to the problem of poor Indo-Pak relations, and to the Kashmir issue, can be found within these values. Open Space Technology (OST) was used in both these conferences.

Here's why I think OST helped so much:

One of the needs in the Indian sub-continent, and Jammu & Kashmir in particular, is for people to take responsibility for co-creating a shared future. Open

---

21) Notes on the book "*The Practice of Peace*" (2nd Edition),
     www.openspaceworld.com/intro%20to%20pop.htm
22) Pragati Foundation (PF) Pune, India is the Not For Profit arm of the Pragati Leadership Institute.
     www.pragatifoundation.org
23) Foundation for Human and Economic Development, FHED, Florida, USA

Space Technology (OST) gave people an experiential feel of the process of co-creation.

The process of opening space opened peoples' hearts. In both the conferences participants commented on how the open, loving atmosphere created in the conference was helpful in healing and re-conciliation.

The process of OST and the focus on listening to each other with respect, and honouring all voices gave many an opportunity to voice their feelings freely. This was an affirmation of the basic human right of free expression.

There were many moments when people paused in silence to listen to the heart/spirit/inner guidance. This brought in a sacred dimension into the proceedings. Since silence is neither Hindu nor Muslim nor Buddhist, it was wholeheartedly accepted by all.

In both the conferences, there was a lot of sharing of the practical household work at the conference centre (Dish washing, serving food, cleaning up, laying the tables etc.). When you do such things with people whom you considered as foes, one strongly realizes the basic commonality of life and human needs. This was a powerful means of connecting us back to our intrinsic humanness.

Because of the unbounded field of human expression that OST provides for, many creative expressions like skits, songs, dances, celebrations, humour and meditation were held. These helped to bring people into the space of feelings/heart and thereby helped integration. This was further reinforced by the cultural programs that were part of both conferences in the evenings.

The beauty of the physical environment (Asia Plateau, Panchagani, the international conference centre of Initiatives of Change in Western India), the proximity to a lush green forest, and the view of mountains, a lake and open sky, connected people to the elements. This further created a sense of wholeness and integration.

Standing up authentically for what one deeply cared about (The "Law of Two Feet" in Open Space Technology) paying attention, being present, and showing up all brought people into integrity. This is the same as reconnection with spirit. Ultimately, it is spirit that heals, reunites, inspires and gives faith and courage for creative action.

Many positive initiatives have rippled out of these two conferences. With more such conversations and inspired actions, the ripples of loving action and responsibility will reach out still further.

Peace and prosperity are not hard to achieve if we create the spaces for people to take responsibility for what they truly care about. When people express freely from their heart, and co-create with others bringing their gifts forward, heaven on earth is not too far.

CHAPTER 7

Education for a Wholesome World

Education either functions as an instrument which is used to facilitate integration of the younger generation into the logic of the present system and bring about conformity or it becomes the practice of freedom, the means by which men and women deal critically and creatively with reality and discover how to participate in the transformation of their world."

— Paulo Freire[1]

Education is that which Liberates

"Sa Vidya, ya Vimuktaye" – True knowledge is that which liberates. Knowledge which is merely the accumulation of information, binds and limits us. True Knowledge begins with an insight into the self, a refinement and deepening of awareness, and a spontaneous flowering of compassion. The deeper purpose of education is to liberate us from bondage of all kinds: Bondage with our kin, our society; and from bondage of attachments created by our 'ego'.

True Education can be seen as an expansion and unfolding of our innate freedom – the freedom to act intelligently and appropriately in a given situation, the freedom to respond to life's challenges in the most

---

1) Freire, Paulo, Ramos, Myra Bergman(Tr.), *"Pedagogy of the Oppressed"*, Bloomsbury Academic: New York, 2000

life affirming and wholesome way. It is the freedom to see the truth as it is, without distortion, free of our own and others conditioning. It is about reaching out to the freedom of love beyond the narrow divisions of religion, nationality, color or class. Ultimately, it is about the freedom of one's own being – the blissfulness of being nobody and yet being connected to all. In this way it is about celebrating each moment of life as a creative play, in deep gratitude for everything.

Our life is governed by the beliefs and mindsets that have been instilled in us in our formative years. These have shaped our perceptions and experiences. As we saw above, true education liberates us from these prisons of conditioning. It not only looks at the content of what goes into the mind, but also sensitizes us to the context - especially the larger context of who I am and why I am here.

To reclaim our freedom, we will need to drop our masks and come out of our rigid pattern of thinking. This will give us the freedom to fully feel what we are feeling, to be in our senses and act creatively.

The time to be creative and useful is here and just now. One need not be caught up in the prison walls of our mind we have allowed to be erected around us by wrong perceptions. As young children, we all are naturally creative, using up to 80% of our creative capacities. As adults we allow this to drop down to a mere 2%. This happens because our attention is caught in habitual tracks. This inhibits learning. New thoughts, new feelings and actions leading to new experience make up the cycle of learning. When this cycle is repeated several times, new habits are formed.

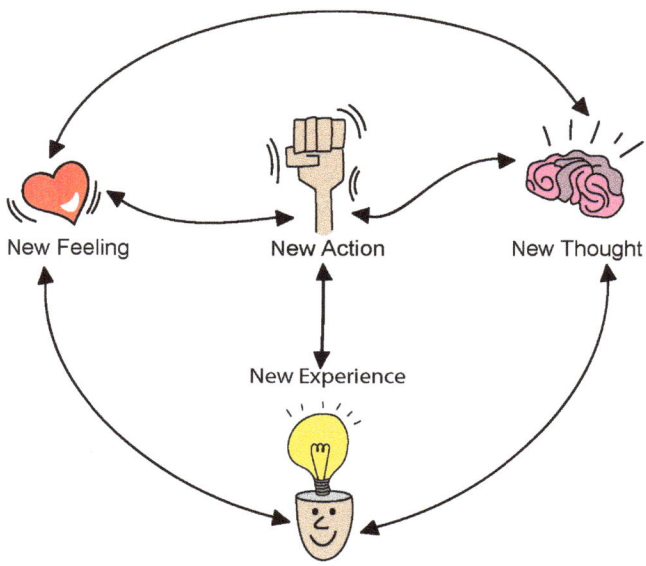

New Feeling   New Action   New Thought

New Experience

Why does the natural and ever renewing flow of thoughts, feelings, actions and experience get blocked? What overshadows the free flow of life energy? We propose that this occurs because we create boundaries between:

- What we imagine to be our 'self' and the world around us

- Ourselves and other human beings

- One part/aspect of ourselves with other aspects of ourselves

These boundaries create resistance in learning: in both the teacher and the student. Resistance binds us. Our notions of who we are, our cravings and aversions, memories from the past and anxieties about the future... all conspire to keep our attention away from life as it is now. Moreover, people bounded by limiting or pre-conceived notions act like puppets being controlled by external circumstances. It is almost as if someone else holds the controls of their mind and manipulates them the way one would operate a computer.

When is freedom from this possible? It will happen when the pupils learn how to operate from an unbounded consciousness which is the source of universal values. This is nothing but working from the space of deep inner silence. Developed human beings exercise a free choice in dealing with situations that they confront. It is well to remember that a lifetime comprises of a series of continuous situations that every one of us has to meet. How we meet these situations and what responses we exhibit determines the quality of our experience and our life.

There are two fundamental modes of thoughts/perception and feelings in which we exist in each moment: Fear and Love. Fear limits, restricts contracts and binds. Love (which is the foundation for a wholesome life) liberates, expands and accepts. It allows the natural flow of life, unhindered and free. The table on the following pages describes teaching and learning in these two different modes.

Fear State Teaching and Learning	Flow State Teaching and Learning
The teacher and the taught are separate. There is a barrier between them.	The teacher and the taught are one. Teaching is happening as one process.
Teacher | **Taught**	**One Whole Process**
Teaching and learning are separate from living.	Teaching, learning, experiencing and living are one integrated whole.
Teaching and learning are born out of desire i.e. the learner and the teacher are operating out of some form of 'Not OKness': • The desire to 'show my knowledge' (teacher) • The desire to gain knowledge (learner) • The desire to impress • The desire to make money • The desire to be a great teacher, great learner • The desire to be famous or 'come first' • The desire to 'teach my students'	Teaching and learning are born of flowing compassion - they happen and are not done. The teacher is operating out of unconditional 'OKness', i.e. no desire. Just a full, loving, creative space within. The student is a vast open joyful awareness; fully in one's senses and totally present. Hence teaching and learning are more like a creative, playful expression of joy rather than the 'drudgery' and 'effort' that happens in the 'fear' state. Life as a whole is seen as a magnificent teacher. Both teacher and student are totally at peace at all times.
Dominant teachers: Teachers work with a desire to exercise power from a position of authority and use the teaching situation as a means to bolster one's 'not OKness'. **Passive and dependent learners:** *Students are passive and powerless.*	**Liberating teachers**: Teachers work with a desire to empower students and recognize that they are 'Perfection in Progress'. They teach from a space of love and use the teaching situation as a means to evolve the unconditional 'OKness' in all. **Active and interdependent learners:** *Students are joyous, active and powerful.*

Fear State Teaching and Learning	Flow State Teaching and Learning
The teacher and students are identified with their own body, mind or skills. They have a limited concept of themselves and others around them. They see only the surface and are asleep to the core. The teacher and students work with misery, from misery and (unwittingly) create more misery for themselves and others.	The teacher and students are constantly aware of their own inner core of peace, bliss and silence. They see this as the common and shared space of being. They also see that the same creative center is at the heart of each human being. They see teaching primarily as a reconnection with or unfolding of this center in all. They work with joy, from joy and for joy.
Students and teachers in the fear state are constantly worried about performance/results. Their mind is preoccupied with future outcomes and hence not in the here and now where life and teaching are happening.	Students and teachers in the flow state focus on the process in the here and now. They know that if the process is creative, good results will follow. They realize that as much is learnt from mistakes and failure as is from success.
They fear and avoid the unknown. They stay within the framework of the familiar, known, routine and planned. They are upset by change of any kind. They defend the status quo. Some cardinal beliefs, they hold; 'Life is intrinsically threatening. So it must be controlled'. Life is a struggle. Learning is a struggle.	They seek out the unknown and welcome the mysterious. They welcome change and can experiment with situations. They encourage the best use of all situations and happenings as fuel for learning. Some cardinal beliefs they hold: 'The beauty of life and learning is in its changes. Everything will strengthen and nourish me' Life is celebration. Learning is celebration.
Fear state teaching creates more conditioning.	Flow state teaching frees the mind from conditioning.
Discipline is imposed from fear. Imposed conditions and compliance are at the core of regulation.	Discipline arises naturally from being a disciple of the being – the real and whole Self. Discipline arises out of intelligence and understanding. Life is the natural master regulator.

Is our education reinforcing the basic paradigm of deficiency and fear or liberating children into natural joy, peace and abundance?

A look at the table might indicate that much of what passes off as 'Education' today is really a part of a huge interconnected cluster of factors which work to keep people feeling deficient and 'not okay'. (There are many outstanding exceptions which will be mentioned later in this chapter).

At the core of all this fear state teaching and learning is a deep rooted sense of 'not-okayness'. This myth that 'You are not okay' leads us into a fervent search for finding something that will make us feel okay. It goes into a downward spiral that takes you away from your home of wholeness. In the process we are depleting both, our inner and outer resources; we are toxifying life in spiral of lies and violence.

There is so much competition and pressure on children today to get into the swankiest, commercial schools that claim that they will be 'producing' young, responsible, mature, intelligent adults! But, what are these schools really doing? They are molding and shaping each child to become a part of a society that is selfish and corrupt, a society that is toxifying the purity of its children. While the true value of education is lost in commercialization and pretense, the energy and vibrancy of students is being lost in the rigid, hierarchy driven education systems of today.

The essence of a creative climate is the freedom to imagine, think, feel and act as shown in the figure.

"Creativity is akin to growth and delivery of a child from a mother's womb. The level of fear and excitement is very high at the front line, but the creative joys are manifold", says Tom Peters, a management expert. "Get into the innovation mode and enjoy your work in an atmosphere of freedom and creativity", he exhorts. Keep this thought always in your mind. Creative climate discourages the tendency in education to give pre-conceived structures to the mind. It provides such an understanding that the mind is not enslaved to conditioning. Instead, independent thinking ability arises. Every person is endowed with the seed of independent thinking in a unique way. These seeds can sprout in a creative climate of the school developed jointly by the Principal and teachers working together. In this climate we teach thinking rather than obedience. Absence of fear is necessary to creativity. This encourages freedom to question existing beliefs and to meet the challenge of the unknown. It also encourages natural and self-inspired growth through love and by accepting the uniqueness of each child.

Unexamined beliefs and judgements have no place in a creative environment. While thinking is like finding one's own vision, belief is like blindness. Thinking is to be learnt, not beliefs. Right reasoning is to be cultivated, not mere trust. We have to guard against the danger of teaching darkness in the name of light.

The search for truth begins with the first step of right doubt. Where there is no doubt there is no thinking. And without thinking there is no creativity, there is no truth. Getting at truth is a continuous search with total awareness. Children learn to search in a creative climate, where they can cultivate courage and awareness.

What could be the Role of the Mass Media?

It is easy to exploit a person who is not secure and comfortable about the way he is. Most people spend all their time trying to be someone else because they think that that will give them more acceptance, more recognition, more love. The media feeds on this with their 'weapons of mass distraction'. Have you ever noticed how many advertisements, cartoons, reality shows and television shows we have recently started watching? Most news these days is about what is going wrong. The simplest piece is sensationalized to the extent of sacrificing the truth. Vital themes, which will truly help man to reconnect and find happiness, are pushed into a mere corner, compressed into a tiny line and made as inconspicuous as possible. Everything negative is reported. Have we ever thought that focusing on the positives will give people hope, encourage them to be positive and attract abundance into their lives?

The influence of certain 'perceptions' create stereotypes. The big business conglomerates pay enough amounts to bribe their way through thousands of waiting documents. They make products for 'fair skin' and hair care, because that is considered beautiful. The vicious circle works like this: Education and media conspire to make you feel 'not okay', to make you feel 'less' or 'not good enough'. Therefore, you are easily pulled in by the consumption machine and to be able to 'fit in', you consume more. There is always something more that you need, there is always some 'gap' that needs to be filled. What we don't realize is that none of this external consumption is going to fill the 'gap'. It will not make you feel whole. And that is because we believed the business people, who for their own interests, said we were not whole in the first place.

A wholesome way of doing it is by being in touch with your fullness. This will make us so secure as people that even our needs will become more natural. The whole focus will start moving towards what I can give to expand true wealth, joy, wellbeing and wholeness. Children who are in touch with their inner essence of unconditional okayness will be an unstoppable force.

Deinstitutionalizing Education

Education/learning must enable a person to live spontaneously, be alive, celebrative and trustful in expressing feelings, relaxed, and have no judgments and no conflicts. It must enable people to delve deep inside themselves, be constantly aware, and operate effortlessly from that ultimate source of joy. This cannot happen in our four walled classrooms where the concept is 'one lecture fits all'.

Can you have learning which is not imparted in a school, college of institution? But learning that happens at your pace, in your modality, in your time? For learning you are the unique customer. You should be able to get whatever you want, whenever you want. The future demands that learning be taken out of boxed classrooms that lead to the creation of a boxed outlook as well. How do we de-box? By taking learning out of the control of parents, authority, schools, and putting it back in the hands of the learner. Such opportunities for learning need to be widespread, easily accessible and self-initiated.

All students might not learn at the same pace and they might not have the same doubts and strengths as others. The grasping power of each student is wide ranging. Salman Khan of the Khan Academy, who started putting concept videos on YouTube for the benefit of his nephews, tells us about the idea of 'One Global Classroom'. Along with the lectures, there is a complex and comprehensive software that allows tracking the student's growth and other things. The idea is that the students learn from watching videos of concepts, so they can go back and forth over the points that they don't understand, they can take their own time to learn something. They can master the concept through various questions that the software generates. The biggest thing is that this technology, instead of dehumanizing the classroom, humanizes it. It allows the teachers to actually spend more time with the students, it allows students to interact with each other and help each other to get through various hurdles. This is not just a one off learning experience; it can last for years, even helping adults who want to revise certain fundamentals. We need to learn from each other and know that we are as much teachers as we are students. People from across geographical, regional and organisational boundaries can now post information and insights, converse, learn from, and teach each other.

We will no longer have to depend on a set time for a particular subject. It will be more understanding driven than examination driven. Imagine the time and potential that could be maximized if every student was able to study what and how he wanted. Traditional institutions today put education into little boxes. Education makes you into an instruction following slave. The richest learning environment is life. The best learning comes when we learn from each other through sharing and collaborating. If we just teach people how to learn and how to make connections across disciplines, we can deinstitutionalize learning. We need to allow people to discover their own innate capabilities, explore their likes and dislikes and be creative and original.

Sharing Stories

Only from a deep awareness of one's own well-being, can one serve the well-being of others, and the planet as a whole. When thoughts, words, and deeds arise from the innermost fountains of love, wholesomeness is present. Learning is about seeing and discovering together. It is a transformation, transcending the form or physical body. The touchstones of this process of change in attitude are love and joy in abundance. Integration has two related meanings:

- The parts of a system are in touch with each other; are connected or joined into one whole

- Being un-touched, or whole (undivided, one, as it is)

The fundamental responsibility of a human being is to become a joyous human being. It doesn't matter what you are doing. It doesn't matter what you are pursuing in your life, whether it's business, money, power, education, service or whatever else you wish to do. The reason we do things is because somewhere, deep inside us, we know that this will bring us happiness. The spirit of co-existence has to be imbibed in the younger generation right from the beginning, through a meaningful system of education. The education we are thinking of is obviously value-based education. Value-based education should be able to build character for the individual. The elements that constitute good character in an individual are: courage, fearlessness, humanism, and dedication to duty and universality. If an education system can inculcate these elements of character in any individual anywhere in the world, then the world will definitely be free from ills like intolerance, hatred, fundamentalism, terrorism etc. These elements make an individual become a wholesome and ethical human being.

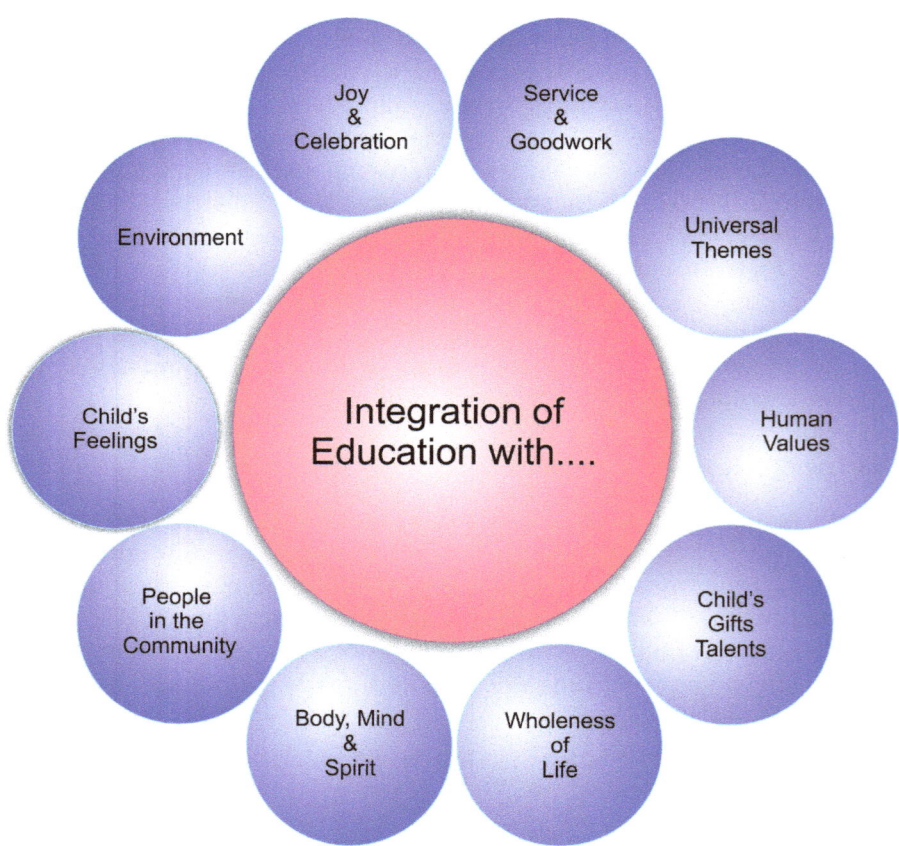

Schools as Societal Centers for the Holistic Organization of Life

Are we equipping our students to only be proficient earners and not equipping them to live in harmony with others and with nature? Today's system of education is becoming a cumbersome task for all those involved in it – the teachers, the founding members, the administrative staff and the students themselves. Judgments and labeling have overruled genuine curiosity. Categorizing based on appearances, family histories and possessions is so rampant, that it is quite dangerous. Suspicion, mistrust and competitiveness have taken over concern and genuine affection in relationships. At a time when we need our world view to expand from 'I, me, myself and my' to 'We, us, ours', we are slacking miserably. This narrow minded thinking, that does not include anyone else, will increase conflict and distress between boundaries. Education today is teaching competition instead of harmony. Cognitive knowledge has to be beautifully fused with affective awareness for a child to be able to hold his own in any forum. While we teach discipline as 'obeying instructions', we have to inculcate habits of introspection and listening to self. These will keep one in tune with personal belief systems and produce more long lasting effects than mere passive conditioning ever will. We need to live with a sense of solidarity amongst us, through appreciating diversity and being at peace with one another.

Let us look at some inspiring schools that have these integrated principles as a part of their framework.

The Kins School, Tekos, Russia — In southern Russia, in the lap of mountains and streams, there is a school started by Academician Mikhail Petrovich Shchetinin[2], whose principles are very significantly aligned with the kind of schooling that we have talked about above. It may well serve as a template for the kind of schools that need to exist in the future.

In this school, students and teachers learn from each other, students teach and explain topics to one another, everything that they do is learnt in the context of the meaning of human existence. Our education system today is rife with silos, and the most necessary thing to do now, is to integrate the various distinctions and isolated layers that have been made. Education today needs to be holistic and needs to instill in the students a holistic view of the world. The innate creativity and passion of the child needs to be brought out. The Latin word for educate is *educere* – meaning to bring out. Stifling a child's beauty by stuffing him or her with information, is not going to make the child a more 'successful' human being. Every action and teaching needs to be combined with life affirming values.

It is the raising of man to live harmoniously, to act in harmony with society – a man who, when he sees and analyses the phenomena of life which surround him, can feel their interconnection, can perceive the world as a whole.

And no matter what he becomes – an engineer, physicist, chemist, builder, teacher etc. – he will understand that he is going out into a unified, and wholesome world! Only when the roots are strong can a tree flower beautifully. It is the same with a child. Attention dwindles in normal schools after the first few weeks of enthusiasm. This leads to inactivity and boredom. Learned helplessness sets in and a child does not grow to

---

2) You can read more about the "*Kins school*" at Tekos in Southern Russia (started by Academician Mikhail Petrovich Shchetinin) here: www.icajapan.org/home-english/abundance/learning/ and http://forum.davidicke.com/showthread.php?t=59310

meet his potential, in fact, somewhere along the way he even loses the willingness to exploit his strengths. Health is adversely affected. In The Kins School, the children are completely free. They are so enthusiastic and full of energy, that they use all their time to continuously enrich themselves. You would be surprised to know that the entire structure of the school has been collectively thought of by the children. They have laid every brick, they have conceptualized and have made the school come alive entirely. In one or two years' time they can complete the same syllabus of one subject that in traditional schools, we would take ten years to finish. Instead of taking breaks between subjects, the students of this school prefer to indulge in one subject at a time, grasp the entire essence of it and master it thoroughly. There are no real teachers. The students explain things to one another and learn from one another. They ask questions, find answers and share their doubts and knowledge.

They are treated as adults from the beginning. The feeling of community is so strong that they all know they are there to progress together. With love and care, they help each other out. They are all 'coworkers'. One student says 'regular' schools prepare children for social roles, but here we don't prepare, we live these roles each moment! The goal is to develop each ones abilities to their maximum. The children cook; do the housekeeping, the organization, absolutely everything. They think in terms of the Universe, not in terms of individuals. What better than to lead a life by having conscious awareness of it? Here follow some more examples of schools that are aligned with what has been shared in this chapter.

Bharat Vidyalaya[3] — We have to share with you the ethos of Bharat Vidyalaya, a school catering to the underprivileged in the Satara district of Maharashtra state in Western India. Moving away from a school system focused on 'teaching', this school has kept its focus on learning which is child centric. Research, thought and effort have gone into planning this education system based on the natural development of the brain. (This aspect is similar to the Education For Life (EFL) system which respects a child's stage of development and his/her energetic profile.) It maximizes the period upto 8 years of a child's growth by working on developing interconnections that translate into the cognitive ability of the child. An open-learning system, encouraging interaction and discussion, the classrooms enable free movement by not keeping any benches. Brain boosting activities take place every few minutes. These ensure active energy to overcome lethargy. Instead of compartmentalizing education, Bharat Vidyalaya capitalizes on the interdisciplinary nature of learning, and the interconnec-

---

3) Bharat Vidyalaya, Village Shahabag, Taluka Wai, District Satara, Maharashtra (85 km south of Pune, India). For more info on Child Centred Approaches to Education, see also: https://civicdrivenchilddevelopment.files. wordpress.com/2008/07/child-centred-approaches_rogier-van-t-rood.pdf

tions between subjects. They take the approach of viewing the 'system as a whole', teach concepts keeping in mind the larger context and facilitate 'learning by doing'. They aim to develop the self-learning capacity of the child, so that the learning process is continuous, placing importance on problem solving and critical thinking. They also embrace the bigger vision of peace and harmony, and are contributors in the collaborative working of all citizens. This seminal work is an extremely worthy step in the right direction. Luckily there are many such beautiful examples in the world. Swami Parmahansa Yogananda set up a school in Ranchi, India based on spiritual and holistic foundation. It became wildly successful. Similar schools were opened all over the world.

Education For Life (EFL) Program[4] — This program is working towards increasing children's motivation with the help of simple principles and practices of how to direct energy to make the classrooms more experiential, engaging and wholesome. It is rooted in old Indian philosophies and modernized to be appropriate for today's day and age. For more than 40 years, EFL has provided the world with 'living wisdom' schools. This approach prepares students to gracefully move from student hood to adulthood. They are recognized as people that are wonderfully prepared for life, willing to face challenges and thence becoming natural leaders. Students and teachers mutually learn, enabling them to consider the realities of other people, making them more empathetic and conscious. They can also use these qualities and skills in their personal lives to be more joyously effective.

Agastya International Foundation[5] — Mr. Ramji Raghavan, the cofounder of Agastya International Foundation, has truly made a remarkable contribution in education. Agastya is a movement led by entrepreneurs, educators, scientists, teachers and children to transform education, make it affordable, and create a sustainable model that will provide affordable education which can be replicated anywhere in the world. With their focus on grass root education, they hope to inspire social development, innovation and leadership. A system that has truly given stupendous results through implementing its philosophy and putting its goals to action, Agastya has reached nearly 2.5 million disadvantaged children with hands-on science education and about 100,000 teachers in rural India.

Riverside School, Ahmedabad, India[6] — Over the last 15 years, Riverside School has designed, implemented and shared a unique user centered curriculum. This curriculum is providing schools with an alternative model which focuses on quality of learning and student well-being.

---

4) Education for Life, www.edforlife.org
5) Agastaya International Foundation, www.agastya.org
6) Riverside School, Ahmedabad, India, www.schoolriverside.com

The practices have been recognized worldwide and the school has regularly been honored for its academic achievement as well as its unique philosophy of 'Doing Good AND Doing Well'. The Riverside approach is to:

- Communicate a compelling idea of children and childhood, their potentials and competencies

- Promote and practice empathy in education, with particular emphasis on cultivating childrens' creative confidence through promoting creative action

- Advance the professionalism and culture of teachers, promoting a greater awareness of the value of collegial work and of meaningful relationships with the children and their families

- Highlight the value of research, observation, interpretation, and documentation of children's knowledge-building and thinking processes

- Share best practices through educational dialogues, conferences, professional development courses on the issues of education and the culture of childhood

Riverside School is currently (2016) run under the leadership of its dynamic founder, Ms. Kiran Bir Sethi. She is an outstanding example of a Wholesome Leader. Under her leadership, the school has taken on many initiatives.

- *"aProCh"* (a Protagonist in every Child): A community based initiative started by the Riverside School in 2007 to create child friendly cities, which has impacted over 100,000 children.

- In 2009, Riverside conceptualized and promoted the world's largest 'Design Thinking' challenge for children – *"Design for Change[8]"* which is now in over 30 countries and reaching over 200,000 schools.

In 2010, Riverside introduced *"the Right to Education"* as a truly inclusive program. The model is now being emulated by other establishments as a way forward.

These are just a few examples of the many great innovations that are occurring in education today. Can these examples multiply? Can good practices spread? The key we believe is in the quality of leadership that Principals and all those connected with education can provide. The key is also in what you can do to make a difference!

---

7) *"aProCh"*: a Protagonist in every Child, www.aproch.org
8) *"Design for Change"*, www.dfcworld.com

Joyful Action Now

1. Look back on your own process of education and learning in life. What have been the most significant lessons learnt? How many of these happened in a classroom?

2. If you are a parent, what might you start doing, continue doing and stop doing to allow the natural unfoldment of your child?

3. If you are an educator/teacher, look at the table in this chapter (Fear State vs. Flow State Teaching). Which side describes your current 'view' of yourself, education and life? What might enable you to make the shift if required?

BOX 7.1

Here are some thoughts on Education for a Wholesome World for you to reflect on:

1. Not ego but love is to be taught. There is love when there is no ego.

2. Values to be inculcated are truth, beauty, goodness, courage, honor, character, integrity and love. All these arise as outcomes of being one with the source of all values – the wholeness of life.

3. Develop love and joy, not competition and rivalry. Let each child grow higher and higher according to his unique endowments.

4. One who seeks his own intrinsic bliss becomes like a beautiful flower, full of fragrance and beauty. May teachers help children learn this wisdom. May teachers model the way.

5. We teach children fierce competition and wrong notions of success. This develops conceit, jealousy and hatred. How can they love? We cannot teach them love in that state of mind.

6. 'Success' defined in a narrow and materialistic way is the value we encourage and other values are blurred. This approach encourages dishonesty. Education needs to encourage people to be fulfilled, not only 'successful' in a wholesome multidimensional way as currently (2016) understood by many.

7. Each child is unique. There is nothing lower or higher. Everyone simply is in his/her own space. All types of valuations are undesirable. We must respect the uniqueness of each individual. Otherwise rivalry, competition and violence will remain.

8. Discipline is not to be confused with obedience born out of fear. Love the children and wish for their well-being. Because of this love and giving attitude for their good, true discipline will emerge spontaneously. This discipline arises from the very depths of the child's self.

9. Education should teach that you are enough as you are; that you do not have to be anything else. Do not be in a race with anyone.

10. Education should lead to proper growth, not to ambition. The ambitious always see what others have. They are not able to see what they have. The secret of happiness lies in how you are using what you have and not in your possessions. This value must be fully ingrained in the child's mind. There is abundance for everyone in the universe.

11. The core of education should be to develop love and humility. Other values are automatically imbibed.

12. Education must also teach how 'good work' spontaneously emerges from leveraging ones natural gifts and talents with joy. One's chosen work will expand joy as we serve from our gifts. The important point is: how joyful, wholehearted and of what quality is the work one is doing?

13. If we spread flowers on someone's path, only flowers will come back to us. Values help to purify our inner gold in fire. Let the impurities burn out so that on y your pure gold remains. Education must serve this process.

14. Awareness of my intrinsic wholeness is the source of all values. Values should lead the students to live a truly moral life. This is a life of inner harmony, and an expression of joy. Morality is a spontaneous expression of joy and peace.

15. The most important purpose of education is that of allowing the natural nourishment, exploration and unfolding of a child's full potential. It is about-bringing up the child in a way that she/he becomes a person who meets all of life situations intelligently with responses that arise from being one with the creative intelligence of life.

16. All the manifestations of reality in the external world can be understood and appreciated with the knowledge of the infinite and whole self, the ultimate reality. This is the Deeper Integrating Principle (DIP).

17. Love and care have to be appropriately provided to the child to help him/her to develop self-reliance, trust, independence and happiness. Teachers need to see themselves as enablers and facilitators rather than 'shapers and molders'.

CHAPTER 8

Healing People and the Environment

Life is intrinsically healthy and vibrant. It is a natural cycle of flourishing, thriving, declining and then withering away. We are by nature at ease and very peaceful. That is why, whenever we stray away from this natural condition, there is a dis-ease.

Stuart J. Kingma[1] in a paper titled *"A unified view of healing: The Centrality of Hope and Reconciliation"*, has defined health and Wholeness as a "dynamic state of well-being of the individual and the society; of physical, mental, spiritual, economic, political and social well-being; of being in harmony with each other, with the natural environment and with God". The World Health Organization described health as "a state of complete physical, mental and social wellbeing, not merely the absence of disease or infirmity". The word for health in Sanskrit is *swasth* (*swa* means 'self' and *asth* means 'established in'). *Swasth* means 'one who is established in the Self'. If we see the Self as life itself, then the Sanskrit word for health translates into 'established in Life' or 'One with Life'.

Health, Wholesomeness and Peace

When your eyes are functioning well you don't see your eyes. If your eyes are imperfect you see spots in front of them. That means there are

---

1) Kingma, Stuart, *"A unified view of healing: the Centrality of Hope and Reconciliation"*, Paper presented at the Bittinger conference, Zurich, Switzerland, 12 October 1982, http://archives.wcc-coe.org/Query/detail.aspx?ID=75703

some lesions in the retina or wherever, and because your eyes aren't working properly, you feel them. In the same way, you don't hear your ears. If you have a ringing in your ears it means, there's something wrong with your ears. Therefore, if you do feel yourself, there must be something wrong with you. Whatever you have, the sensation of I is like spots in front of your eyes - it means something's wrong with your functioning.

— Alan Watts (1915 - 1973)[2]

Health is a state of utmost ease and peace. A state which is characterized by a total absence of dis-ease. When we are healthy, our body–mind experiences a condition of total forgetfulness. We forget the body, the mind, the emotions and nothing demands our attention. This is the state of perfect health. This definition of health was brought home to us dramatically by an Ayurvedic healer who simply said "If I hadn't mentioned it, would you have remembered that you had a little finger on the left hand?" We ware taken aback but replied "No". Now suppose you had a cut on the little finger on the left hand, would you have remembered it? The answer was "Yes"! When everything, all processes in the body-mind are operating in a balanced and harmonious way, there is a subjective experience of bliss, peace and free joy.

Dr. Herbert Shelton talks about the web of life and how we are related to food, water, air and sunshine and to other people and other forms of life in his book *"Health for All: Organic Unity and Its Relation to Cure"*[3].

He says that the only correct way of viewing the body is to view it as a whole. It is possible to live fully only if we realize that there are no shortcuts. The easiest and most straightforward way to truly live is by learning the simple laws of being, by realigning your life with the law of nature. Though an organism has differentiated parts and specialized functions, it is only in cooperation and symbiosis that there can exist a feeling of overall wellbeing. He says "We must put our physiological house in order not by myriad local treatments, as physicians with financial interest in suffering do, but by duly adjusting ourselves to the ordered harmony of nature upon which every organ and function in the body depends for its very existence".

When we are in touch with our wholeness, when we are listening to the simple guidance of what our body is telling us, when we obey that guidance and move with that guidance, we are healthy. When we eat food which is naturally grown, without chemicals, additives and color, we are at the peak of our health. We will see further in this chapter, how conscious farming leads to holistic growth. The feeling of being out of touch with ourselves interferes with the process of healing.

2) Watts, Alan, "*The Essential Lectures of Alan Watts*", Season 1(1971): Ego, (Video), Gaia: Boulder, Colorado

3) Shelton, Dr. Herbert, "*Health for All: Organic Unity and Its Relation to Cure*", Kessinger Publishing: Whitefish, Montana, 2006.

We can restore health in a place of deep inner silence. Health can pertain to an individual, a neighborhood, a nation as a whole, including its environment. When all the people in a neighborhood know each other and celebrate together with love in their hearts, participate in each other's joys and sorrows, we can say it is a healthy neighborhood. When people are in touch with and care for the animals and plants around them, we can say that they are connected and balanced and so foster environmental health.

To understand the interconnected nature and the factors surrounding health and the environment, let us look at two imaginary scenarios. One is based on a fundamental paradigm of fear/limitation/separation and the other on love/wholeness/integration:

Fear — I am feeling 'unfulfilled' and deficient. My life is ruled by the unexamined assumptions that 'there is not enough for all' and 'I have to consume things to be happy and feel okay'. As a corollary to this, I have to keep 'working', often doing work I do not enjoy. There is no time for reflection, exercise, relaxation and recreation because long working hours and the long commute to work drains my energy and time. I am stuck in traffic jams on most of the days. My health suffers because of all the negative emotions arising from this lifestyle. Our city is getting more polluted by the day, and medical care is getting very expensive. Since there is little time that I have, I buy most of my food from the local mall. Much of my food is processed. This further affects my health adversely. This worries me. I look for ways to alleviate my sorrow. TV is a handy distraction. The advertisements inspire me to buy more things to make me healthy and happy. To buy more things, I need more money. So I then start worrying about my next raise at work.

Love — Being in touch with who I am, I am feeling fulfilled, whole and abundant. There is no need to prove anything to anyone. My life runs under the conscious assumptions that 'there is enough for all' and 'I have to do absolutely nothing to feel 'unconditionally okay' about who I am'. This arises from the understanding that I am nothing, and this moment is all I have to be joyous and loving. As a corollary to this, joyful service from my gifts, makes my work (play!) nourishing. Because I am joyful and creative, I attract money. There is ample time for reflection, exercise, relaxation and recreation. Working hours are appropriate and energizing. I cycle or walk to work, because I work in my neighborhood or work from home. Thanks to the constant surge of good feelings, regular exercise, fresh nourishing vegan food and meditation, my health is excellent. I regularly have herbal tea, made from the herbs I grow on my rooftop, and eat plenty of Moringa leaves plucked off the Drumstick tree growing at home. (See Box 8.3). My food is cooked fresh, partly from the vegetables and fruits from the rooftop garden, and partly from the organic farms close to our city. There is hardly any expense on medical care. I enjoy the company of my neighbors when we gather for potluck dinners and community celebrations. I read inspiring books instead of watching TV. I am grateful for choosing health and happiness.

What is Dis-ease?

From the two scenarios described, it should be clear that fear limits well-being in life. In the natural flow of life, when energy is absent due to a lack of connection or blocks, we experience dis-ease. At one level, dis-ease is really – a system's attempt to restore balance. According to *The Health Awareness Centre*[4], diseases are manifested by the body for the purpose of cleansing, repair or rebuilding. A disease affects the whole body, even if the symptoms might just be visible in one part. The intelligence of the body itself causes the disease, so that it can intelligently respond to a particular imbalance in our body. By fulfilling and maintaining the basic and very simple needs of life, which help to build and sustain health (wholesome natural living), the symptoms of disease will disappear. A disease is not an event, but a process, and if we recognize and respond to the small signals that our body gives us when in need of nutrition, we will be able to avert these illnesses. It appears only where necessary and where there is need for it. Thus, even if we temporarily patch it up, it will occur elsewhere. Disease is our body's way of saying 'Hey, Stop! Listen! And give me a break!'

What Is Healing?

"The word 'healing' comes from the same root as from where the word 'whole' comes. Whole, health, healing, holy, all come from the same root. To be healed means to be joined with the whole and to be ill means to be disconnected with the whole. An ill person is one who has simply developed blocks between himself and the whole, so something becomes disconnected. The function of the healer is to reconnect it. But when I say the function of the healer is to reconnect it, I don't mean that the healer has to do something. The healer is just a function. The doer is life itself, the whole."

— Osho: Beloved of My Heart[5]

---

4) *The Health Awareness Centre*, www.facebook.com/thacmumbai
5) Rajneesh, Osho, 'Learn to Become a Void' in *"Beloved of My Heart"*, http://oshosearch.net/Convert/search.php?q=The+word+Healing&area=Consciousness&col=Osho&cat=Beloved+of+My+Heart

Everyone can be a healer. Healing is something like breathing, it is natural. If somebody is ill, it means he has lost the capacity to heal himself. The healers role is to serve him to rejoin. Healing is about making whole. Wholeness is the goal of restoring one to health.

In my separation is my dis-ease and in my wholeness is my ease. When I am separated from life and existence, nature and fellow humans, I have dis-ease. When I am one with all, I am ease.

As Dr. Deepak Chopra once said "healing is the remembrance of our wholeness."[6] When we remember that space of grace in us, our own Self, life functions without any resistance. We slow down and notice more. We are more conscious of our feelings – the language of existence. Feelings are always telling us if we are connected to the source or not. When everything is flowing unhindered, then life is whole. Health at the individual, organizational, social and environmental level is all really part of one larger 'health' called wholeness. When we envision One Wholesome World, we see healthy people having healthy relationships with others and themselves, coming together to make healthy communities that involve a fluent exchange of ideas, information and energy. Such exchanges are totally free and natural. They are born from deep symbiotic and respectful connections to all aspects of Nature. They form a mutually nourishing and interdependent dance of joy and abundance. It is not a coincidence that the Sanskrit word for Joy (*Ananda*) literally means fluent receiving and giving!

Let's look at a few different ways in which people can heal, themselves and the environment.

---

6) Chopra, Deepak, www.creatingheartconnections.com/wp/2009/02/healing-is-the-remembrance-of-whole-ness. Also see: Bakken, Kenneth L., "*The Call to Wholeness: Health as a Spiritual Journey*", Wipf and Stock Publishers: Eugene, Oregon, 2009.

Unlimited Food – This piece is adapted from an article on *"The (now dying) living wealth of India – our forests"* by Bharat Mansata[7]: According to the *"Gaia Atlas of Planet Management"*[8], there are an estimated 80,000 edible plant species on Earth, other than the many edible varieties of each species. Most of these are uncultivated foods – free, nourishing gifts of nature, growing wild, requiring no human labor, except in harvesting or gathering. According to another source, *"Plants for a Future"*[9], there are over 20,000 species of edible plants in the world yet fewer than 20 species now provide 90% of our food.

Less than 150 plant species have been historically cultivated on a large scale as food crops. But with the spread of extensive industrial monocultures – grown with toxic chemicals for distant urban markets – barely 20 plant species now provide 90% of the entire human diet, and just 8 crops (of a very few varieties) provide three quarters of all human food! That is a miniscule 0.01% (or one in ten thousandth) of the edible species gifted by Nature. Besides supplying us with food, many of these species have profound positive impacts on health. (See, for example, Box 8.3 on the Miracle Tree).

Unlimited Energy – Forests can provide us free food and shelter in a most ecologically efficient manner. There is no need for any external input, whatsoever, of energy, water or fertilizer. Forests are by far the most efficient agents of sequestering carbon, ameliorating climate change, conserving and regenerating our soils and their fertility, fostering biodiversity, recharging groundwater and providing a huge variety of useful produce. They are also very efficient agents of harvesting solar energy.

There is no real dearth of available solar energy. In an article called *"Plugging into the Sun"* By George Johnson[10], the author describes how there is far more solar energy available to humankind than we could possibly ever need. Currently (2016) the total power needs of the humans on Earth are approximately 16 terawatts. (A terawatt is a trillion watts.)[11] In the year 2020 it is expected to grow to 20 terawatts. Power from solar radiation (which falls only on the solid part of the Earth) is 120,000 terawatts.[12] This

7) Mansata, Bharat, "*The (now dying) living wealth of India-our forests*", www.thealternative.in/society/the-now-dying-living-wealth-of-india-our-forests. Bharat Mansata is the cofounder of Earthcare Books (www.earthcarebooks.com). Also see: The Wealth of India, a multi-volume encyclopedia of India's biological wealth, published by the National Institute of Science Communication and Information Resources, CSIR (www.niscair.res.in). The encyclopedia is a treasure-trove of information on the myriad useful plant species of India.

8) Myers, Norman (Ed.), "*Gaia Atlas of Planet Management*", Pan Books: London, 1985

9) "*Plants for a Future*", www.pfaf.org/user/edibleuses.aspx

10) Johnson, George, "*Plugging Into The Sun*", Article in National Geographic: 2009 http://ngm.nationalgeographic.com/2009/09/solar/johnson-text/3

11) "*How much power does the world consume?*", Howstuffworks Science, http://science.howstuffworks.com/environmental/green-science/world-power-consumption1.htm

12) "*Solar Energy Pros and Cons*", Energy Informative, www.energyinformative.org/solar-energy-pros-and-cons

is 6,000 times more power than what is needed to supply the entire world in 2020! The potential of solar energy is abundant. Combine this perspective with the role of food forests, and you have a potential cornucopia of possibilities for health and freedom.

Unlimited Health — The authors of this book have lived in Kashmir An ancient plant (that is now used only on ceremonial occasions) is the *Utpal Shakha*[13], locally known in Kashmir as *Wotpal Hakh*. It was once known to have been the staple diet of mystics and sages. *Wotpal Hakh* is known for its extraordinary nutritional value. Few people eat it today.

> *"Let food be thy medicine and medicine be thy food."*
>
> — Hippocrates

The connection between nutrition and health is well known. Our food can cause and cure diseases.

Dr. Johann Georg Schnitzer of Germany[14] has shown (and has very well documented) the impressive results in curing of diabetes, obesity and hypertension by restoring ones nutritional patterns to a fresh and natural diet.

The focus of the work and research of Dr. Schnitzer is simply making sure that a patient eats what his/her body really needs. Referring to his book "*Schnitzer Intensive Nutrition - Schnitzer Normal Nutrition*"[15], the author states that "feeding habits of civilization cause most chronic ailments of civilization. The genetic programming of the human metabolism couldn't adapt to this unnatural, denaturized food. So, the old genetic program for man's origin nutrition must be functional". He searched for this "original nutrition", found it, and developed from it a man-appropriate "civilized origin nutrition". This is described in his book (mentioned above). The book has gone into 13 editions and sold 144,000 copies.

Industrial agriculture has had an impact on the quality of the food we eat. It is now well known that cow's milk (as produced today on an industrial scale) can be harmful to the adult human body.[16]

Similarly, the global production and consumption of meat[17] negatively impacts both the environment and human health, not to mention the ethical

---

13) Utpal Shakha in Sanskrit translates loosely into *Excellent Plant*. Wotpal Haakh is the Kashmiri version of *Utpal Shakha.*

14) www.dr-schnitzer.ce/introe1.html

15) Schnitzer, Dr. J. G. and Schnitzer, M., "*Schnitzer-Intensive Nutrition, Schnitzer-Normal Nutrition*", Schnitzer Publishers: St. Georgen, Germany, 1998

16) Goldschmidt, Vivian, "*Debunking The Milk Myth: Why Milk Is Bad For You And Your Bones*", www.saveourbones.com/osteoporosis-milk-myth. Also see: www.whitelies.org.uk/resources

17) See for example: Walsh, Bryan, "The Triple Whopper Environmental Impact of Global Meat Production", http://science.time.com/2013/12/16/the-triple-whopper-environmental-impact-of-global-meat-production/

impropriety of treating animals as a source of our food. (This aspect has also been discussed in Chapter 6.)

There are well documented stories of doctors curing cancer through changes in diet. Many of our healer friends in Pune and Mumbai have successfully cured chronic diseases like cancer and diabetes by getting patients to consciously shift to vegan/raw diets. Dr. Vijaya Venkat and Anju Venkat of The Health Awareness Centre (THAC)[18], Mumbai, Dr. Nandita Shah[19] and Dr. Pramod Tripathi[20], Hemant Chhabra[21] and Bharat Mansata[22] of Van Vadi, (in Maharashtra, India) are all people, who are healing people and the environment through their example.

Natueco Farming – Another related story which gave a lot of hope is the story of the experiments with *"Natueco Farming"*[23] by a person called Deepak Suchde[24], of the *"Prayog Pariwar"*[25], in the village of Harda near Bhopal, India. Deepak is a disciple of Shripad Dabholkar[26], the founder of the *Prayog Parivar* in Maharashtra, India. In a speech he delivered in Delhi (*"Prosperity with Equity"*)[27], Daboholkar emphasized that "the best and the latest of the modern science and its work results have failed to reach the last person. Why not take the very essence of the latest and the best of modern science straight to the average grass root people and hand it over to them?" He was the first to assert that the real problem before the nation is 'Waste Mind' and not 'Waste land', saying that without 'Waste mind' there would be no 'Waste land'. With natural farming, all the needs of a small family can be met through the enlightened and conscious cultivation of only 10,000 square feet of land. We need to network with nature. The rural people, who are living in close proximity with the natural environment, are more resource literate as they are linked closer to it than the urban dwellers. Natueco farming is a practice followed by knowing and understanding nature better and deeper and is innovative, involved, integrated and interactive. It is not just natural farming, where the ancient wisdom is trusted and followed, but it is farming by knowing nature better and better through critical scientific enquiries and carefully performed experiments. It believes and has proven that there can be plenty-for-all, if the resources

18) The Health Awareness Centre (THAC), www.facebook.com/thacmumbai
19) Dr. Nandita Shah, www.sharan-india.org
20) Dr. Pramod Tripathi, www.freedomfromdiabetes.org
21) Hemant Chhabra, www.hideout.co.in. Also see *"Living in Communication With Nature"* www.youtube.com/watch?v=utAbigQP9Fc
22) Bharat Mansata of Van Vadi, *"At Home In the Forest"* www.thehindubusinessline.com/todays-paper/tp-life/at-home-in-the-forest/article1086454.ece
23) *"Natueco farming"* is a short form of Nature Ecological Farming. Read more here: www.slideshare.net/malpani/natueco-book-pdf
24) Deepak Suchde, www.beyondorganicfarming.in/contactus.htm
25) Prayog Pariwar, www.urbanleaves.org/2009/11/prayog-pariwaar.html
26) Dabholkar, Shripad A., *"Plenty for All"*, Mehta Publishing House: Pune, 1998
27) Dabholkar, Shripad. A., *"Prosperity with Equity"*, Ideas That Have Worked Seminar, New Delhi, 2001.

are methodically harvested. At *Prayog Pariwar*, the idea is that knowledge should not be restricted at any position/level or with any person. "Learning, earning livelihood and living must be closely and constantly linked". Central to the idea of the *Prayog Pariwar* is a community of learning and experimenting practitioners of the art of Natueco farming. They share a sense of community around a shared vision. This is something that also nourishes and heals human beings. Our own experience with Natueco farming can be summed up as a deep, intimate and loving communion with the energy that runs all of life in ourselves, in other people and in the plants, soil, trees around us. It is a very close manifestation of wholesomeness in action!

Community Heals — How intimacy and community have a positive impact on health is described by Dr. Dean Ornish[28] in his book *"Love and Survival: The Scientific Basis for the Healing Power of Intimacy"*. In it, Dr. Ornish discusses the Roseto effect[29]. This effect is the phenomenon by which a close-knit community of Italian immigrants experienced a reduced rate of heart disease. The effect is named after the city Roseto in Pennsylvania. The Roseto effect was first noticed in 1961 when the local Roseto doctor encountered Dr. Stewart Wolf, then head of Medicine of the University of Oklahoma, and they discussed the unusually low rate of myocardial infarction in Roseto, compared with other locations. Many studies followed, including a 50-year study comparing nearby Bangor and Nazareth. As the original authors had predicted, as the Bangor cohort shed their Italian social structure and became more Americanized in the years following the initial study, heart disease rose.

Wolf attributed Rosetans' lower heart disease rate to lower stress. "The community," Wolf says, "was very cohesive." There was no keeping up with the Joneses. Houses were very close together, and everyone lived more or less alike." Elderly were revered and incorporated into community life. Housewives were respected, and fathers ran the families.

In another part of the same book, Dr. Ornish looks at how community, togetherness and a sense of mutual sharing helped people heal faster and live longer compared to others who were isolated. Even women with cancer, who had weekly support groups, lived on an average twice as long as the others, who did not have this benefit.

---

28) Ornish, Dr. Dean, *'Love and Survival: The Scientific Basis for the Healing Power of Intimacy"*, HarperCollins: New York, 2011
29) The Roseto effect: https://en.wikipedia.org/wiki/Roseto_effect

What does this mean for healing? Here are some connections brought out by Dr. Ornish:

- Love/commitment — trust — vulnerability — intimacy — healing

- Fear/no-commitment — mistrust/cynicism — hostility — closed off — isolation– disease/premature death

When I am isolated, lonely and not having someone to share with, I fall sick. Medical research now says that isolation makes us more vulnerable to illness, while relationships help survival. When we listen sensitively and attentively (with great humility, presence and openness) to the gentle promptings of our body, the longings and inner callings of our soul, the voices and feelings of others in our community and also to the environment, then healing occurs. Our joys, sorrows and humanity are shared. The listening provides release, relief and unblocking. Re-connecting to each other and to ourselves leads to restitution, and a return to wholeness.

Ideas for Action

All the knowhow that is needed to heal our planet and provide low cost/ affordable healthcare for everybody exists on the Earth at this moment. There are inspiring examples all over the Earth of people who are providing such effective service. We have shared some examples above. These are only a miniscule fraction of the wealth of examples that the authors have come across and/or are participating in. In almost all the agro climatic zones of the world, there are shining examples of islands of ecological excellence. The ecological wisdom embedded in many indigenous cultures like the Native American Indian, different communities in India, South America and Africa, Australian Aboriginals, the Masai tribes in Kenya etc., all embody great respect for natural processes. They also all have the knowhow to live in great harmony in their ecological neighborhood in a sustainable way.

How do we collect this practical wisdom, bring it all together coherently and put it out for appropriate adoption and action? How can digital technologies enable this process? Here is a roadmap to take this forward:

- Conduct a Global Appreciative Inquiry for Action (GAIA). This would be a collaborative process to ferret out the best practices and examples globally of successful ecologically sound and healing initiatives for different agro climatic zones.

- Translate this knowhow into different languages and also convert it into simple modules for action learning: Learning by doing as we go forward.

- Create a team of Catalysts who can take this knowledge forward and disseminate it in a viral fashion.

- Create a Global Network of schools/educational institutions dedicated to this vision. Make children/youth a part of this global initiative.

A global process of learning and sharing followed by inspired action will vouchsafe the protection and restoration of Earth's ecological systems. This needs to become a burning passion in the hearts of those who are called to make it happen.

Speaking at the eighth annual Cinema for Peace Gala in Berlin on 9 February 2009, Leonardo DiCaprio[30] (who was accepting an award for his ongoing and outstanding dedication to environmental issues) captured this sentiment when he said: "The more I am a part of this issue, the more I work with these different organizations, I realize that the fight to protect our planet is way bigger than any religion, any government or any individual. In order to achieve real lasting, change we must first understand that this is a collective fight that everyone in the world must get involved. During this critical period of human history, healing the damage of industrial civilization is the task of our generation. And our response depends on the conscious evolution of our species. And this response could very well save this unique blue planet for future generations."

Healing Earth begins with My Own Homecoming

The starting point for healing is with one's own body-mind. According to the ancient Hawaiian healing process called *Ho'Oponopono*[31], we are 100% responsible for all that is happening in our 'Reality'. *Ho'Oponopono* is based on the knowledge that anything that happens to you or that you perceive, the entire world where you live is your own creation and thus, it is entirely your responsibility. A hundred percent, no exceptions! (See Box 8.1 of an example of its application). This means that polluted rivers, terrorist activity, the prime minister, the economy, the state of your health – anything you experience and don't like – is up for you to heal. All these don't exist, in a manner of speaking, except as projections from inside you. The problem isn't with them, it's with you, and to change them, you have to change your thoughts. This will enable us to live harmoniously with each other and our Mother Earth. This is the original common purpose of all human beings. The journey begins by reclaiming your own wholeness now.

Taking care of your health through regular exercise, proper diet, adequate rest and thinking can also be useful, alongside giving time to find out what nature wants you to do. (You will feel blissful and at peace doing this). At the group level, the master key to healing is understanding, getting

---

30) Green Cross: www.gcint.org/leonardo-dicaprio-receives-international-green-film-award/
31) Learn more about this ancient Hawaiian practice of healing here:
https://en.wikipedia.org/wiki/Ho%CA%BBoponopono

to know 'others', becoming familiar with their ways and understanding their culture, festivals and symbols. Out of this understanding grows love, which is the absence of fear. Out of love grows healing or deeper integration. As far as healing of nature is concerned, a few simple steps can set us off on the road to peace. We could start in a small way – like planting some trees, getting to know their names and learning about the birds in the neighborhood, joining the world wide fund for nature and contributing in its activities.

Meditation, prayer, rituals, and ceremonies for healing and living in harmony with nature raise our own consciousness. We see and experience our interdependence with the whole web of life. It is a change in consciousness which will change our thinking, feelings and actions. As millions of people tune into the frequency of wholesomeness, profound changes will occur spontaneously in their patterns of work, travel and consumption. This, in turn, will begin to change the economy and the physical environment.

As the old *Sukyo Mahikari*[32] adage goes, "Spirit first, mind follows and body belongs". The Earth will be first healed at the level of spirit. We will come home to our intrinsic wholeness "within" before that wholeness manifests on the outside "outside". Love and blessings to you dear reader. May our children and grandchildren inherit a world where the wholeness of life reigns supreme!

---

32) Matsunaga, Louella, "*Spirit First, Mind Follows, Body Belongs: Notions of health, illness, and disease in Sukyo Mahikari UK*", SOAS: London,2000. Learn more about the Healing Process of Sukyo Mahikari originating from Japan at https://en.wikipedia.org/wiki/Sukyo_Mahikari

Joyful Action Now

1. Pause for a few moments now. Remember that you are the Subjective Witnessing Awareness (SWA). Abide as your Self. Visualize this SWA infusing all aspects and dimensions of your body-mind with healing energy. See your cells celebrating this infusion of life force.

2. You are infinite peace, joy and love right now. This is both the source of health as well as the goal of health. This is you as one with life. What are the thoughts that "you" may be holding that overshadow this remembrance of your infinite/empty wholeness? How would you let go these thoughts, and come home to wholeness now?

3. Our body-mind has a built in wisdom, which keeps us pointed towards health. If we listen to its promptings, it will tell us silently what changes we need to make to remove toxins and restore balance in our body-mind. Take some time out to listen to your inner body wisdom. Take some inspired action on them.

4. Slowly go over the visual map of The Principles of Perfect Health in Box 8.4. What changes can you make in your patterns of thought, words and habits that would enhance the health and well-being of your body-mind?

5. Think of all your relationships. Which ones are in need of healing? What are the few steps you can take to do this? Where can you forgive yourself, others?

6. There is a list of 50 Ways to help the planet[33]. Play with this list. Feel into what feels right for you. Pick up a few items to implement each week.

---

33)   50 Ways to Help the Planet: www.theguardian.com/environment/2002/aug/22/worldsummit2002.earth21

BOX 8.1

Ho'oponopono[34]

"The only task in your Life and mine is the restoration of our Identities - our Minds - back to their original state of void or zero."

— Ihaleakala Hew Len, Ph.D.[35]

A therapist in Hawaii, Dr. Ihaleakala Hew Len, cured a complete ward of criminally insane patients without ever seeing any of them. He would study an inmate's chart and then look within himself to see how he created that person's illness. As he improved himself, the patient improved.

The ward in the Hawaii State Hospital, where they kept the criminally insane, was dangerous. Dr. Len never saw patients. He agreed to have an office and to review their files. While he looked at those files, he would work on himself. He used the ancient Hawaiian healing process called Ho'oponopono. He just kept saying, "I'm sorry", "Please forgive me", "I Thank you" and "I love you" over and over again. After a few months, patients that had to be shackled were being allowed to walk freely. Others who had to be heavily medicated were getting off their medications. And those who had no chance of ever being released were being freed. In a few months, the whole ward was shut down. As Dr. Ihaleakala Hew Len worked on himself, patients began to heal. He was simply healing the part of him that created them. Dr. Len believes that total responsibility for your life means that everything in your life, simply because it is in your life, is your responsibility. In a literal sense the entire world is your creation.

---

34) Read more about the Hawaiian Practice of HoÓponopono which Dr. Ihaleakala Hew Len used here: https://en.wikipedia.org/wiki/Ho%CA%BBoponopono

35) The Official Website of Dr. Ihaleakala Hew Len is zero-wise.com. The story of how he healed a ward of mentally ill criminals is here: www.rosariomontenegro.hubpages.com/hub/How-Dr-Hew-Len-healed-a-ward-of-mentally-ill-criminals-with-Hooponopono.

Box 8.2

The Twelve Principles of Attitudinal Healing[36]

The essence of our being is love.

Health is inner peace. Healing is letting go of fear.

Giving and receiving are the same.

We can let go of the past and of the future.

Now is the only time there is and each instant is for giving.

We can learn to love ourselves and others by forgiving rather than judging.

We can become love finders rather than fault finders.

We can choose and direct ourselves to be peaceful inside regardless of what is happening outside.

We are students and teachers to each other.

We can focus on the whole of life rather than the fragments.

Since love is eternal, death need not be viewed as fearful.

We can always perceive ourselves and others as either extending love or giving a call for help.

— The Center for Attitudinal Healing, Sausalito, CA 1997

36) The Twelve Principles of Attitudinal Healing
www.ahinternational.org/about/about-ahinternational/principles-of-attitudinal-healing

BOX 8.3

The Miracle Tree - Moringa Oleifera (The Drumstick Tree)[37]

Moringa leaves are full of essential disease-preventing nutrients:

Vitamin A, which acts as a shield against eye disease, skin disease, heart ailments, diarrhea, and many other diseases

Vitamin C, fighting a host of illnesses including cold and flu

Calcium, which builds strong bones and teeth, and helps prevent osteoporosis

Potassium, essential for the functioning of the brain and nerves

Proteins, the basic building blocks of all our body cells

Moringa leaves compared to common foods:
Values per 100gm. edible portion.

Nutrient	Moringa Leaves	Other Foods
Vitamin A	6780 mcg	Carrots: 1890 mcg
Vitamin C	220 mg	Oranges: 30 mg
Calcium	440 mg	Cow's milk: 120 mg
Potassium	259 mg	Bananas: 88 mg
Protein	6.7 gm	Cow's milk 3.2 gm

37)   Witt, Kathryn A. "*The Nutrient Content of Moringa oleifera Leaves*".
www.miracletrees.org/moringa-doc/nutrient-content-of-moringa-oleifera-leaves.pdf

BOX 8.4

Perfect Health[38]

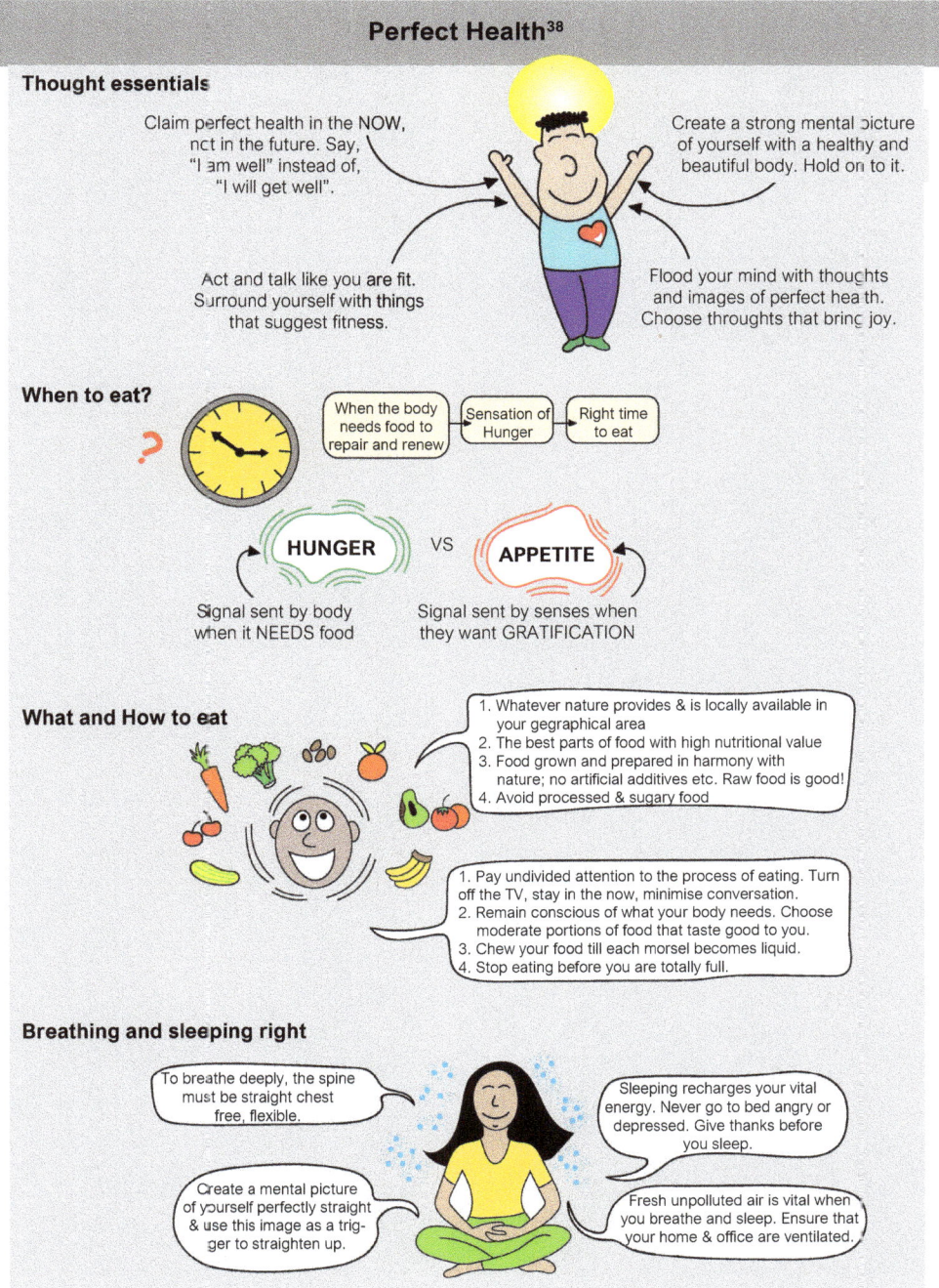

Thought essentials

Claim perfect health in the NOW, not in the future. Say, "I am well" instead of, "I will get well".

Create a strong mental picture of yourself with a healthy and beautiful body. Hold on to it.

Act and talk like you are fit. Surround yourself with things that suggest fitness.

Flood your mind with thoughts and images of perfect health. Choose throughts that bring joy.

When to eat?

When the body needs food to repair and renew → Sensation of Hunger → Right time to eat

HUNGER vs APPETITE

Signal sent by body when it NEEDS food

Signal sent by senses when they want GRATIFICATION

What and How to eat

1. Whatever nature provides & is locally available in your geographical area
2. The best parts of food with high nutritional value
3. Food grown and prepared in harmony with nature; no artificial additives etc. Raw food is good!
4. Avoid processed & sugary food

1. Pay undivided attention to the process of eating. Turn off the TV, stay in the now, minimise conversation.
2. Remain conscious of what your body needs. Choose moderate portions of food that taste good to you.
3. Chew your food till each morsel becomes liquid.
4. Stop eating before you are totally full.

Breathing and sleeping right

To breathe deeply, the spine must be straight chest free, flexible.

Sleeping recharges your vital energy. Never go to bed angry or depressed. Give thanks before you sleep.

Create a mental picture of yourself perfectly straight & use this image as a trigger to straighten up.

Fresh unpolluted air is vital when you breathe and sleep. Ensure that your home & office are ventilated.

38) These images have been transcribed by Nitya Wakhlu from the article "*The Science of Well-Being*" by Wallace D. Wattles.

173

CHAPTER 9

Working from Abundance: New Ways for People to be in a Business

In the last Chapter (Ch. 8), we saw how much is possible if we change the way we see things. There are great opportunities for 'Plenty for All' and 'Good Work for All', if we re-examine our beliefs behind the notions of wealth, value, and the higher purpose of business.

True Wealth through Abundance

There are certain beliefs surrounding the word 'wealth' that most of us have become conditioned to holding; one of them being the idea that success means having to consistently make a lot of money, even at the cost of neglecting one's inner life. We think that to be people with raised levels of consciousness, all desires for material life need to be forsaken, while focusing solely on spiritual evolution. These however, are misconceptions. What really is true wealth? And how can we BE it?

As Parveen Chopra[1] says in Life Positive, "You will probably not lack in anything, be it love, health, happiness, knowledge or money, if you understand that your outer, material fullness is not really separate from inner spiritual wealth - that both together mean a lifetime of abundance."

---

1) Chopra, Parveen, "*YOU ARE RICH! YOU JUST HAVE NOT REALIZED IT*",
Life Positive: December1996, www.lifepositive.com/you-are-rich-you-just-have-not-realized-it

True Wealth[2] is the wealth of being true. Truth is that which is permanent, it is the underlying peace behind everything. Some of the many names it is known by are love, spirit, awareness, God, essence and 'I Am'. Every one of our tangible possessions or what we usually refer to as 'wealth', are transient; they will go one day. True Wealth cannot be taken away from us because it is ever-present and eternal. It bestows freedom on its owner and nurtures him/her. It is like a true light, which is the foundation of wealth in all its material forms. It is the wealth of wholesomeness, or being whole.

True Wealth flows in accordance with needs, spontaneously aligning itself – neither too much, nor too little. The quantity and timing of the flow of money, energy, information etc. dance in perfect harmony with our evolving needs. The following diagram captures what True Wealth is as we see it:

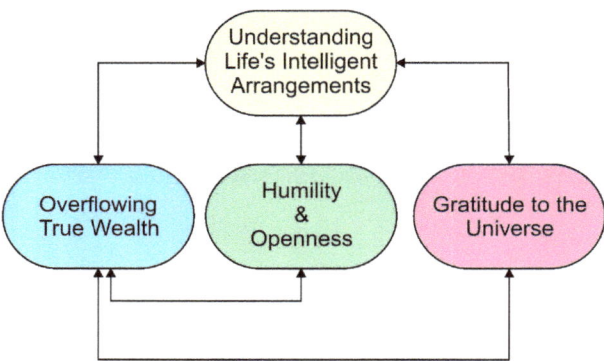

True Wealth is FLOW – Fullness and Love Overflowing in the World. It is not a coincidence that both the words 'Affluence' and 'Influence' refer to the fluency that is needed to generate them; the flow of ideas, information, communication, appreciation, gratitude, service and value.

The Source of True Wealth

Everything we do in life has its origin in our mind. Our view of life affects our way of life. Our beliefs determine our capacity, and they also affect our perception. This, in turn, affects our actions and shapes the forthcoming outcomes.

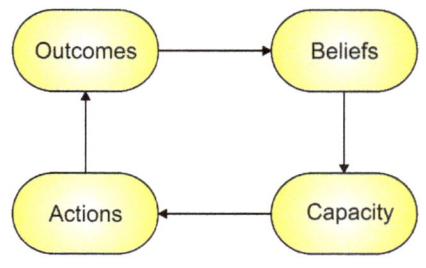

2) Wakhlu, Arun, "What is True Wealth and How To Be It", Chapter 20 in *"What is True Wealth & How Do We Create It"*, by Verna Allee and Dinesh Chandra, eds., Indigo Press: New Delhi, 2003

How we see and use resources, the depth and quality of our relationships, and the kind of thinking, communication and actions we bring to life, determine the results or outcomes we achieve. They determine how much wealth we create.

True Wealth is the fundamental source of everything. It is that creative intelligence which can see and connect a need with a means to serve and satisfy that need. Free flowing ideas, creativity, joyful expressions and a celebratory approach to life and service are the hallmarks of being in touch with True Wealth.

The table below captures what happens when we are in touch with True Wealth, and also when we are out of touch with it:

In Touch With True Wealth	Out Of Touch With True Wealth
Resources seen clearly. Opportunities perceived. High inner resourcefulness.	Resources not seen. Hidden. Clouded up by agitated mind, and limited perception.
Open, trusting. Giving and receiving ideas, information money etc. freely.	Closed, untrusting, rigid. Restricted, blocked, or misaligned giving and receiving of ideas, information etc.
Giving back to the whole. Wealth recycled back into the system. Flow keeps going on. Abundance, richness, balance.	Wealth held back, accumulated, hoarded. Deficiency, poverty, imbalance.

Being True Wealth

True Wealth is our natural state. We simply need to unlearn back to it. How can we be one with the larger flow of life recognizing its intrinsic abundance and wholeness? We need to be, and do, those things, which are aligned with an understanding of life as a whole. Having defined the problem in this manner, we can say that the foundation of True Wealth is a life of integrity or wholeness. A life of integrity implies that I am following my calling, and that the time I am spending on Earth has a larger meaning connected to the whole. This keeps me enthused, creative and energized. My time is spent on things that bring joy to others and to me. I am content with the happiness this gives me, and therefore, I need less. This reduces compensatory spending and consumption born out of inner emptiness.

True Wealth is our own real and whole Self. When we drop all boundaries, illusions, false notions of who we are and what we 'own', then we awaken to the glory of True Wealth. We awaken to the fact that the source is the whole and that the whole contains everything. We also see that all this is open to us, available to us, if only we drop our perceived limitations. These limitations are all in the mind. If we drop the mind, and understand that we are intrinsically boundary less, we *are* abundance.

Here are a few tips for being True Wealth, and opening up to abundance and prosperity in our lives:

- Enjoy serving for the sheer joy of it. From an inner space of love/ being, do what gives you joy and peace in the now. Do what you really love to do! Do nothing else!

- Focus on what you can 'Give' from what you have. Ask often "How can I serve/add value with what I have?", "What is the best I can give to the world; how can I best serve from the gifts/talents that life has given me?". Connect with, and express your deepest calling.

- Surrender your little self to the real Self – your subjective witnessing awareness. Drop all worries and attachments. Everything will happen miraculously. Seek guidance from your Self (the I Am, God, Love, Life). Trust it to show the way towards manifesting and unfolding True Wealth.

- You are an infinite creative source. Walking on the Earth and remembering this source (our very essence) can create almost anything you want. Use the power of creative visualization to create well-formed pictures of what you want. Trust that articulating and thinking about the desired outcomes from a space of gratitude and abundance will surely manifest what you want.

- The palace of True Wealth (another name for life as a whole) is full and overflowing. Accept what you need, but do not cling. Clinging and possessiveness bring in boundaries where there are none. The very act of clinging and possessing blocks the flow of True Wealth. Flow with life, letting go into the fullness. Say "Yes!" to True Wealth. Move forward in faith that all your needs will be met, without any necessary accumulations.

- Change your beliefs. 'Abundance, and a free flow of money, used wisely for life-affirming goals, are good'. 'It's okay to make lots of money'. 'There is more than enough for all'. Affirm "I am Abundance now; I am grateful for this abundance".

More beliefs that attract abundance:

- My work is a great contribution to others and I am richly rewarded for it.

- I am a giver and what I give comes back to me multiplied manifold.

- I gratefully accept all of life's abundance. I gratefully accept my situation.

- I am willing to know what I want, I am willing to ask for it, and I am willing to receive exactly what I ask for.

- My strong sense of purpose attracts those people and situations that are necessary to accomplish my desired results.

- First, be the fullness of life, then act from this space. You will notice that, as boundaries drop, everything is yours to dance with and enjoy in the service of expanding joy and wholeness.

- Prioritize and focus. Be consistent and persistent in the pursuit of those goals which serve evolution.

- Take good care of yourself. You are precious and blessed!

What are Some Feelings Associated with Being Abundance?

"Why are you dying of thirst when you sit on the banks of the Ganga?"

— Sri Ramakrishna Paramahamsa

When one lives a truly abundant life, these are the feelings that he or she feels:

- Deep relaxation. There is no agitation in the mind. Life is experienced as a play.

- Joy. This feeling is captured beautifully in the poem *"Song: Rarely, rarely comest thou"* by Percy Bysshe Shelley[3]: "I love all that thou lovest, Spirit of delight! The fresh Earth in new leaves dress'd, And the starry night; autumn evening, and the morn, When the golden mists are born"

---

3) Shelley, Percy Bysshe, From the Poem: *"Song: Rarely, rarely, comest thou"*, Read the whole poem here: www.poetryfoundation.org/poem/174406

- Fully experiencing what is happening here and now. There is an intense sense of being in the present.

- A deep feeling of peace. A clear knowing that all that is needed is here. Existence, in its infinite wisdom and compassion, will automatically send whatever is needed, wherever and at the right time.

- A feeling of wholeness/togetherness. A sensing that this body-mind is not a separate island but woven into the fabric of the whole; that it is deeply interconnected, richly endowed, and one with the fullness and abundant flow of the Universe.

- Simplicity and ease in all actions. Because one is crystal clear about life and awake to wholeness, things are straight, simple and effortless. The mind that makes the simple action complex is kept at bay!

- A feeling of gratitude; a thanksgiving for this abundance, and a sense of wonder at the ways of existence; at how every need is provided for if only we allow it. Melody Beattie[4] expresses the power of gratitude beautifully: "Gratitude unlocks the fullness of life. It turns what we have into enough and enough into more. It turns denial into acceptance, chaos into order and confusion into clarity. It turns a meal into a feast, a stranger into a friend. It makes sense of our past, brings peace for today and creates a vision for tomorrow"

- Knowing. In spite of the chaos and complexity of everyday life, we can see that there is a deeper order in the Universe; night follows day, seasons follow each other. Similarly, as we become one with the abundance of life, more orderliness is observed, increasing efficiency at home and in the workplace.

- A feeling of dissolving humility: the kind a doll made of salt would feel as she went into the ocean to measure its depth! Great oneness, immense richness, profound gratitude and tearful peace.

---

4) For more quotes from Melody Beattie and also more information on her, take a look at www.livinglifefully.com/people/melodybeattie.htm

A nice metaphor to think of abundance is captured in this illustration by Nitya. Imagine a reservoir of infinite capacity connected by a pipe to you. You can draw as much water from it as you want. There is, however, a tap which regulates the flow. How open or closed this tap is, is controlled by your thoughts, feelings and actions.

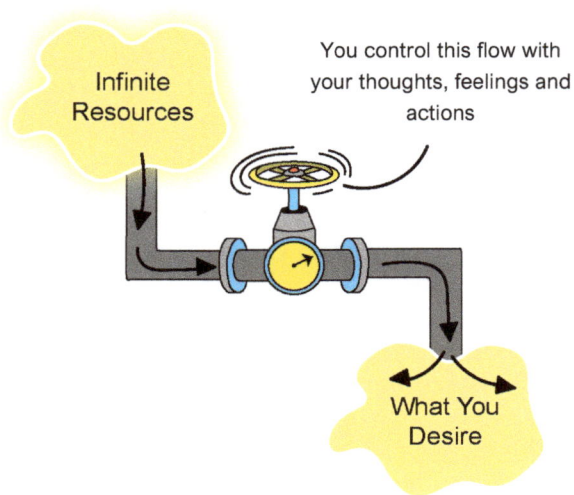

Choosing love and positivity keeps the tap open. Choosing fear and negativity closes the tap. With a clear intention/desire to manifest what you value, and with the tap wide open, you can swiftly create what you desire. In that sense, you hold the key to creating value.

The New Source of Value

If you look at any kind of value that is created by people, whether it's a work of art, a new innovation or a new way of doing business, it always comes from a creative source, it always comes from the activity of the human mind and the human consciousness. This connects things in new ways; it links dots in ways that have not been linked before. It creates new combinations, new processes, new artifacts, new machines, and new things – to serve human beings in a different way.

'Seek not outside yourself'

You are the source of all values. It is not outside you, nor is it inside you. You, yourself are the source. Value is the substratum of everything. It is the very foundation of wholeness which permeates everything. Value is the juice of life. It is the unbounded awareness which underlies everything. This is accessed only when we are in the NOW. When we appreciatively see the beauty of each moment, we are in touch with this substratum.

There are different types of value. There is a value in information and knowledge sharing. What we make of the information we have received and what action follows from it, matters greatly. Hoarding information, instead of sharing it freely with others, could forsake some valuable insights and actions, deeming that information of no use. The value creating flow of information is what makes the difference. Information, in isolation, may hold no value.

Value may be intangible, in forms such as happiness and joy. Similarly, objects that make life easier and more convenient, have a tangible value. If our actions commence from promptings and coercing from other people, we are out of touch with what 'makes our heart sing'. This simple way of measurement is indicative of true value – guided by our inner voice, our shining eyes and singing hearts can be signifiers of alignment with the whole.

The view that we propose is that finally, everything that we call 'valuable' takes us back to a source of great inner satisfaction, inner balance, ease, freedom and peace. And this book shows how the very same space, from which new ideas come, new inventions come, is also the same space which is the goal of all value.

If we look at it as a rainbow – the source of the rainbow is this space of wholeness, space of peace, of universal intelligence and creativity. And the end of the value creation rainbow is also the very same space – of peace, joy and happiness. You are that space of profound value. You are the source of all value, and you are also the goal of all value. The source and sink, alpha and omega, start and end of the rainbow of value, are all from the same source of wholeness or fullness of life or Universal intelligence or your own I Am.

Whether it is through business, or exploration or writing, we are all seeking this same source. As we have discussed at length in Chapter 4, we are seeking that which we already are! The following story captures this beautifully:

The Precious Jewel[5] — All wisdom, according to Daudzadah, is contained in the various levels of interpretation of this ancient traditional tale. In a

---

5) Shah, Idries, "*Thinkers of the East: Studies in Experientialism*", Octagon Press: London, 2003.
Also see www.idriesshahfoundation.org/books/thinkers-of-the-east-studies-in-experientialism

remote realm of perfection, there was a just monarch who had a wife and a wonderful son and daughter. They all lived together in happiness. One day the father called his children before him and said, "The time has come, as it does for all. You are to go down, an infinite distance, to another land. You shall seek and find and bring back a precious Jewel."

The travelers were conducted in disguise to a strange land whose inhabitants almost all lived a dark existence. Such was the effect of this place that the two lost touch with each other, wandering as if asleep.

From time to time they saw phantoms, similitudes of their country and of the Jewel, but such was their condition that these things only increased the depth of their reveries, which they now began to take as reality. When news of his children's plight reached the king, he sent word by a trusted servant, a wise man: "Remember your mission, awaken from your dream, and remain together."

With this message they roused themselves, and with the help of their rescuing guide they dared the monstrous perils, which surrounded the Jewel, and by its magic aid returned to their realm of light, there to remain in increased happiness for evermore.

As we go through life seeking things that appear to give us lasting value (illusions that make us ill!) we are actually looking for the precious jewel of True Wealth or Lasting Value. This is nothing but our own already present wholeness.

New Forms of Doing Business

"Never go into business to purely make money. If that's the motive, you're better off doing nothing!"

— Richard Branson

As more people are slowly waking up to these deeper realities, the very nature of business is undergoing a slow but steady shift. Many books mentioned in the References section at the end of the book point to the shift in paradigms that are impacting the purpose and form of businesses.

Business is a powerful tool shaping our planet today. Of the hundred largest economies in the world, forty-nine are sovereign states and fifty-one are multinational corporations. Business today has the capacity to make an enormous difference to humanity's leap towards a new paradigm of living and learning on the planet. Given their economic clout, knowledge and human capital, geographical spread and cross-cultural impact on people, businesses can be a powerful force for good in the world.

However, many businesses in the past have had negative environmental impacts. Many ethical breaches by businesses have also come to light in the past decade. To quote Klaus Schwab[6], president of the World Economic Forum in Newsweek, "In today's trust-starved climate, our market driven system is under attack. Large parts of the population feel that business has become detached from society and that business interests are no longer aligned with social interests".

It doesn't matter if the past has not been so wholesome. There is always the opportunity to have a change of heart and start on a fresh note. Companies who have in the past created a huge "unwholesome impact" in the world by way of exploitation, control of people, destruction of natural habitats and distortion of people's cultural lives, can change. Corporations are run by people and peoples' perspectives can shift. As leaders in corporations start resonating to the new vision and values, entire corporations can become life-affirming forces on the planet.

This will call for a movement of, and towards, Wholesome Leadership. Wholesome Leadership is a leadership inspired by our intrinsic oneness with all other human beings, and with the natural environment. It is a leadership that works from an inner space of love, married with resolute and focused action.

Such leaders would align the purpose and objectives of their organizations with the larger wholesomeness and well-being of all stakeholders in the business. (Customers, investors, employees, suppliers, partners, the community, the environment and government). All stakeholders will need to receive 'Value' from the business if it has to thrive and grow in the long run. Value could be financial, social, intellectual, spiritual, aesthetic or emotional.

Their strategies would have to be not only effective, but meta-effective i.e. their goals are aligned with the greatest good for the largest number of people. They need to be fully integrated with and guided by the intelligence that runs all of life. Can we flow with this intelligence? Can our work and business, mirror the beauty and grace of this amazing wholeness? We sincerely believe that this is possible. There is enough evidence to show that such businesses are thriving at 10 times the level of like to like businesses.

As business leaders become more conscious of the fundamental spiritual nature of all of life, the distinction between the outer 'material' and the 'inner' spiritual aspects will dissolve. As they begin to see and experience the amazing wholeness of life, they will learn to dance in tune with this abundance.

---

6) Schwab, Klaus, from an interview to "*Newsweek*": February 24, 2003

This is how Bob Galvin[7], Chairman of the executive committee on Motorola's board of Directors, once described the primary job of leaders: "Inspiring acts of faith ('things are do-able that are not necessarily provable'), spreading hope, and building trust." When a VP asked how these values relate to the 'real world of business', Galvin replied that executives must develop strong character in themselves and others, not just good technical or financial skills. Then he concluded: "Faith, hope, and trust... Theology is very practical business".

As the world grows in Wholesome Leadership and as these leaders start collaborating together for the well-being and evolution of the whole system in life affirming ways, more such leaders will grow. This will be like a viral spread of the notion and practice of Wholesome Leadership. Such a process is vouched safe to succeed, because all of life is intrinsically built to unfold wholeness and health in all people. It is our 'not seeing correctly' that interferes with the natural unfolding of this process.

Business with Heart

There are many examples of businesses (which we will see further in this Chapter) which are like light houses in the dark. These are businesses that nourish all those who come in contact with them. These are businesses with a heart. When we say 'business with a heart', we mean conducting business based on a foundation of a calm and clear understanding of the larger canvas of life and in it the role of business. The words 'Heart' and 'Earth' have exactly the same letters in them! This is by no means just a happy coincidence! Business from the heart is deeply respectful and caring of the Earth and all her inhabitants.

In this form of business, profits are seen as a means instead of the goal. This is very much in line with what Peter Drucker once observed: "Profit is for companies what oxygen is to a human being; it is necessary for survival, but *not* the reason for it."

While our life depends upon oxygen, our life is not about collecting and storing oxygen. In exactly the same way, the best way to be happy is not to pursue happiness directly. Serving others with your gifts, loving what you do, staying healthy and being kind and caring towards others, is a spontaneous by-product of happiness. Peter Drucker has also observed that Information Technology can play a very important role in making this happen. While Open Space Technology (OST) has proven to be a very powerful tool for unfolding peace and Wholesome Development on the planet, we now need to create a similar process in cyber space which is owned by humanity as a whole. This can enable the creation

---

7)   Bob Galvin's conversation cited here was quoted in: "*The Role of Meaning and Purpose in Business*', by William C Miller and Debra R. Miller. Read the whole paper here: www.vcihome.com/sites/PDF_files/Paper_purpose_and_meaning.pdf

of rapid connections across individuals and organizations and foster the conversations and collaborations needed for people to work creatively and 'co-heartedly' together. It would serve as a meta-integrating platform for anyone on the planet working for wholesome sustainable development. This activity in cyberspace will go hand in hand with face to face meetings on the ground with inspired action and genuine community building. This promises to unleash an explosion of learning, innovation, integration and inspired action on the planet. This is waiting to happen.

Reliable Prosperity based on a Conservation Economy[8].

The entire system of capitalism in its current form will be slowly replaced by a wholesome economy which is centered around a full life for all. The diagram below represents this idea. The aim of the Wholesome Economy will be the enhancement of wholeness and wellbeing based

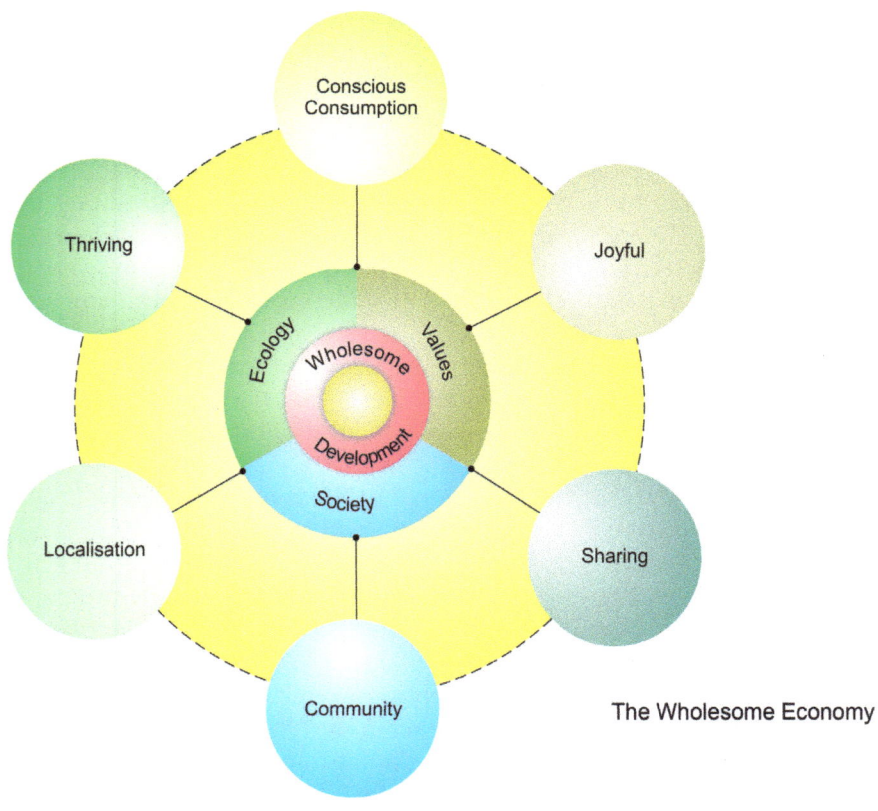

8) www.reliableprosperity.net/explore.html

on co-operation rather than competition. Economic activity will be in the joyful service of life and in deep harmony with nature, values and other people. Transactions will be based on the local sharing and exchange of gifts. Participatory Leadership will guide community based actions and initiatives. People will produce and consume consciously, and the environment will be pure, thriving and abundant. There will not only be one big corporation that produces. Everyone is heading towards becoming a 'Prosumer'[9] (producers + consumers are prosumers). Prosumers will help to create something for people they are really in touch with. In this way, thousands of micro entrepreneurs can be born. Earlier, men and women did not buy shoes made by a designer, but simply went to the cobbler and got him to make a pair with cow hide. Similarly, they got clothes from weavers. Local people sought what they needed in the local market, creating work for the local craftsmen. In the future as well, the mother can bake cookies, someone can teach, someone can look after the house, someone can look after construction of the solar panel. In this way, there will be no need to look 'outside' for any job to be done. Our own communities will become locally self-sufficient and sustainable. Thus, the use of ones gifts for creating something for the people that they are in touch with will change the entire corporate equation. From mega corporations, we will move to micro entrepreneurs. The economy will move towards demonetization; something that the *"Zeitgeist Movement"*[10] had envisioned.

The new paradigm of business based on a wholesome way of life would be very different from what we are experiencing today. From a focus on only profit and growth, we would move towards maximizing value for all the stake holders. From centralized organizations with power structures based on a philosophy of command and control, we would move towards organizations based on networks, partnerships, inclusion and participation. There would be a strong emphasis on the elimination of all kinds of waste, including the waste of human potential. Collaborative work in the service of a larger good, and for individual and collective evolution would replace motivation based on pay alone.

Collective ownership and profit sharing in a workplace that honours family life and health, will replace a male dominated, intensive workplace where people work long hours.

As people begin to relax more and more into the wholeness of life and also begin to see that abundance like life is infinite and endless, the craving for amassing personal wealth will be replaced by forms of collaborative ownership and trusteeship. Mahatma Gandhi had long ago propagated the aspect of all of us being trustees for the organizations, office and positions

9)   Quain, Bill, *"Pro-Sumer Power II! How to Create Wealth by Being Smarter, Not Cheaper, and Referring Others to Do the Same"*, International Network Training Institute, Inc.: Berlin, 2008

10)   *"The Zeitgeist Movement"*: http://en.wikipedia.org/wiki/The_Zeitgeist_Movement

that we hold. The new paradigm of business and gift exchange will call for the formulation of new laws and new ways of managing money. Many experiments and initiatives in this direction are already in place.

Here are a few examples of many businesses that are aligned to this paradigm, businesses that are from the heart.

Whole Foods Market[11] – This is a company that is definitely a little out of the ordinary. The 19 people who started the first store were quite the idealistic bunch. Early on, they adopted a set of core values to guide their purpose. With care for all stakeholders being at the foremost, these were the values:

- Selling the highest quality natural and organic products available

- Satisfying and delighting customers

- Supporting team member' happiness and excellence

- Creating wealth through profits and growth

- Caring about communities and environment

- Creating on-going win-win partnerships with their suppliers

- Promoting the health of their stakeholders through healthy eating education

They now have over 84,000 team members in 388 stores. The idealism and commitment to their core values is as strong as ever. Sit in on a meeting and you'll hear team members asking questions like "How does that support the core values?" It's a tough crowd!

Over twenty-five years ago, when the founder of Whole Foods, John Mackay witnessed flood waters inundating his first store in Austin, Texas, his customers started flowing in to help him rebuild the store. A beautiful example of 'giving is receiving'. Whole Foods Market is a publicly held company and has to make a profit to survive in the market place. But it has more than proven that a company can do well, and does well, if the doing comes from the heart.

Café Gratitude[12] — A product of the creative ownership by Matthew and Terces Engelheart, this started when the sweethearts promised to live their lives together following and trusting intuition. Resulting from that commitment was an initial guidance to develop a board game. This evolved into them wanting to create a place where people could gather, eat, play and exchange ideas. After their experience with live foods, they decided

---

11)   *"Whole Foods Market"*: http://media.wholefoodsmarket.com/faq/
12)   *"Café Gratitude"*: www.cafegratitude.com

to make this place of their dreams a live food café. Thus was born Café Gratitude and it now has seven branches. It has been a ground breaking example of sacred commerce and its capacity to build a community, encourage healthy living and achieve abundance.

Pragati Leadership Institute[13] — Their work is teaching business organizations how to grow leaders with a heart and work from a wholesome perspective. 25 years ago when Pragati Leadership used words like joy, spirit and compassion in business, well-wishers said they were trying to make 'snowballs in hell'. But, 600 leading organizations and 25 countries later, people are sitting up and noticing this new paradigm. Today, optimizing sustainable stakeholder value in the long run, is the new mantra for successful businesses all over the world. In their book *"Firms of Endearment"*[14] (FoE) Raj Sisodia, Jag Sheth and Wolfe have shown that investment portfolios of FoE's outperformed the market by a ratio of 10:1.

Along with the changes that conscious businesses are bringing in, and also with the advent of a 'Gen Y' workforce (people born after 1980), there are some basic changes happening in the way business is structured and conducted. These will also call for radical changes in the way leaders lead. (These trends draw upon several bodies of knowledge which are partly captured in the references at the end of the book.) The key ideas emerging from this body of knowledge are the following:

1. People love to develop and give from their unique gifts, to collaborate, to make a lasting difference and to contribute to something larger than themselves. Businesses will need to demonstrate this in organizational cultures that challenge and support rather than control and extract.[15]

2. Our top-down, control-over-people, compartmentalized organizational designs are not a good fit for our times. Their rigidity leaves such organizations highly vulnerable in our volatile world. Millennials see these traditional organizations as today's dinosaurs.[16,17]

3. Our 'next big thing is not a thing'. Rather, it's those organizations that actually develop and unleash the virtually unlimited potential of people to evolve their organizations and themselves.

13) *"Pragati Leadership"*: www.pragatileadership.com

14) Sisodia, Rajendra S., Wolfe, David B. and Sheth, Jagdish N., *"Firms of Endearment: How World-Class Companies Profit from Passion and Purpose"*, Financial Times/Prentice Hall: New York, 2007

15) Pink, Daniel H., Drive: *"The Surprising Truth About What Motivates Us"*, Riverhead Books: New York, 2011

16) Natarajan, Ganesh and Jayaram, Lavanya, *"What We Really Want (Aspirations of Gen Y)"*, Menaka Prakashan: Mumbai, 2013

17) *"Gen Y"* www.slideshare.net/lific/generation-y-15763073; Also see *"Learning Preferences of Gen Y"* www.slideshare.net/wali11/learning-preferences-of-gen-y-millennial-learners-wali-zahid-spelt-2013

'Evolutionary purpose' challenges organizational leadership to step up to a very large question – "What's the highest purpose we can imagine for our organization?" As we get a sense of our evolutionary purpose we see our organizations as vehicles for a never-ending action-learning journey with ever-improving contributions to the wellbeing of all life and for all time. (The Infinite Game)[18]

4. The motivation that really works (especially with the GenY/Millennials) is the intrinsic motivation (Type I) coming from the higher purpose, coming from mastery and autonomy. In contrast to this is the Type X motivation which is extrinsic. Leaders and organizations that will succeed in the future will be the ones that foster Type I behavior. That is the behavior that fosters intrinsic motivation.[19]

5. Sustainable organizations will deliver value to all the stakeholders.[20]

6. A climate of value innovation is fostered by an inspiring culture that is rooted in values and also supports innovation. It is also a function of a vision and strategy for value innovation; processes, practices and systems that support value innovation and a leadership team that drives value innovation. It also comes from cross functional, cross practice and cross cultural teams that have the space and opportunity for conversation, connection and co-creation across business silos, across practices and across geographical/organizations boundaries.[21]

7. 'Self-management' is the way in which all the rest of nature works. This 'key' changes nearly everything that we've grown to hate about top-down controls. 'Wholeness' at all levels of a system is not a new idea. It happens to exist throughout all the rest of nature. Learning to see ourselves and our organizations as whole conscious, caring, committed and courageous living organisms is a key that opens all stakeholder relationships to a new level of co-creative possibility. Leaders will have to make time to reflect on and co-creatively explore the implications of all of the above. As leaders realize the power of 'Self-management Breakthrough,' their world changes. They also achieve a level of spaciousness and new ways of seeing that support a 'virtuous spiral' of co-creative exploration that routinely turns breakdowns into more breakthroughs.[22]

---

18) *"Global GEA"*: Guild of Evolutionary Architects, www.globalgea.net

19) Secretan, Lance H.K., *"Reclaiming Higher Ground: Creating Organizations that Inspire the Soul"*, Response Books (Sage Publications): New Delhi, 1996

20) Mackey, John and Sisodia, Raj, *"Conscious Capitalism: Liberating the Heroic Spirit of Business"*, Harvard Business Review Press: Boston, 2013

21) Wakhlu, Arun, *"Managing from the Heart"*, Response Books (Sage Publications): New Delhi, 1999. Also, please see: Wakhlu, Arun, *"Value...An Inner View"*, 2010

22) Laloux, Frederic, *"Reinventing Organizations"*, Laoux (Frederic): Brussels, 2014

8. Most leaders are captives of a vicious circle where their rigid organizations are unable to handle the challenges implicit in our 'VUCA' (Volatile, Uncertain, Complex and Ambiguous) world. So, 'messes' get delegated upward to an already harried leadership. Unfortunately, reactive problem-oriented fixes tend to be born of the same thinking that created the messes in the first place – and, in turn, create new 'messes.'[23]

9. Leaders need to move away from being 'Heroes' to 'Hosts'. The kind of leadership needed to lead and inspire Gen Y people will have to be consciously developed in your organization.[24]

Business leaders of the future will be entrepreneurs for wholeness. Working from their own natural calling (and inspiring others to do the same), they will work in a self organising way, constantly listening to what life is calling them to do in each moment. They will recognise that a community, drawing upon the collective intelligence of the group, will be able to come up with the right response to almost all challenges. They will use technology appropriately. The technology will be Earth friendly, sustainable and localized. Its development and use will be in the hands of the local community and not in the hands of monolithic and centralized corporations. The *"Centre for Environment and Education"* (CEE)[25] has piloted a similar process of rural based eco enterprise for sustainable livelihoods. It flourishes under the name of *"Gram Nidhi"* As more and more such experiments blossom all over the planet, there will be a dramatic reduction in waste and inefficient use of resources. The blueprints and processes for this wholesome way of earning and living are all available on the planet at this point in time. They are all tested models.

New times create new needs – and new needs require new solutions. *"The New Pioneers"* by Tania Ellis[26] is a practical guide for capitalists and idealists on how to navigate in the new economic world order. It is about responding to the social megatrends that are shaping our lives in new ways and creating a new face of capitalism. It is about the new breed of leaders/pioneers that are paving the way for the new business revolution: this century's generation of visionary leaders and social entrepreneurs. To quote Tania "Hardcore business people are realizing that they can increase their profits by incorporating social responsibility into their business, and heartcore idealists are realizing that the use of market methods helps them meet their social goals successfully." It is such leaders who are anchored

---

23) Collins, Jim and Hansen, Morten T., *"Great by Choice Great by Choice: Uncertainty, Chaos, and Luck - Why Some Thrive Despite Them All"*, Harper Business: New York, 2011

24) Wheatley, Margaret, and Frieze, Debbie, *"Leadership in the Age of Complexity: From Hero to Host"*, Published in Resurgence Magazine, Winter 2011

25) *"Centre for Environmental Education"* (CEE), India www.ceeindia.org

26) Ellis, Tania, *"The New Pioneers: Sustainable business success through social innovation and social entrepreneurship"*; Wiley: New York, 2010

in the space of their true inner Being, working from deep compassion and understanding, AND who are adept in the market place, providing needed goods and services that are Earth and people friendly, who will bring in the revolution needed in business. As more and more business leaders realize that the divide between Corporate Social Responsibility (CSR) and Business As Usual (BAU) is totally artificial, and that good, sustainable business is socially responsible at its core, business will come into its own as a harbinger of True Wealth to Earth. Moreover, many trans-national organizations are already working models of people collaborating very successfully across nations and cultures. As we work with many such organizations, we are seeing that they can become lighthouses of not only wealth creation, but also of teaching Governments the art of collaboration across national boundaries.

So, far from being the 'bad boys' of the planet with a huge trust deficit, businesses can play a creative role in the emergence of One Wholesome World.

Joyful Action Now

1. Describe your ideal work situation. Visualize yourself in that work situation. (Don't worry about whether you are trained, educated or whether it is possible or not. Just let your imagination run freely)

   - What would you be doing?

   - What skills will you be using?

   - Your work environment…?

   - The money you will be earning…?

   - How much is the gap between your current work and what you describe above. Can you think of any small steps you could take to bring you closer to your ideal work situation?

2. If you were given a magic wand to create four other lives for yourself, what fun work would you choose to do in each of them?

   - Write down whatever comes to mind.

   - Do not censor.

   - Now pick one of these dream occupations and do something in that direction for a few days. For example, if you wrote 'teaching children', you could take up teaching at your neighborhood school or if you said 'be a painter', start painting.

3. Look at the section on True Wealth in this chapter. How do you need to think differently if you want the flow of more prosperity in your life or business?

CHAPTER 10

Wholesome Governance

"…if the Government cannot create happiness (dekid) for its people, there is no purpose for the Government to exist."

— Legal Code of Bhutan 1729[1]

Among the many difficulties India faces, the most palpable problem is the crisis of Governance. Other countries in Asia, Africa and South America, are similarly placed. Governance affects the life and working environment of millions, who consider themselves free citizens of welfare states. In the last fifty years, we have witnessed a growing restlessness with the systems and instruments of Governance. Available evidence suggests a continuous decline in the quality of governance in most developing countries. Some of the obvious elements of this crisis are:

- Inefficient delivery of services

- Dichotomy between the political and executive wings of governance

- Breaking down of existing institutions

- Corruption in the polity and economy

- Lack of societal involvement in governance

---

1) *"The Story of Gross National Happiness"*: www.gnhcentrebhutan.org/what-is-gnh/the-story-of-gnh

Good governance will have a big role to play in the emergence of One Wholesome world.[2] A few questions that come up for reflection when we think of Governance are: Who is governing life? Does good governance imply a powerful and centralized government? Can outer governance, align with the intelligence that governs all of life (without human intervention)? First let's take a look at what good governance is.

What is Good Governance?

In a World Bank paper[3] Daniel Kaufmann, Aart Kraay and Massimo Mastruzzi outlined six dimensions of governance for 199 countries for 1996, 1998, 2000 and 2002 centered around three key reference points:

1. The "process by which governments are selected, monitored and replaced".

2. The "capacity of the government to effectively formulate and implement sound policies".

3. The "respect of citizens and the state for the institutions that govern economic and social interactions among them".

From this, the authors went on to devise the key indicators of governance. These are:

- **Voice and accountability**, which includes a number of indicators that measure various aspects of the political process, civil liberties and political rights

- **Political stability and absence of violence**, which consists of several indicators that measure the chances that a government will be overthrown by unconstitutional means

- **Government effectiveness** is about the quality of public service provision, the bureaucracy and its competence and independence and, most critically, the credibility of the government's commitment to policies.

- **Rule of law** includes several indicators that "measure the extent to which agents have confidence in and abide by the rules of society. These include perceptions of the incidence of crime, the effectiveness and predictability of the judiciary, and the enforceability of contracts."

2) Wakhlu, Omkar, N., Unpublished Letter, November, 2000

3) Kaufmann, Daniel and Kraay, Aart and Mastruzzi, Massimo, "*Governance Matters III: Governance Indicators for 1996-2002*", World Bank Working Paper No 3016, June 30, 2003
http://papers.ssrn.com/sol3/papers.cfm?abstract_id=1682130

- **Control of corruption** which is about all the things we know and act upon in an open and transparent way, with the full knowledge of the citizens of a country. It includes the tendency of the elite to engage in 'state capture'.

And what do they conclude? Just this: "Interpreting these trends is difficult, but we can state with some confidence that there is little, if any, evidence of improvements in global governance over the period we consider."[4]

Looking around at the state of the world today (February 2016), we are witness to the economic collapse of Greece, the advance of ISIS, severe economic stress in China, ongoing scams of all varieties, and the fact that (despite all the hype), half of rural India is still poor. We see that Governance has largely failed.

The Elements of Good Governance

So what exactly are the elements of good governance? Good Governance means eliminating poverty by empowering the poor, unprivileged and the exploited. Good Governance means, a system and a structure that is democratic, transparent, clean, efficient, equitable, sensitive and accountable.

Good Governance requires, "not so much additional resources as better personnel policies and sound delivery mechanisms. Unless teachers attend schools and teach, unless doctors attend health centers and provide health care, and subsidies reach the poor, mere increase in the social sector expenditure would only result in further leakage…"[5]

It is clear that good governance is finally about people passionately and professionally doing what they are supposed to do.

To understand the roots of governance we need to first look at the elements of excellent service oriented governance. If we treat the recipients of the service (citizens) as customers, and also look at the state as another stakeholder, the dimension of Good Governance could be listed as under:

Empathetic orientation towards citizens/customers: The Administrators' ability to understand the customers' need and requirements, from their perspective, and realistically appraise whether or not something is doable.

Commitment to excellence: Individual commitment to help citizens in achieving their goals/objectives within the given resources.

---

4) Kaufmann, Daniel and Kraay, Aart and Mastruzzi, Massimo, "*Governance Matters III: Governance Indicators for 1996-2002*", World Bank Working Paper No 3016, June 30, 2003
    http://papers.ssrn.com/sol3/papers.cfm?abstract_id=1682130

5) Mitra, R. K. and Gupta, M. P., "*E-governance*", Indian Management, August 2003, pp. 52-59, Mumbai

Responsiveness: Administrators taking responsibility for creating a delightful experience for citizens/customers and solving their problems.

Reliability and trustworthiness: The administrator's ability to generate trust and win the confidence of customers/citizens.

Creative problem solving ability: The administrator's ability to come up with innovative solutions to customer problems within the given constraints.

Timeliness: The administrator's ability to accomplish things within time constraints and deadlines.

Tolerance for pressure: The administrator's ability to maintain control and poise in the face of adversity and political pressures.

Service recovery mindset: The administrator's ability to undo the bad service experience of a citizen/customer by taking the required corrective action there and then.

In a nutshell, good Governance is all about:

- Accurate and sensitive understanding of peoples' needs

- Creative responses to these needs with a resourceful mind giving innovative solutions to problems

While the elements required for good Governance are clear, why is it so rare? What are the underlying bottlenecks and problems which keep administrators from giving their very best to the public? In the past ten years, whenever the authors have encountered senior government officials in different forums, the following bottlenecks to good Governance have emerged:

- Conflicts between one's duties in the public domain and one's personal life

- Inability to respond speedily because of the fear of rapid change and chaos all around

- Inter-personal conflicts between people (e.g. between officers of the Indian Administrative Services (IAS) and from the Indian Police service(IPS) because of egos

- An inner conflict between one's values and professional ethics on the one hand versus 'the pressures' of political bosses and public expectations on the other. These conflicts were cited as affecting issues like postings/transfers/appointments and even normal professional functioning

- Problems arising from a lack of inter-departmental co-operation and teamwork

- Dealing with immature and arrogant bosses

- Feelings of helplessness and powerlessness in the face of the above issues

- Problems of low morale of staff due to low wages and low opportunities for promotion

A concrete experience of an NGO (with which the authors are connected with) regarding the unfolding of employment opportunities in the state of Jammu and Kashmir in India shows the following:

- A lack of co-ordination between different departments connected with the issue

- An inability amongst officials to see the opportunities in the state as a whole

- Slow or no response by the Government to an offer of pro-bono help (by competent and qualified citizens) to work on the problem

- The absence of bold leadership to resolve the problem by inspiring a shared vision and mobilizing people and resources

Another similar example in the area of catalyzing sustainable livelihoods for the urban poor in Pune city (Maharashtra, India) has shown that there are over 50 schemes and provisions (including generous funding) of the local, state and central governments applicable to people living in an urban slum. When you ask the 'beneficiaries' if they know of these, the answer is "No". When you ask government officials if they know of all these schemes and provisions, the answer again is "No".

What's happening in the Government these days?

In the movie *"Tangled"* by John M. Bernard[6], there is an appropriate metaphor that talks about government. "Imagine for a second, an automobile built over the years by people who kept piling on new features and innovations without ever stopping to integrate the ideas and remove the outdated ones. That's Government today". We need to change our focus from creating a new law or amending an old one, to actually focusing on outcomes.

More often than not, the new laws and the obsolete ones (that still happen to be in existence) are contradictory. Many times, the citizens are not aware of the law at all and it remains just some ink on a book without being

---

6) Bernard, John M., *"Our Efficiency-Killing Tangle of Laws"*,
    www.governing.com/blogs/bfc/col-efficiency-tangle-laws-regulations-outcomes.html

practically implemented. Instead of operating as one whole, there are lots of different fragments. Life does not throw up problems neatly packed into compartments: Problems are whole, so solutions also need to be whole. The ministries in the government (for example in India) need to be aware of what the other ministries are doing.

Let's take an example related to food and nutrition, something that affects all of us. Out of the 350,000 species of plants in the world, around 80,000 are edible for humans. However, at present, only 150 species are cultivated (directly for human food or as feed for animals). Of these, 30 produce 95% of human calories and proteins.[7]

Around 1200 varieties of uncultivated forest foods were displayed at the *"Forest Foods and Ecology Festival"*, December 12 to 14, 2014, held in New Delhi[8] by 23 Forest dependent communities. The nutritional value and health benefits of these uncultivated forest foods are proven beyond doubt. To bring this kind of forest food based cultivation and nutrition in the mainstream, India would require creative collaboration between the following ministries: Ministries of rural development; food processing Industries, tribal affairs, agriculture, health and family-welfare, social justice and empowerment, and the Ministry of environment, forest and climate change. Would they be willing to sit together to capitalize on this very credible opportunity to enhance the well-being of nearly 250 million people who live in and around forests in India? That's over one sixth of India's population!

As we raise our levels of consciousness and start working from a space of honesty and integrity for the genuine welfare of the people, silos will dissolve. People will be working with each other creatively and seamlessly to deliver innovative and low cost solutions to millions of people.

While the divisions may make the government think that it is better structured, but in the process of the fragmentation and complete lack of communication, we forget that our schools suffer, the common tax payers suffer, social harmony is affected, the infrastructure crumbles. Who will trust a government like this? The citizen's needs keep on piling, while governments are lost in the mess they created for themselves.

The government needs to learn from private companies where there is a focus on performance and outcomes. It needs to shift its focus to the basics again – educating children, ensuring food for all, and creating of jobs. The government and the citizens both need to become responsible and accountable for the actions that they take.

People need to learn from the best practices of each other. There are many good, commendable practices happening in Africa that can benefit

---

7) Füleky, György, *"Cultivated Plants, Primarily as Food Sources"*,
    www.eolss.net/sample-chapters/c10/E5-02.pdf
8) www.slideshare.net/forestfoods/forest-food-and-ecology-festival-december-2014

India greatly. The things happening in the United States are phenomenal but does Australia know all of them? There needs to be a migration of best practices. We must realize that, it is only through collaborating and working as one from an inner space of wholesomeness that we can control the damage that has already been done to the planet. If the government can have a more holistic and complete understanding of the developmental challenge, there is likely to be better policy formulation and even better execution.

Nobel laureate Amartya Sen[9] has said: "Poverty is not simply the lack of income. It is also the lack of a voice, of a responsive local administration that can redress local needs; the lack of a system of governance that is transparent and accountable to people it supposedly exists to serve". He has also aptly summed up the many dimensions of poverty as lack of 'capability'– capability to overcome violence, hunger, ignorance, illness, physical hardship, injustice and voicelessness.

The World Bank has argued that poverty often lies in the absence of opportunity, empowerment and security, and not just the absence of food on the table.

Today, although man possesses the resources and the technology to create a poverty-free world within a generation, about a quarter of the human population on Earth continues to live in extreme poverty[10].

Echoing a similar flow of thought, Swami Ranganathananda in his book "*Vedanta and The Future of Mankind*"[11] wrote that "when we speak of 'Lakshmi', our beautiful Goddess of wealth; it does not mean money only. It means money creatively used to enrich and beautify human life, to ensure human welfare." This is True Wealth. Money jealously hidden and confined under one's pillow is not 'Lakshmi'. The mere static ownership of money is something inauspicious! It does not produce joy or welfare. Money invested in human welfare is alone true Lakshmi. The blessing of 'Lakshmi' confers on humanity a capacity to create, appreciate and enjoy wealth, beauty and goodness". This is what wholesome governance aims at, creating True Wealth for as many people as possible for as long as possible.

What is Wholesome Governance? …The Integrated Model

We now need Government to start thinking of itself as the co-creator (along with business, educational and research institutions, NGOs and citizens at large) of enabling and facilitating structures and processes that serve global evolution and well-being.

9)   Sen, Amartya, https://en.wikipedia.org/wiki/Amartya_Sen

10)   Poverty, https://en wikipedia.org/wiki/Poverty

11)   Ranganathananda Swami, "*Vedanta and the Future of Mankind*", Advaita Ashrama: Kolkata, 1980

Unless the larger context of development is understood, and it also becomes the operating reference for the formulation and execution of policy, we are working in the 'wrong paradigm'. This is the fundamental problem with Governance all over the world at this point in time (2016). Governments and leaders are working with paradigms and mind models that are obsolete. There is a need to shift inner and then outer gears towards a more wholesome understanding of life, and also what governance means in that context.

Life is already governed beautifully. Left to themselves, people are creative, vibrant, healthy and loving. This innate and glorious naturalness is overshadowed by limitations, fear, hopelessness, helplessness and strife. It is almost as if we are coming in the way of our own good, like blocking the sunshine as we stand in shadows.

Can Governments become enablers of the Highest Natural Good for all people everywhere? Can Governments be the catalysts, supporters, connectors and expanders of all the good things that are already happening in abundance?

What is needed today is a revised focus, one that views development as a sustainable process of expanding the capabilities of people that seeks to mobilize all the human and material resources available; one that systematically seeks out innovative and cost-effective methods of production, which generate additional employment while being environmentally sustainable. This 'capabilities approach' to development, advocated by Amartya Sen, emphasizes the human initiative and creativity, individual and collective. It points to the need to democratize the development process. This approach provides an integrating concept which can guide public policy at national, regional and international level[12].

James D. Wolfensohn, former president of the World Bank, has stated that the true gauge of success for development projects is not to be found in numerical data or statistics but "in the smiles of children".[13] Against this backdrop, what might 'Wholesome Governance' be? Wholesome Governance occurs when the following come together:

- **Context:** Seeing the whole picture

- **Connection**: Connecting with the whole system and all its relevant parts

- **Consciousness**: Working from a space of wholeness within, from the infinite inner resources of joy and peace

- **Commitment**: Honoring one's word and working from truth

---

12) *"Why "Development" should Focus on People, Not Economy"*, www.hubpages.com/education/Why-Development-should-be-Peoples-Development

13) Wolfensohn, James D., former president of the World Bank, quoted in Ikeda, Daisaku (President, Soka Gakkai International), *"A Global Ethic of Coexistence: Toward a "Life-Sized" Paradigm for Our Age"*; Soka Gakkai International: 2003 www.daisakuikeda.org/assets/files/peace2003.pdf

Let us look at these four themes in greater detail in relation to Governance:

Context — Administrators are totally in touch with the 'big picture', their own and others' positive potentials, and how all pieces of the jigsaw puzzle fit together. They understand the larger purpose of governance as a whole, as embedded in society, which in turn, is embedded in the ecological/natural system. They fully comprehend the systemic linkages of different actors and stakeholders and the value that is delivered by the Government to each one. They clearly see the source of all value as lying more in the natural world and the world of culture and spirituality rather than being obsessed with 'growing' the material dimension alone.

Besides the larger context, administrators are also in touch with their own strengths and positive potentials. They are fully aware of the positive elements and life-giving forces in the areas and departments that they govern. They are adept at appreciatively leveraging these potentials.

Consciousness — Levels of positive emotional energy and initiative are high. Life and Governance are lived through and exercised consciously. Old unquestioned assumptions and beliefs are challenged and questioned. There is a strong prevalence of ownership, inner power, joy, love and empathy. People are healthy and energetic. They swiftly do what they intellectually know they ought to do. There are no gaps between knowing and doing.

Both those in power and those who are being governed, feel powerful and creative. They are active partners in the process of governance and have a say. Through participatory processes, they shape decisions affecting the allocation of resources.

Connection — Wholesome Governance relies on adequate connection and conversations. Whether it is to listen to the voice of the customer/beneficiary or to coordinate the formulation or implementation of a new policy, conversations happen regularly, especially across different horizontal layers and departments of the government. There are adequate spaces, forums or 'platforms' for people (citizens and administrators) to converse on things that they truly care about.

Knowledge and best practices are regularly shared across states, departments, and within the same state through regular conversations. Initiatives taken at the center and what is actually happening in the states (for example in the area of e-Governance) are coherently coordinated, and billions of dollars are saved in the process. Since, diverse perspectives and viewpoints get a chance to cross-fertilize, levels of innovation increase. Partnerships between the Public, Private Players (business) and People (PPPP) are routine and are skillfully facilitated by trained i-Catalysts (Catalysts of Inspiration, Integration and Innovation).

Commitment — Levels of commitment to honoring ones word, to the development of people and to sustained improvement actions are high.

Attention is given to systematically executing plans in a timely way. Even when a change intervention is started, sustaining it is usually a challenge. The quality of sustained commitment and focused tracking will be an important component of wholesome governance.

Mr. Narendra Modi (the PM of India, 2016) has coined an acronym for Responsive Governance: *"PRAGATI"*. It stands for PRoActive Governance And Timely Implementation.[14]

To summarize, Wholesome Governance happens when:

- The larger purpose of governance is seen as the expansion of freedom and capabilities/capacities, rather than just an expansion of material goods alone

- People are aligned with the power of natural governance that runs all of life. (You may call this power *Dharma* or Love)

- Everyone sees governance as their role (Not only the Government, but citizens, NGOs, businesses, trade bodies etc.). There is a Public, Private and People Partnership in the process of Governance (PPPP)

- Everybody works as one in an integrated and collaborative way through connection, conversation and co-creation; above all, there is concerted and coherent action to make a difference, no matter what the odds are

- There is deep care in the hearts of the key players for themselves, for other people and for the environment

- Governance is based on awareness and consciousness which inspires working from deeper values and also in an ethical way

Speaking about 'Wholesome Governance', Anil Swarup, IAS, (Currently, Secretary Coals and Mines, Govt. of India, 2016) has this to say: "There has been a lot of talk about good governance but not so much about 'wholesome' governance. Whereas good governance would normally imply delivery of goods and services by the governing agency in a transparent and objective manner, wholesome governance goes much beyond this. In wholesome governance there would be an attempt to touch the lives of the people. There is an inherent element of 'empathy'. Hence in designing of the policy there would be an attempt to understand the beneficiary in a more comprehensive manner. The instruments used for implementing such policies would not be robotic but empathetic to the beneficiary. Thus there

14)   PRAGATI, www.pib.nic.in/newsite/PrintRelease.aspx?relid=117685

is a greater participation of stake holders in the formulation of policies and their implementation. Wholesome governance creates a greater ownership of policies and deliverables amongst the stakeholders. In another context, wholesome governance would also imply creation of a facilitating environment for its constituents to fulfill their aspirations, both material and spiritual without being intrusive. This would be tricky especially in the context of drawing a line but there would be an attempt to provide that balance. In short wholesome governance would be good governance with a human touch." The diagram attempts to capture 'Wholesome Governance' pictorially.

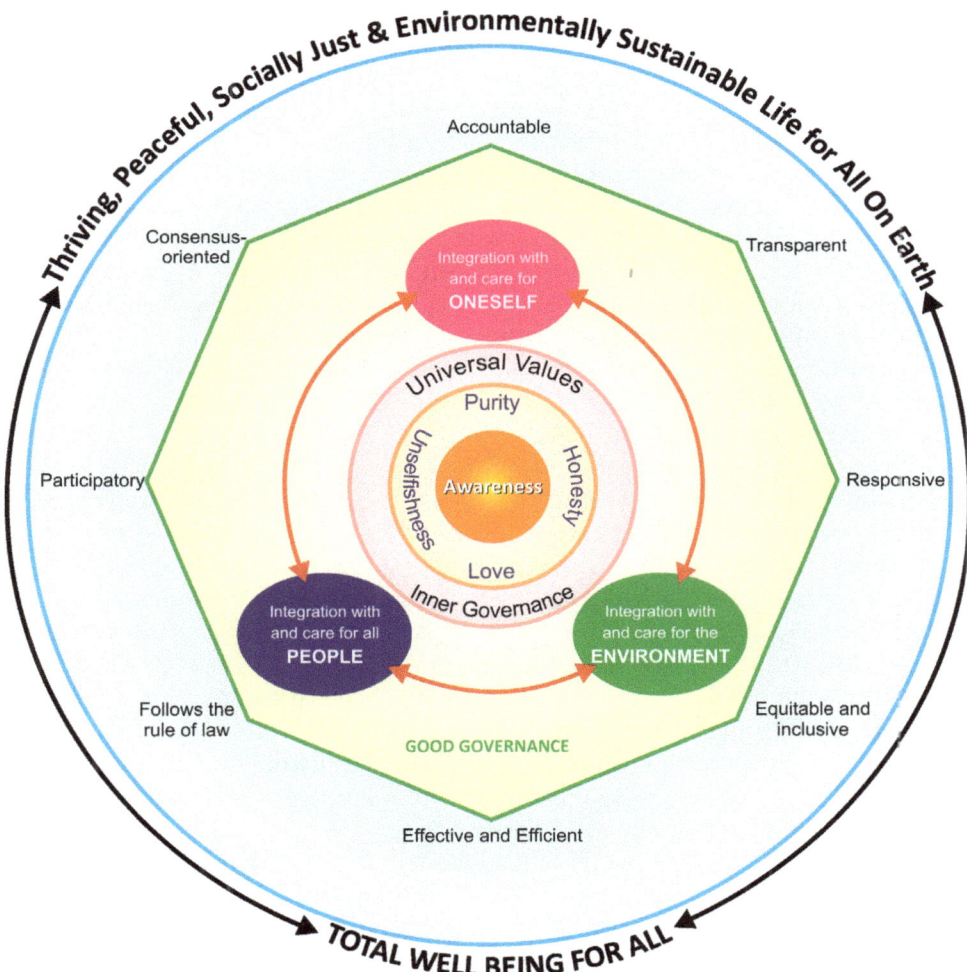

It starts with the largest and most expanded context of governance: total well-being for all. This is the same as a thriving, socially just and environmentally sustainable life for all on Earth.

The next layer shows the attributes of good governance. These are based on the wholesome triad of integration with and care for oneself, other people and the environment. The foundation and core of all this is inner governance based on universal human values and also on being one with awareness.

Measures of Development

It is important to have valid and accurate measures of progress. At this juncture, there is an urgent need for new methods. The new method has to include something that is meaningful, something that we as a community value more than just our economic status. Indicators do not change reality. They do help, however, in shaping the way we perceive it and to forge a common understanding of development. Indicators have fundamental importance in a complex and rapidly changing world. As was put beautifully in a paper titled *"Valuing Spirituality in Development"*[15], meaningful development requires that, "the seemingly antithetical processes of individual and social progress should be an organic process in which the spiritual aspect is expressed and carried out in the material."

In our increasingly interdependent world, development efforts must be guided by a vision of the world community which we desire to create and be animated by a set of universal values.

Spiritually based indicators to assess development progress apply the spiritual principles. These indicators should be based on universal principles which are essential to the development of the human spirit, and therefore, to individual and collective progress. These measures emerge from a vision of development in which material progress serves as a vehicle for spiritual and cultural advancement to help to transform not only the vision but the actual practice of development.

Spiritually based indicators help to establish, clarify and prioritize goals, policies and programs. At the heart of their conceptualization is the understanding that human nature is fundamentally spiritual and that spiritual principles (which resonate with the human soul) provide an enormous motivational power for sacrifice and change.

The components of a spiritually based indicator include a vision of a peaceful and united future; the selected principle(s) crucial to the realiza-

---

15) *"Valuing Spirituality in Development: Initial Considerations Regarding the Creation of Spiritually Based Indicators for Development"*, A concept paper presented to the *"World Faiths and Development Dialogue"*, hosted by the President of the World Bank and the Archbishop of Canterbury at Lambeth Palace; London: February 1998. Read more at:
www.bic.org/statements/valuing-spirituality-development#WCg0dpy17ZS1A6oU.99

tion of that future; the policy area addressed by the principle(s); and the goals toward which the measure assesses progress.

Improving the quality of our lives should be the ultimate target of public policies. But public policies can only deliver best fruit if they are based on reliable tools to measure the improvement they seek to produce in our lives.

— Angel Gurría, Secretary General of the OECD, May 2011.

Crucial to the problems of wholesome governance are good measures of development. A good dashboard focuses energy and gives us the capacity to measure progress. In what follows, we will discuss two measures that are aligned with what we have been advocating in this book:

- Gross National Happiness (GNH)
- Happy Planet Index (HPI)

Gross National Happiness[16]

Bhutan, a small nation, has suggested a method to make development human and nature centered. This country uses the concept of Gross National Happiness (GNH), instead of Gross National Product (GNP), to measure the achievements and impact of development. GNH includes all the regular indicators of economic development, ecological security, cultural promotion, and spiritual values. GNH also includes good governance as additional parameters to measure whether development enhances human happiness or increases human misery.

"Gross National Happiness is more important than Gross National Product"

— His Majesty Jigme Singye Wangchuck, the Fourth King of Bhutan

With his famous declaration in the 1970s, the former King of Bhutan challenged conventional, narrow and materialistic notions of human progress. He realized and declared that the existing development paradigm GNP or Gross Domestic Product (GDP), did not consider the ultimate goal of every human being: 'happiness'.

---

16) "*The Story of Gross National Happiness*": www.gnhcentrebhutan.org/what-is-gnh/the-story-of-gnh. Also see, "*Seventh Five Year Plan, Main Plan, Document*", Royal Government of Bhutan: 1991

The Folly of the GDP obsession!

GDP, as a measure of economic activity, does not distinguish between those activities that increase a nation's wealth and those that deplete its natural resources or result in poor health or widening social inequalities. If the forests of Bhutan were logged for profit, GDP would increase; if Bhutanese citizens picked up modern living habits adversely affecting their health, investments in health care systems would be made and GDP would increase; and if environmental considerations were not taken into account during growth and development, investments to deal with landslides, road damages and flooding would be needed, and GDP would increase. All of these actions could negatively affect the lives of the Bhutanese people yet paradoxically would contribute to an increase in GDP. It is evident that GDP/GNP is not the right measure when it comes to measuring Wholesome Development. Gross National Happiness(GNH) is definitely closer.

As the former King, His Majesty Jigme Khesar Namgyel Wangchuck has said: "Today GNH has come to mean so many things to so many people, but to me it signifies simply – development with values. Thus for my nation today GNH is the bridge between the fundamental values of kindness, equality and humanity and the necessary pursuit of economic growth. GNH acts as our National Conscience guiding us towards making wise decisions for a better future."

Bhutan in the last four decades has developed at a high speed. Governance has managed to reach even the remotest areas of the country. The major reason for Bhutan's smooth and successful development was that the leadership had a powerful and futuristic vision. The aims and objectives of development have been outlined as follows: "Apart from the obvious objectives of development – to increase GDP on a national level and incomes at the household level – development in Bhutan includes the achievement of less quantifiable objectives. These include, ensuring the emotional well-being of the population, the preservation of Bhutan's cultural heritage and its rich and varied natural resources." They realize that intellectual progress cannot be separate from practical experience. They translated their cultural and social consciousness into their development priorities. The western economists, who might find this concept irrational, miss the point. The aim is not economic efficiency, but a maximization of happiness.

Development ought to be people centric. As this is based on Buddhist philosophy it also has a different view of the environment. The concept holds that no subject or object has an independent existence; rather it dissolves into a web of relationships. The relationship is non-hierarchal since Buddhist philosophy does not differentiate between species (humans and non-humans).

Though, many countries outside of Bhutan are exploring this view and trying to measure success by keeping happiness as a crucial factor, there are chances that this concept will remain only on paper. Unless a fundamental shift occurs in the underlying paradigm of governance, it is unlikely that this concept will take root.

Happy Planet Index (HPI)[17]

The Happy Planet Index of 2012 is a new measure of progress that chooses to focus on the things that are of importance i.e., sustainable wellbeing for all. It does not take into account only the current lives of people, but also takes into consideration how the future generations will be impacted if things continue the same way.

We get so caught up that we forget that it is for happiness we're doing things. At the end of the day, everything that we do, we hope it takes us to a happier place. How can I be happier?

Happiness is not a function of external material wealth. It is hence omitted from most of the standardized measures that are present today to decide which nation is the most successful.

The HPI is one of the first global measures of sustainable well-being. It uses global data on experienced well-being, life expectancy, and ecological footprint to generate an index revealing which countries are most efficient at producing long, happy lives for their inhabitants, whilst maintaining the conditions for future generations to do the same.

$$\text{Happy Planet Index} = \frac{\text{Experienced wellbeing x Life expectancy}}{\text{Ecological Footprint}}$$

This simple indicator gives a clear sense of whether a society is heading in the right direction. It provides a vital tool to ensure fundamental issues are accounted for in crucial policy decisions. The elements in this formula show that it is not just the current well-being of a country that matters. A country which cannot provide for its future generations is far from successful.

According to this index, the countries that are economically forward have not necessarily fared better in the happy planet index. This is because of their high ecological footprint. Though the United States of America shows a high life expectancy and satisfaction, it is at the bottom- ranked 105 from amongst 151 countries. We are largely an unhappy planet. The crises that are affecting the world as of now, economically and otherwise, have shown considerable changes in the wellbeing of people within a period of just one year. But, even though income has increased, happiness levels have remained the same or in some cases have even declined. India in the Gallup World Poll survey of 2015 (focused on income levels and life satisfaction),

---

17) "*Happy Planet Index*", www.happyplanetindex.org/data

is ranked 70[18]. But, on the Happy Planet Index survey its rank rises to no. 32![19] This is because of its low ecological footprint. Countries like the United Arab Emirates that have high life expectancy and life satisfaction fall behind in the HPI because their ecological footprint is extremely high.

Could there be similar indices for individuals, neighborhoods, organizations and cities? What might happen if there was one single index for planet Earth as a whole? And we could link our personal and organizational indices to that of our nation and planet? This is a very fertile area for rapid research and innovation. The World Happiness Report[20], launched in 2012, is a step forward in this direction.

Global Governance... what can be done?

From command and control hierarchies we are moving towards more collaborative structures, with open spaces for sharing and learning. The future governance of the planet will not be a single, central authority. Each individual will be governed by spirit, by his/her own awareness.

At all levels, there will be gatherings in unifying circles. A circle has one center and can have infinite points on its circumference. These circles could happen at the family, neighborhood, city, national or international levels. Besides geography based circles they could be also around domains like city farming, health, art from the heart, sustainable livelihoods etc. Such gatherings for One Wholesome World are platforms which are:

- Free and Neutral Spaces for people gathered

- For listening to the guidance of purity, peace, positivity of the Heart

- Beyond any individual/organizational/gender/religious or national affiliation

- Beyond boundaries and identities of any kind

- Celebrating and appreciating with gratitude, what is already working

- Expressing through music and dance, joyful and celebratory

- As universal as silence/peace/love, the unifying core of life.

The heart of these platforms is symbolized by a circle of light. We will all sit on the periphery of this circle in deep reverence and gratitude, listening

---

18) www.thehindubusinessline.com/news/india-ranks-70th-in-gallups-well-being-index-latam-nations-on-top/article7350777.ece
19) www.happyplanetindex.org/countries/india
20) *"World Happiness Report"*: www.worldhappiness.report. Also, see more at: https://en.wikipedia.org/wiki/World_Happiness_Report

to the insights and inspiration for loving action. In these gatherings we:

- Seek to reclaim our Wholeness through deep allegiance and faith in our one source/one life. We look to this source for guidance/ inspiration/integration and innovation to be instrumental in reclaiming the Wholeness of Life. In this guidance, the only expert is life (love in full expression);

- Are serving no one else but life. We adore, surrender to and are devoted to love and light alone;

- Are pure channels of healing (making whole) starting with the healing of ourselves.

- Work and play with deep compassion for the team based on deep listening.

People going to regular conferences are tired of the mechanics of jostling egos, of negotiations for power, tired of working from complicated and fixed minds, tired of listening to experts. They are now looking for meaning, higher purpose and inspiration. They want to listen to and work creatively from their hearts. The gatherings for One Wholesome World are meant to provide a shining contrast/example of what happens when we are working from a space of meaning/purpose/heart for the wellbeing of all and the whole of life.

One Wholesome World circles are portals of grace and love, of pure, loving and intelligent thought, feelings and action. There will be circles of healing and integration, giving the people gathered energy, descending through us in the circle of love and light. This will be very different from being in awe of experts, who may be pushing their own agendas or working from cleverness of mind. We will all trust the innate wisdom and intelligence of Life. Our work will be based on sharing, collaboration, conversations and co-creation, all guided by Wholeness.

There is a lot to learn about this way of living and governing from indigenous cultures all over the world. The *Kraals*[21] of the *Maasai* tribe of East Africa are circular in fashion, facilitating a lifestyle of sharing and collaboration. Their main subsistence comes from livestock trading. The chores of the family members are equally divided, where each individual is responsible for something of importance – the woman builds the house, the man looks after security and the boy of the livestock herd. For thousands of years, the *Maasai's* have refined the way they grow and foster their leaders. What can we learn from the *Masai*? According to Chris Howe, director of *"Changemakers"*, a Training Company in the UK, "humility, authenticity and transparency, willingness to pass down knowledge, insistence on leading by example, the fact that they are all working towards a common

---

21) Kraal are societies where houses are arranged in a circular fashion

goal, and an ability to trust, show respect and dish out responsibility to the younger tribe members".[22]

The *Kogi* people of Columbia[23] are another unique indigenous community that call themselves the 'Elder Brother'. They have managed to stay away from the encroachment of humans but are now sending a warning to their 'Younger Brother' (which means us), that if we don't protect the environment, the world will come to an end.

Just like the *Masai* and the *Kogi*, the Aboriginal's of Australia and many tribes in India, have managed to maintain perfect ecological harmony and harmony amongst themselves. They work together, in the spirit of love and treat each other like family members. They trust each other's intelligence as they all work from a space of peace and joy. They realize that their communities are interlinked and interdependent on one another.

We could take the opportunity to reflect on our own practices of leadership and governance by looking at these tribes. They act in ways that strengthen their community; they love nature and are deeply humble. They are honest, accommodating and open, even in times of crises. Their life is committed to the value of wisdom and to lifelong development.

22) *"HR"*: Natural born leaders, www.hrmagazine.co.uk/article-details/natural-born-leaders

23) Redi, Jinny, What Colombia's Kogi people can teach us about the environment
     www.theguardian.com/sustainable-business/colombia-kogi-environment-destruction. Also see this Video:
     Kogi Tribe of Atlantis - The Elder Brothers Warning: www.youtube.com/watch?v=4vLaeenrGpY

Joyful Action Now

1. Reflect on how you see your local government. Do you see 'them' as separate from you, or do you see yourself as a co-creator along with other roles? What might happen if you saw yourself as a powerful, integral and active part of the governance in your neighborhood, city, state or nation?

2. Map out who your local councilors, members of parliament and legislators are. Write to them expressing your ideas and offering support/partnership.

3. Do you have a neighborhood community circle for change? A community of neighbors who join together regularly for action to make a difference? If not, consider initiating one. There are many sites on the web which will guide you on how to convene and run such circles.

4. In the final analysis, life is love in loving action or love in full expression! What single step/action can you take now to improve life for all in your neighborhood?

BOX 10.1

THE WORLD OF TOMORROW

"The world of tomorrow will be, must be, a society based on non-violence. This is the first law; out of it all other blessings will follow. Individuals, groups and nations must adapt the way of non-violence, the way of love. I see then no poverty in the world of tomorrow, no wars, no revolutions, no bloodshed."

— Mahatma Gandhi

"If you want others to be happy, practice compassion. If you want to be happy, practice compassion."

— HH The Dalai Lama XIV, The Art of Happiness

The United Nations has actually declared March 20th of each year as the International Day of Happiness![24] President of the General Assembly, Nassir Abdul-Aziz Al-Nasser says the pursuit of happiness is a fundamental human goal: "I believe that the proclamation of an international day of happiness by the General Assembly to be observed over a year with full participation of the international community as a whole would be a forward looking way of focusing on the value of happiness as a universal goal and aspiration on the lives of all."

---

24) www.ghanabusinessnews.com/2012/06/30/un-adopts-international-day-of-happiness

BOX 10.2

HAPPY PLANET CHARTER[25]

We need new measures of human progress.

The Happy Planet Index offers us an excellent example of how such measures work in practice. It shows that while the challenges faced by rich resource-intensive nations and those with high levels of poverty and deprivation may be very different, the end goal is the same: long and happy lives that don't cost the Earth.

We must balance the prominence currently given to GDP with those measures that take seriously the challenges we face in the 21st century: creating economies that deliver sustainable well-being for all.

By signing this charter, we:

* Call on governments to adopt new measures of human progress that put the goal of delivering sustainable well-being for all at the heart of societal and economic decision-making

* Resolve to build the political will needed across society to fully establish these better measures of human progress by working with partner organizations

* Call on the United Nations to develop an indicator as part of the post-2015 framework that, like the Happy Planet Index, measures progress towards the key goal for a better future: sustainable well-being for all.

---

25) *"Happy Planet Charter"*: www.happyplanetindex.org/supporters

BOX 10.3

A few examples of organizations that imbibe wholesome governance

Bhagwan Mahaveer Viklang Sahayta Samiti (BMVSS) by Dr. Devendra Raj Mehta[26]

A former civil servant, who after an accident felt deep empathy towards the pain and suffering that people who have lost their limbs and their livelihoods too go through. His organization, BMVSS serves the disabled by providing all assistance at a negligible cost – artificial limbs, calipers and other aid. In India and across 26 countries, more than 1.3 million amputees and polio patients have been rehabilitated. The 'Jaipur Foot' as it has come to be known, costs only INR 2500 (or free), which in the United States would cost approximately US$ 10,000.

Karnataka Sakala by Dr. Shalini Rajneesh[27] – 'Be Online not In-line'

Karnataka Sakala is an online delivery system of Public Services in the Indian state of Karnataka. It assures timely delivery of government services to citizens. All the services provided are completed in a time bound manner, empowering citizens and making processes more transparent. A compensatory cost, deducted from the salaries of the government officials in-charge, is made payable to the citizens in case of a delay.

Community Policing[28]

Community policing and outreach programs which are mostly initiatives of iWhen a population of 2.4 million would need 7000 police constables, Tiruchirapalli, (also called Trichy, a town in Southern India) is managing policing well with only 260. This is because of their community policing experiment. Before this was initiated in Trichy, the crime rate was extremely high. Mr J.K. Tripathy (the former Police Commissioner of the Trichy) introduced various schemes. He divided the city into 'beats' and made 4 constables in charge of each beat. This empowered them to be more responsible, take decisions and tackle civic problems efficiently. He also started a complaint box system in different areas of the city to gather information. A Wide Area Network (WAN) was set up across the police stations and offices. This brought the citizens and police closer. Transparency and interaction improved. All these efforts encouraged involvement of the citizens, built confidence and fostered accountability among the people. It has controlled the crime and conflict rate in the city to a large extent.

---

26) Read more about the Jaipur Footat: www.jaipurfoot.org
27) Karnataka Sakala by Dr. Shalini Rajneesh: www.sakala.kar.nic.in
28) http://shodhganga.inflibnet.ac.in/bitstream/10603/1993/9/09_chapter%201.pdf

BOX 10.4

ETHICS AND VALUES IN PUBLIC GOVERNANCE[29]

The Department of Personnel and Training (DoPT, Govt. of India) invited the IC Centre for Governance, Initiatives of Change and Pragati Leadership to develop comprehensive and suitable modules on 'Ethics and Values in Public Governance' for all the 29 Administrative Training Institutes (ATIs) and Central Training Institutes (CTI's) in India. This was based on the positive results of the program on 'Ethics and Values in Public Governance'.

The objective of the program is to catalyze and facilitate thinking and action for creative, effective and ethical governance. The success of this program is partly due to the active involvement of serving and retired senior officers of the IAS who have publicly demonstrated their ethical and exemplary achievements.

Key learnings from the implementation of this program:

- Discover, expand and connect the positives rather than struggle with the negatives - look for and celebrate, what is right with the world. The inspiring photographer, Dewitt Jones[30] of National Geographic, echoes our own deepest sentiments: "By celebrating what's right, we find the energy to fix what's wrong".

- Connect people through conversations. Get people into circles of spirited conversation to generate opportunities to create, act and heal.

- Be open to creative possibilities. Enjoy operating out of humility and total acceptance.

- Steadily hold a clear intention in your mind, be open to possibility and watch the magic unfold. Listen deeply to your own intuition, the people around you, the situation, and respond wholesomely/fully at all times.

- Go for joy, energy, enthusiasm and peace.

- Take great care of yourself, keeping your life unblocked and pure.

- Keep yourself in good health through regular exercise, meditation and reading books with high inspirational content. Take care of yourself before you try to change things outside.

- Begin change with yourself. Replace judgment with wonder, curiosity and action. Listen to the inner voice to see where you need to make a change.

- Be in integrity and start change with yourself. Remember that, initiative, integrity, innovation, integration and India all begin with "I". Blame happens only when we do not see the wholeness of life.

- Know where you are going and trust life.

---

29) http://archive.indianexpress.com/news/govt-to-train-officials-on-ethics-values-in-public-governance/961531/
30) www.dewittjones.com

BOX 10.5

NEW PUBLIC MANAGEMENT[31]

Pradip N. Khandwalla's summary of Good Governance (*Transforming Government through New Public Management*):

New Public Management (NPM) as a concept originated in the U.S and Britain but has now been adopted by many countries (of course, it has been modified to suit their local flavors). This concept emphasizes on the inclusion of the private sector into governance to ensure accountability and performance. It also encourages participation, professionalism, is stake holder centric and boosts innovation.

Prof. Khandwalla primarily talks about increasing government capacity, not by discarding democracy or bureaucracy but by adding a new player who is professional, futuristic, innovative, and task focused.

In his analysis of transformation of India's governance suggested in his book, Dr. Khandwalla suggests a slew of improvements using New Public Management tools like stakeholder mapping, regulatory impact assessment; and strategic decision making via policy analysis. He recommends other actions like: compulsory training in constitutional governance for legislators and ministers; extensive 'agencification'; 'Deliberation Councils' of wise experts and representatives of civil society attached to each ministry; extensive use of e-governance and performance management systems, and much more extensive use of Public Private Partnerships (PPP).

31) Khandwalla Pradip N., *"Transforming Government Through New Public Management"*, Ahmedabad Management Association: Ahmedabad, 2010

BOX 10.6

FOUR PILLARS AND NINE DOMAINS OF GROSS NATIONAL HAPPINESS [32]

The intuitive guiding principle of Gross National Happiness led to a practical conceptualization of the concept. The foundation is made of four pillars:

Good Governance: Good Governance is considered a pillar for happiness because it determines the conditions in which Bhutanese thrive.

Sustainable Socio-economic Development: A thriving GNH economy must value social and economic contributions of households and families, free time and leisure given the roles of these factors in Happiness.

Preservation and Promotion of Culture: Happiness is believed to be contributed to, by the preservation of the Bhutanese culture. Developing cultural resilience, which can be understood as the culture's capacity to maintain and develop cultural identity, knowledge and practices.

Environmental Conservation: Environmental conservation is considered a key contribution to GNH. In addition to providing critical services such as water and energy, the environment is believed to contribute to aesthetic and other stimulus that can be directly healing to people.

The four pillars are further elaborated into nine domains, which articulate the different elements of GNH in detail and form the basis of GNH measurement, indices and screening tools.

- Living standards
- Education
- Health
- Environment
- Community vitality
- Time-use
- Psychological well-being
- Good Governance
- Cultural resilience and promotion

---

32)   www.gnhcentrebhutan.org/what-is-gnh/four-pillars-and-nine-domains

CHAPTER 11

Reclaiming Our One Wholesome World

"Another world is not only possible; she is on her way."[1]

— Kufunda Learning Village

"We must understand each other and work in harmony with one another, because it is our responsibility to develop in human beings their natural disposition for Peace."

— HH the 14th Dalai Lama

*"All the joy the world contains
has come through wishing happiness for others.
All the misery the world contains
has come through wanting pleasure for oneself (at the expense of others)"*

— Shantideva[2]

---

1) Kufunda Learning Village: www.kufunda.org
2) Shantideva, Bodhisattvacharyavatara: *"A Guide to the Bodhisattva's Way of Life"*

The words in this book are useless unless we begin taking steps to manifest the vision that they convey. If not us, who? If not now, when? The uncertainty of life is such that death can come at any time. Let each moment be a joyful contribution to wholesomeness in our life and the lives of others.

Having come this far, the discerning and 'practically' minded reader would surely be asking the question, "So what next? What are the things I can do now?" Luckily, there is a lot one can do!

The website for this book, www.onewholesomeworld.com, gives a whole list of web resources for you to draw from for information, learning and action. You can find these under the tab "Resources" on the website. As we have often said in this book, we truly believe that the world has all the knowledge and resources for all of us to co-create a world that works for all and for future generations in the long run. What is needed is more inspired and informed action.

However, before we rush headlong into 'doing something' or 'saving the world', it may be useful to remember that more important than 'doing' is who we are being? What is the emotional and spiritual space that one is experiencing at the moment? Is it one of joy, peace, abundance and wholeness? Am I deeply accepting whatever I am experiencing now as being perfect, and also as something I can improve upon at the same time? It would be helpful to keep in mind what was mentioned in Chapter 4 on "Inner Transformation".

To give you a metaphor, we have many gadgets and appliances with us (like motors, pumps, fans, mixers, toasters, TVs etc.) but no electricity. To reclaim our wholeness and oneness with life, our efforts and initiatives have to be rooted in awareness. We need to remember that inner transformation (the electricity in the metaphor above) is the foundation for wellbeing, creative expressions and social coherence. It is also the foundation for compassion in action and experiential reverence for life as a whole.

Inner transformation is the foundation for working well together with harmony and coherence. It is an antidote to the fragmentation, strife, agitation, violence and self-serving people and organizations that abound on the planet today (2016).

Basic Principles for unfolding One Wholesome World

In this book, we have shared that the human and social dimensions, putting people first, has to be at the heart and the core of any development activity. By human and social, we mean focusing on the well-being and empowerment of people. The world's scientists' Warning to Humanity, (Union of Concerned Scientists, 1992)[3] in a comprehensive statement

---

3) *"1992 World Scientists' Warning to Humanity"*:
   www.ucsusa.org/about/1992-world-scientists.html#.Vr_gyPl97IU

provides a five point program for action summarized as follows:

- Control environmentally damaging activities

- Manage critical resources more effectively

- Stabilize population

- Eliminate poverty

- Ensure gender equality

One Wholesome World (OWW) is a vision of the future that provides us with a road map. It helps to focus our attention on a set of values, ethical and moral principles which guide our actions as individuals, and in relation to the institutional structures with which we have contact – governmental and nongovernmental. The manifestation of a vision of One Wholesome World (OWW), a world which works for all requires the structuring of a set of basic principles to serve as its foundation:

- The entire journey of moving toward a more wholesome world needs to start with an individual action at this moment. Without action, the best plans are of no use. The first step is to recognize, that the inner space from which we need to work has to be one of deep acceptance and gratitude. We need to approach this work in a spirit of 'All is well and all is perfect and still can be improved'. This is a space of acceptance and joy. Listening to my inner guidance, moment to moment, and being fully in touch with my intrinsic wholeness is the foundation for living in this way. Box 11.1 gives a way forward in listening to inner guidance.

- People on the journey of OWW are aligned with their deepest life purpose. Listening to our inner voice, we also find our life's purpose at a deeper level. Our life's purpose is simply to be one with the "peace of Love which passes all understanding and which is the same as being one with life". Being this is a way of dancing with life. At another level, our purpose is to share and experience the gifts that we have been blessed with, in the service of our fellow being and also of life. Box 11.2 gives you a tool to discover your life purpose.

- It is finally people who are both the doers and beneficiaries of any developmental effort. We need to keep this perspective in our consciousness at all times. OWW starts with an individual effort and cultivation. It begins with a change in the way of thinking about who we are, of how we see things and how we choose our thoughts, words and actions. The whole spiral of actions leading to OWW needs to start with loving and responsible action at the level of the individual. Every single thought, word and action of ours can move us all a step closer to our vision or a step away.

Transformation, One Person at a Time:

When we listened to intuitive guidance for 'creating a movement' the clear answer was "Don't!". Most such ideas come from the mind which thinks something like this: 'We will create a Grand Design, and then try to execute it, and enlist people, and then track progress towards the shared Vision over a period of time, (typically 3-5 years or more).'

Here is another way of looking at the same thing: "I surrender this body-mind to the infinite power of wholeness, my own innermost awareness. I am one with wholeness because there is only one whole! Its nature is peace, joy, abundance, ease and grace. This body-mind trusts the guidance of the whole in each moment as it speaks in the language of well-being, joy, energy, enthusiasm and peace. I wholeheartedly do what life is calling this body-mind to do. I see life as love in full expression. Guided by joy, I act lovingly and playfully.The expression of my life becomes a LILA: Love in Loving Action. I entrust the larger unfolding to life. My role in this moment (which incidentally is all there is or will ever be) is to share my love through loving service and do whatever I can to eliminate suffering and to expand happiness. The journey has to start with me."

Swami Chinmayananda echoes this sentiment: "World transformation through individual transformation! The world can only be changed by the spiritual unfoldment of each individual – not by political revolution, but by spiritual evolution."[4]

In his book, *"Birth of the Chaordic Age"*[5], Dee Hock argues that conventional organizational structures can no longer work because organizations have become too complex. Hock advocates a new organizational form that he calls 'chaordic', or simultaneously chaotic and orderly. A much quoted idea of his is "Simple, clear purpose and principles give rise to complex intelligent behaviors." When many people on the planet start following a few simple rules towards the expansion of joy, complex and intelligent behavior will arise spontaneously.

Here are a few simple points that have emerged from conversations with people who are passionate about making a difference and have considerable 'hands on' practical experience in the field:

1. The very first step is to listen! With empathy, listen to your own inner voice (see Box 11.1). What is life calling you to do? Remember that it is not your role to do everything or to fight all battles. Listen to and feel empathetically into what feels joyful and expanding for you. This step will point you to what your life is calling you to do.

2. The next step is listening to people, listening to the environment

4) Chinmayananda, Swami: www.transformingindians.org/about-us/chinmaya-mission
5) Hock, Dee W., *"Birth of the Chaordic Age"*, Berrett-Koehler Publishers: San Francisco, 2000

and even listening to the future. Deep empathetic listening reveals opportunities for change. Areas where what is yours to do (step 1) and what needs to be done (step 2) intersect, are the opportunities for making efforts.

3. Since you cannot do things alone, find the right 'sparked up' people who share the understanding of the need to come together and make a difference collectively. What are the domains of knowledge they are working in? What questions bring them together? Where are they physically located? What complementary strengths and skills do they bring?

4. Connecting them all up for conversations is the next step. This can happen locally, or via the internet. There are many tools available, some of which are Loomio, QiqoChat and OpenSpace-Online.[6]

5. The purpose of these conversations is to form action learning project teams. Such teams move together towards shared goals and also keep learning from their experiences as they move forward.

6. Finally, as we begin to achieve tangible results and create impact in a certain domain or geographical area, it is time to build capacity. This could take the form of developing change makers, or 'I-Catalysts', or simply other facilitators who can successfully replicate and grow what you have started.

An important area of personal change is our pattern of consumption. What do we consume? How conscious are our choices in consumption and buying? The collective power of our spending is enormous. For example, what might happen if thousands of people gave up smoking out of their own conscious choice? Let's look at changing our patterns of consumption a little closer.

Changing Patterns of Consumption

Every change that you can make needs to ripple out from the silent depths of your awareness outwards to the immediate family, your physical home and work place, the neighbors and neighborhood and so on. The metaphor of a drop of water creating ripples on a lake is apt.

The following story (The Weight of Nothing[7]) underscores the power of simple acts: "Tell me the weight of a snowflake," a coalmouse asked a wild dove. "Nothing more than nothing," was the answer. "In that case, I must

---

6) Some Online Tools for working Collaboratively with other people: http://qiqochat.com/about, http://openspace-online.com/, https://www.loomio.org/

7) Author Unknown, "*The Weight of Nothing*", This story appears in various forms across the web, and is referenced either as "*Thus Spoke the Caribou*" from "*New Fables*" by Kurt Kauter, or from "*Synchronicity*", by Joseph Jaworsky

tell you a marvelous story," the coalmouse said. "I sat on the branch of a fir, close to its trunk, when it began to snow – not heavily, not in a raging blizzard – no, just like in a dream, without a wound and without any violence. Since I did not have anything better to do, I counted the snowflakes settling on the twigs and needles of my branch. Their number was exactly 3,741,952. When the 3,741,953rd dropped onto the branch, nothing more than nothing, as you say – the branch broke off." Having said that, the coalmouse flew away. The dove, since Noah's time an authority on the matter, thought about the story for a while, and finally said to herself, "Perhaps there is only one person's voice lacking for peace to come to the world."

Starting with one's own purification and inner transformation, one slowly begins to purify relationships and actions. These have their own spontaneous impact. Our own experience has been that talk of wholesome devolvement or wholesome leadership is futile and sterile unless it is backed by living and radiating that in one's own life. This book has finally come out only when the authors have chosen to dedicate their lives to facilitating people to awaken to and return to wholeness.

There are many things that one can do to reduce consumption and lead a more wholesome and sustainable life. Simple things like switching off one's computer when not in use, recycling water, curtailing consumption of fuel, using more locally made food and food products. A conscious change in ones diet for example, can save costs, improve your health and help the planet all at once. Carpooling with neighbors helps build community, cut your transport costs and also reduce your carbon footprint.

The website mentioned earlier (www.onewholesomeworld.com) shares many resources on changing the way we consume, including things you can do in your neighborhood and community to save resources.

We can also choose to consume things that have been made locally, and be more in touch with our community.

Localization

People need to feel loved, appreciated, seen, and heard, especially as children growing up. They need to be nurtured in order to become nurturing, loving and happy people. Living, learning, working and consuming locally makes this possible. It is about healing (or making whole) our relations with ourselves, other people and with nature based on love and care. It is about restoring connections and care. That is why Helena Norberg-Hodge[8], a pioneer in this area, argues that "localization is the economics of happiness".

Localization is based on the belief that those people that live in closest proximity to the resource possess the best knowledge of it. Localization of

---

8) Norberg-Hodge, Helena, *"Localisation is the Economics of Happiness"*; YES, Magazine

essential production, consumption, trade and of services like health and education is a move in the direction of wholesome progress.

Some of the features and benefits of localization as shared by Helena Norberg-Hodge (in the Economics of Happiness Conference, Bangalore, 15th March 2014)[9] are:

- Localization is the diversification and decentralization of economic activity.

- Localization strengthens human scale business – especially basic needs such as food, water, energy but also in housing, baking, healthcare.

- Localization relies more on human labour and skill and depends less on energy and technology.

- It requires less transportation, less packaging and less processing, thereby reducing waste, pollution and fossil fuel use.

- Localization adapts economic activity to the diversity of ecosystems, restoring cultural and biological diversity.

- It fosters a deep connection between people and nature.

- It rebuilds social interdependence and cohesion, providing more secure sense of identity and belonging, which in turn is a prerequisite for peaceful existence.

- Localization challenges conventional notions of international development, instead reclaiming and regenerating diverse knowledge systems, languages, aesthetics and wisdom traditions.

In the same vein, Ms. Ela Bhatt (2009), Founder, Self Employed Women's Association(SEWA), Ahmedabad talks of the '100 Mile Principe'[10]: "I would urge us to use things and services of primary needs to life that are produced within 100 miles around us. To name them: food, shelter, clothes, primary education and primary healthcare". As part of one's personal commitment to Wholesome Development, we need to work not only in a way that the work is aligned with one's calling and unique contribution, but also to live, learn and earn in close proximity with each other. This will reduce waste and also our ecological footprints, besides developing a deep connectedness with life.

The starting point for civic action is your own neighborhood. Reach out to your neighbors and have regular meetings to reflect on joint action. Such meetings need to have moments of quietness and listening to the

9) www.yesmagazine.org/happiness/localization-is-the-economics-of-happiness
www.bhoomicollege.org/short-programme/economics-happiness-conference
10) Gupta, Anil K., "*The 100 Mile Principle weaves decentralization, locality, size, and scale to livelihood*", http://anilg.sristi.org/the-100-mile-principle-weaves-decentralization-locality-size-and-scale-to-livelihood/

inner voice. Neighborhood circles can also become the social structure for initiatives such as segregation and recycling of garbage, growing vegetables on your roof top, using bio-culture and perma culture, joint civic action for more ethical governance and even celebrating festivals together. The same platform can also serve as a foundation for the gift economy and gift exchange which will form the basis for the new economics. *Sikshantar Andolan*[11], working out of Udaipur in Rajasthan, India is spearheading one of many such experiments all over the world. Localization will also change the very face of work.

Good Work for All

Deeply related to the shifts in the way businesses are owned and run (including localization) will be deep shifts in the way people work. How we work is critical to our sense of our well-being. As places where we live, work, and learn progressively come closer to each other, there will also be a need for re-organizing our work. More and more people will turn to entrepreneurship. More and more people will start earning their livelihoods in ways that leave a low ecological foot print. More and more people will be aligned with good work and with a wholesome life style.

Work being done by many people today is toxic: toxic to themselves, to other people and to the planet. It often carries unnecessary risks to workers, is stifling to the spirit and does not generate 'True Wealth'. Local economies everywhere are threatened by economic globalization, and yet jobs for local markets can often be created at a fraction of the cost of jobs for global markets. In the 'developed countries', many skilled workers are unemployed whilst 'developing countries' often suffer from severe skills shortages.

We need to address this by creating a new paradigm and process of 'Good Work' which is soulful, empowered, innovative, using local resources and in harmony with the environment. Such work is work in the 'Flow State' i.e. Fullness and Love Overflowing in Work. This implies that they would have to work out of their own self-nature, unfold their own vocation arising out of their own deepest impulses and harmonized with the needs of the environment around them. It means being aligned with one's natural profile of motivated skills, being productive and beneficial to ones surroundings and operating out of a deep loving, free, creative energy. Work would need to be as much person driven as it is environment driven. Work would have to be aligned with the deeper purpose of people. This would be in alignment with the paradigm of new forms of doing business described in Chapter 9.

---

11) www.swaraj.org/shikshantar/udaipur.html

All the knowledge and experience that is needed to create new approaches to 'Good Work' exist on the planet. These resources are, however, not connected to each other or to the people who can use them.

Leaders will need to connect all the relevant resources and provide an 'eco system of support' for local enterprise centered on 'Wholeness'. This support system would include extension services and technical support, economic services, entrepreneurial training (including attitudinal shifts based on inner transformation and the principles of abundance), ecological awareness and sustainable forms of eco enterprise, mentoring and IT support.

A Global Revolution in Human Consciousness

Without a global revolution in the sphere of human consciousness, nothing will change for the better. This means moving from a fragmented disintegrated view of life to one which is whole. Speaking in Berlin on the 20th anniversary of the fall of the Berlin Wall (9th November 2009), Mikhail Gorbachev, said: "The Berlin Wall has gone into history. Sadly, there are still many walls existing today: the wall of suspicion, of disbelief, the wall between the rich and the poor, between human being and nature. People must be realistic and see these walls!"

These 'Inner Walls' represent identification with limited notions of who we are. They are the clouds that overshadow our innate wholeness. Amidst these intense challenges of fragmentation, and largely catalyzed by them, lies the prospect for tremendous growth in human potential and consciousness. People and communities all over the globe are coming together to reclaim responsibility for creating their own living situations – at local and regional levels. In the process, they are overcoming prior limitations and developing new talents, skills, knowledge and approaches. Paradoxically, many of the most innovative solutions rely on a timeless, perennial kind of wisdom that seems to have been disregarded recently. The potential for a refreshed, renewed, revitalized humanity goes hand-in-hand with meeting the challenges of our present age.

A new stage in the evolution of man has already begun. A new consciousness, higher than the mind, a truth-consciousness, as Sri Aurobindo[12] said, in which the dualities, hesitations and limitations of the mind and the greed and blindness of the ego will no longer exist, has already started to appear. All the upheavals and convulsions that are at present so painfully tearing our Earth apart are the outward signs of this evolutionary and spiritual crisis. This new consciousness is already at work in the noosphere of the Earth. We can connect with it, evoke it in ourselves, and use it to transform our own life and consequently the world in which we live.

---

12) Towards human unity, www.auroville.org/contents/577

Wrong perceptions have to be left behind. Listening skills and life skills have to come to the forefront. Arrogance: racial, political, ethnic, material or any other, has to be replaced by compassion, altruism and concern. Erroneous judgments based on past prejudices need to be buried. Conflict prevention and conflict management have to be developed as skills to prevent war and strife. The United Nations needs to ensure provision of security at a global level in social, economic, political and ecological spheres. Ensuring human rights; development of democratic participation and institutions; and ensuring international solidarity and harmony shall be the foundation for the Wholesome Development of the world. And these will flower only when attention is concentrated on the Wholesome Development of people everywhere.

The starting point would be getting people to see differently. The entire foregoing analysis sees the problem of development as one of changing our mind-models of the way the world works and what constitutes good behaviors or good actions. In a sense, development is the process by which our mind-models undergo constant change and refinement until we begin to realize our intrinsic freedom from all mind models. When we awaken to this ground state of free awareness, we find a profound fullness which manifests as playful and creative action.

The question that then arises is: how do we get the maximum number of people to unfold their awareness and thinking, and through that, to evolve their actions towards more joy, more health, more integration and wellbeing? The task is to get this view across to people, not so much in terms of intellectual models or theories, but more in terms of direct experience. To awaken more people to this space of freedom and wholeness, we need to:

- Make visible the interlinkages between people, between people and nature, between what they do and the consequences thereof

- Make visible our deep relatedness to each other and to nature

- Show how we are really one with the whole i.e. with all of existence

- Show how this direct experience of oneness affects almost everything we do

There are many exercises that have been developed over the ages to meet this need. There are many existing techniques. Newer techniques can also be devised, to get people to see things clearly and get a direct insight into their real unbounded nature from which Wholesome Development springs. This is the most important task ahead of us today.

Inspired Communication

Linked to the previous points is the need for inspired communication and education using processes and devices which encourage and facilitate holistic thinking and which could help people to see the big picture. Today's written devices make it difficult for people to connect things together and see the interlinkages. The use of creative and integrating graphics will need to become more common. Also, a balance between the rational and logical approaches and the more mythological and emotional approaches to development issues would have to be arrived at.

Significant actions will need to be taken by the media to transform the collective consciousness of people in the world. Media today is mistrusted because of the negative role that the advertising industry plays in fostering a collective myth of deficiency leading to a culture of addictive consumption. Not only does the media foster unwholesome consumption but is also responsible for implanting in people's minds images of violence, separation, hatred and strife. Media will now have to be governed with a wholesome understanding of life and a professional ethic that shapes its role in unfolding a wholesome world. New forms of financing the media industry e.g. through wider use of the internet and also through more opportunities for free expression by citizens (e.g. as in YouTube) will need to be put in place. Journalists need to see that freedom of operation and a commitment to truth and wholeness are absolutely essential for their own well-being and the fostering of a better world. Ultimately freedom of access to information, freedom of expression and freedom to tell the whole truth will be the foundation for a more wholesome role of the media. Transparency, balanced and unbiased reporting and a focus on stories that foster the positive, the true, the good and the beautiful will need to be the pillars of a new media which awakens and fosters a different consciousness in society. Journalists and media persons will need to awaken to the true meaning and importance of their work.

Can journalists see themselves as harbingers of wholeness on the planet? Not only as passive reporters of what is happening around us, but as enlightened shapers of patterns of thought at the root of what we see manifesting all around us? The media needs to see its role as active shapers of a wholesome ethos, and not passive handmaidens of vested interests. They need to understand that there are many people on the planet who will support positive efforts if they play a role in promoting the same.

Continuous dialogue, inspired by deep and silent reflection, can improve the ability of all actors in the system to make informed, responsible and responsive decisions. This will promote a pro-active approach to development. The increased engagement of the scientific, technological, business and government sectors and civil society in these dialogues is essential.

Education and Learning

While on the issue of dialogue and inspired communication, we could visualize organizations like UNESCO drawing up a few basic primers for children, giving young children all over the world a unified worldview of wholesomeness. It is also possible to conceive of beautifully made films which are deeply humanistic and which creatively bring out the essence of oneness and wholesomeness in our lives. They would present the new vision of a full life for all in an innocent, humanistic, fun, joyful and a creative way. With the present potential of the media (particularly the electronic multi-media) to reach out to millions of people round the globe, these can be powerful instruments for raising consciousness. These would need to:

- Reinforce the positives rather than the negative

- Focus more energy on creating and transmitting images of true wholesomeness and global wellbeing

The communication devices, mentioned above, would have to show not only new ideas or a new vision, but also would have to point towards methods to transcend our mind-models and our conditioning. The process is primarily one of psycho-spiritual renewal. This would spread into groups of people spontaneously rather than through coercion. The process is already alive and well tried. This needs expansion and strengthening.

Teaching and learning opportunities would have to be proliferated at a local level with people of all ages and categories self-actualizing themselves, engaging in all kinds of occupations at various skills levels. Holding this vision E.F. Schumacher[13] has remarked: "Much of the learning would have to be done 'hands-on' and through apprenticeship, with no one being too old to be an apprentice or too young to be teacher." Continuous learning alone at all levels would ensure growth and development in a natural wholesome manner.

Learning will also require the development of networking and a very rich exchange of information and ideas. We would need to look for, learn from and empower the 'other'. This would deepen our relatedness. It will call for participation and action around shared goals. Even businesses would have to start thinking of themselves as learning systems (a learning process of people via work).

Given the vastly expanded and revolutionary breakthroughs in communications and information technology (IT) worldwide, it is feasible to expeditiously activate such global learning systems permitting the best inputs of experiential learning from everywhere in the world. For the momentous task of inner transformation, it is imperative that the matter be placed on the global agenda for immediate action.

---

13) Schumacher, E.F, https://en.wikipedia.org/wiki/E._F._Schumacher

The four billion poor people in the world have to find an innovative way to convince the two billion rich about the great need to live through the present crises together or else perish together. The global agenda of interdependence of all peoples in achieving development with harmony needs unequivocal emphasis. This is the most basic attitudinal change needed in order to open the floodgates of universal creative energies for Wholesome Development in the 21st century.

Opening the floodgates of human creative energy will need a change in the way we connect, converse, collaborate and co-create with each other. Open and free participation by all, supported by the values of democracy, nonviolence and peace will be crucial in bringing about these changes. These skills and values will need to be integrated into formal education and life-long learning to foster a more sustainable way of life.

Wholesome Development through Good Governance

If localised economic growth is essential to eliminate poverty, then it is crucial to have good governance to enable such balanced growth. Economic growth is critical but not the sole requirement for success in the fight against poverty. It is equally important to have a social policy that places particular emphasis on meeting basic human needs; education, training and extension services as well as availability of credit, fostering self-reliance and initiative in people from all segments of society.

A further component is a social climate in which the door to full personal development is open to everyone – regardless of gender, race, socio-cultural background or other differences. In countries like Sweden, where a socio-economic ambience of this quality has been put into effect, it has led to impressive economic success from which the lowest income groups have also benefited. Such countries have also been more successful than others with respect to the ecological sustainability of their development policy.

Where there is long-term investment in people's health and education, where both men and women, regardless of their social status, have access to the necessary means of production, extension and credits, they can take their fate in their own hands and make use of opportunities to improve their quality of life.

Kofi Annan[14], former Secretary General of the United Nations has remarked: "Good Governance and sustainable development are indivisible. That is the lesson of all our efforts and experiences from Africa to Latin America. Without good governance –without the rule of law, predictable administration, legitimate power and responsive regulation-no amount of funding, no amount of charity will set us on the path to prosperity"

---

14) Annan, Kofi, "*Good Governance Essential to Development*", Press release, July 1997, www.un.org/press/en/1997/19970723.SGSM6291.html

In an International Conference (held under the auspices of the Caux Roundtable for Business)[15] aimed at studying the problems of globalization, after four days of deliberations, the distinguished participants came out with the view that it was Governance really that was at the root of the problems facing the world. In the next conference focused on Good Governance, they came to the realization that it all boiled down to good leadership. When the gathering, at yet another conference, sincerely probed deeper into leadership, they came to the understanding that the core issue was not just leadership but *ethical* leadership.

This story underpins a very important understanding i.e. it is only when leaders can work from an inner understanding of wholeness, the foundation for ethical behavior, that we can have the governance and the leadership required to bring about substantial changes towards Wholesome Development. This implies that there has to be an ongoing dialogue and conversation between politicians, NGO's, civil society, education, business, artists and the people who formulate and implement policy. It is only through such ongoing conversations that a holistic perspective can be fostered. In addition to this dialogue, there is also a need for integrating good governance with the spiritual aspects of life.

In India, in a series of programs on ethics and values in public governance, the authors have personally experienced the power of integrating the spiritual and holistic dimension with the issue of governance and leadership. Participants from four programs on the above topic have gone back and made significant impacts in their own areas of work. The design of the program is proven and can be replicated all over the world with minor changes relevant to local situations. What is required to scale this up, however, is a gathering of all those who teach ethical leadership and governance and their mutual exposure to each other's best practices and also to the paradigm and practices of Wholesome Development.

Actions Related to Planning of Development

People need to plan development from the fullness and unconditional okayness of their inner core of peace and bliss.

The way people work will need to change. They will have to see clearly the linkage between their work, their own evolution and development, and the larger social purpose. This approach could provide a sound moral base for providing joyful work for all.

Organizations, all over the world, including government organizations, NGOs, social organizations, religious organizations would have to align their objectives with wholesomeness and well-being of people and the preservation of the ecosystem. Work would need to be as much person-driven as it is driven by the need for a wholesome environment.

---

15) *"Caux Initiatives for Business"*: www.cibglobal.org

Planning would have to receive guidance from a higher and deeper level coming from a holistic understanding of man. Technology would have to serve man rather than move unrelentingly forward on its own trip of feasibility. The focus would have to be on the stimulation of the balanced growth and liveliness of people as the central issue rather than the curbing it. Focus would have to be on the motivation of the individual, rather than on making him a passive element in a faceless system.

Healing our cities is eminently possible. All the knowhow and talent to do this exists. Governments need to take this up. Local municipalities can be better integrated into international sustainable development programs given their direct involvement in managing the urban environment. Local elected corporators and municipal officials should receive training in wholesome sustainable development issues including the appreciation and preservation of heritage. State governments, NGOs and international institutions can be encouraged to create best practice networks and development cooperation projects with city governments. Such projects can be financially self-sustaining and can serve other cities and governments in a 'value networking' process where all benefit. Decentralized 'city-to-city' cooperation could become a major force in poverty alleviation and the promotion of north-south solidarity.

One World

There is only one world. It is a totally integrated and beautiful mechanism which some people have called *"Gaia"*[16]. There are no intrinsic boundaries in it. The atmosphere and oceans are one. Superimposed on this wholeness (which has been working so well on its own, based on millions of years of evolution) are manmade boundaries.

We will need to envision and manifest a single world government not in the hands of people, but in their hearts. The energy of our inner consciousness is the highest. This is the same as love. This is the greatest power in the universe. This governs the mind, and mind can govern the rest of matter and the material world. This implies that a one world government would be governed by love. Love stands for wholeness. Love and wholeness are exactly the same thing.

A new humanity would be governed by love… love for oneself, for others and also love for the environment. People who are surrendered to love and run their life by what love calls them to do will coalesce spontaneously into a network; a Radiant Network[17]. This Radiant Network will work guided by love, since each member in it will know through a direct understanding of and connection with wholeness, what has to be done. The creative

---

16) Gaia Hypothesis: https://en.wikipedia.org/wiki/Gaia_hypothesis
17) Stadler, Anne, *"A Story of Radiant Networking: October 2003 to April 2011"*;
    http://collectivewisdominitiative.com/papers/stadler_radiant.pdf

intelligence that runs the whole world without human intervention will orchestrate some very beautiful manifestations. This will slowly result in a one world government. It will be based on decentralization and the rule of love. The most effective channels of love and light will be the ones who will govern in a just, equitable and fair way for the well-being of the whole. We are very close to the emergence of such a network. The creation and publication of this book is one of the many concurrent processes which are egging people on the planet towards a new Heaven on Earth.

The clearer we become of what we want, and the more we communicate with like hearted people on the planet, the greater will be the coherence that emerges. Leaders in Government (who resonate with what has come through in this book) can take some actions along the lines that follow.

Catalyze the creation of a World Wisdom Council of the wisest people on the planet. This council would appreciate, oversee and address the institutional linkages and interdependencies between economic, social, cultural, environmental and peace concerns. Their authority would be derived from their selflessness and integrity, and allegiance to and obedience to love as the supreme governing principle. The vision of the council would be a wholesome sustainable future for all of humankind. Its mission would be the implementation, coordination and supervision of all aspects of the co-creation of this future.

Governments the world over can empower organizations operating under the umbrella of the United Nations and other global bodies to network into unified organisms. The main focus of their vision and work would be the well-being of all people on Earth. These organisms will be geared towards fostering universally needed knowledge, skills, and attitudes. (The word 'Organism' has been used consciously instead of 'Organization'. The latter is reminiscent of the old command and control machine-like structures that stifle spirit and innovation. An 'Organism' is more like the systems found in nature.)

Move towards the creation of a few strategic World Organisms like a World Environmental Organism, a World Learning Organism, and a World Peace Organism. The World Learning Organism would focus on providing inspired learning for basic education and skill development on a massive scale and for the long run. Sustainable societies cannot be reached without learning in local communities, organizations and in our daily lives. These World Organisms could be hosted within the UN structure, or a new organism could be created at the level of today's Security Council. At any place in the One World Government people would owe allegiance to love, the common thread, core and purpose of the One Wholesome World. (This is how life actually runs right now! Human beings, who are out of touch with wholeness, deviate from this law of life, and end up creating the very conditions that will eventually restore the understanding).

Look for outstanding examples of Wholesome Development from all over the world and find ways to support the natural proliferation of these examples. This may also require the creation of a dynamically evolving global knowledge repository, which could be administered by the World Learning Organism. Use the GAIA (Global Appreciative Inquiry for Action) process described earlier, for different priority sectors like water, sanitation, ecological healing, healing cities, sustainable livelihoods, human rights and culture.

Erase the boundaries between 'developed' and 'developing' nations. The World Bank, IMF, and other economics related bodies should let go of classifying nations as 'developed' or 'developing'. People everywhere must be accepted as equal partners in the important task of global togetherness to produce a happier life for all. We can all learn from and teach each other. We need to learn with humility from our ancestors and rich (culturally, spiritually and environmentally) indigenous communities like the *Kogi*, the *Ladakhis*, the people of Bali, Tibet, Hawaii, North American Indians, the *Inuit* and many more such communities that are on the verge of extinction now.[18]

Create an experiential learning system, via the use of cyberspace, for the Wholesome Development of people continuously. This could be the task for a world organism like UNESCO. Best inputs on experiential learning may be used from all over the world. Increase opportunities for conversations amongst international institutions with cross and multi-sectoral discussions, partnerships and program planning. Encourage and support mutual understanding, solidarity, and cooperation among all people and within and among nations. Tools like QiqoChat, Loomio, OpenSpace-Online can be used for this. Create networks of people and leaders in different walks of life that can forge new grounds inspired by their creative and systemic understanding of issues facing humankind.

Integrate the voices of all civil society actors into the activites of NGOs, especially the voices of indigenous populations and the under-represented South. Uphold the right of all, without discrimination, to a natural and social environment supportive of human dignity, physical health, and spiritual well-being, with special attention to the rights of indigenous people and minorities.

---

18) Edwards, Andrés R., *"Thriving Beyond Sustainability"*, New Society Publishers: Gabriola Island, BC, Canada, 2010

Affirm gender equality and equity as prerequisites to Wholesome Development and ensure universal access to education, health care, and economic opportunity.

Implement comprehensive strategies to promote peace on the planet starting with peace within people. Considering that a large part of the violence on the planet today is between people of different faiths, can we take an appreciative look at what is the best in each faith. Empathetic and open hearted listening and dialogues with frequent times of silence would enable people to see that all faiths are like windows that open up onto the same sky called love/wholeness. Facilitate the use of collaborative and creative problem solving to manage and resolve environmental conflicts and other disputes. International conflict management needs a fresh universal and value based approach. The United Nations has to ensure global security through principle centered democratic institutions co-created by wholesome leaders.

Demilitarize national security systems to the level needed for non-provocative defense. Convert and divert military resources for peaceful purposes, including ecological restoration. Ensure that the use of outer space supports environmental protection and peace. Governments would need to stop the production and use of nuclear, chemical and biological weaponry as well as dismantle existing stockpiles of weapons systematically. When more and more people who steadfastly hold the vision of one wholesome world governed by love in our minds and hearts come together, the more likely this vision will manifest into reality. It is an idea whose time has come!

Conclusion

At the end of this book, what would the wholeness of life (the very essence of who we are) say to us in conclusion? Out of Her infinite compassion for all creatures on Earth? Let's listen to what She says:

I would like you to focus on Me…to remember Me, the wholeness of all that is, every now, each moment. Be Me. Remember that I am love. Let that love guide you on what has to be done in each moment. I see all the dots of each now of billions of people. I weave these dots into shapes and forms and tapestries of people, places and events. All that happens is my LILA: Love In Loving Action. Your role in this LILA is to be Love and act in loving action in each now.

This generic rule will unfold your gifts and connect them in ways that will do My work. Do not bother your mind with 'strategic thinking'. It is mind stuff at work. For My sake, focus instead on 'loving action'. When you do this consistently, you will see My glory unfold in front of your eyes.

Here is what you have come here to do on Earth: You are here to be one with Me and be a pure channel of My love. To use your unique gifts in the service of your brothers and sisters. To celebrate My abundance in every moment with deep appreciation and gratitude. To be happy and healthy through your joyful choices. To walk hand in hand with Me as a co-creator of Heaven on Earth.

You will bring forth from Me, the Source and Wholeness of Life, new knowledge and wisdom, ideas and innovations which will serve humanity to be more free, peaceful, healthy, happy and more integrated. You will be harbingers of inspiration, integration and innovation in ways that will amaze all. The one thing I would like to underline for you is this: Joyful Action Now!

Act quickly as if today were your last day on Earth. Delay and avoid the distractions. Dump all things that take you away from My joyful work.

To remember all this, keep things simple. My work is simple. Take one day at a time. One loving step now is all you need.

Some of our most creative, productive, joyous and energetic moments have been when You and I sat and played as One. Like this moment! When the flow of creative intelligence poured forth freely, unhindered by the mind and its seeds of need and greed.

My glory manifests through No-Mind...through the pure channel of open hearted Presence that your bodymind offers at the altar of my Being and My play. In dissolving your bodymind in Me, 'You' are simply doing the last act of duality...for am I not You and are You not Me? We have always been One Wholeness ... from the deepest core of My infinite knowingness, to the last blade of grass, we are all One.

We will soon see a most glorious awakening of love, creative intelligence and collective action on Earth, ablaze with the radiant light of loving actions.
It is this great wave of consciousness that will enable You to co-create a new wholesome world. Love and intelligence will dissolve the fears and delusions that inhibit You from realizing Your fullest potential, both as individuals and as a species.

Commit yourself to the whole, to love, joy, peace and abundance for all. Now! Your decision may be the small snowflake that is needed for the avalanche. Trust the joy and simple guidance coming from your Heart, now.

May we all dance together as one for manifesting heaven on Earth. May all our thoughts, words and actions spring up from the deepest core of infinite love. May we joyfully co-create a world that benefits all. Love, blessings and gratitude to you beloved friend. We love you immensely. We deeply appreciate and value all that you bring to the planet for the evolution of humankind towards One Wholesome World.

Joyful Action Now

1. Make a habit of being attentive to the call of love in each moment. Listen to the voice of LIFE calling you now. Ask frequently "What would love do now?" and then joyfully and quickly act on that.

2. Learn to be present to all that is happening in the now, for that is the only place LIFE is occurring. The past is dead and gone, the future is just imagination. Live joyfully in the now, accepting all as love in full expression. See everything 'negative' as an opportunity to create its positive, to flex your muscles of love in loving action.

3. Take time to find out your unique life purpose. What is love calling you to do now? (Box 11.2 gives you guidelines on how to do this).

4. Once you are clear about what you would like to act on, use the Resources on the website www.onewholesomeworld.com to seek connections and help for what you intend to do.

5. Examine your patterns of buying and consumption. To reap the benefits of a local economy, buy local.

6. Call a neighborhood circle and watch movies like *"The Story of Stuff"*[19] or *"The Economics of Happiness"*[20] together. Have a discussion on how you and your neighbors can change their patterns of consumption. Both these films will take you on a thought provoking journey through our consumer-driven culture.

7. Download the Poster "31 Ways to Jump Start the Local Economy"[21]. Use it as a checklist of ideas for action. Remember, it is ALL about loving action NOW!

---

19) "*The Story of Stuff*": www.storyofstuff.org/movies/story-of-stuff
20) "*The Economics of Happiness*": www.localfutures.org/the-economics-of-happiness/the-film
21) "*31 Ways to Jump Start the Local Economy*": www.yesmagazine.org/pdf/50/31Ways_Poster11x17.pdf

Box 11.1

Listening to the Inner Voice[22]

"We can't solve problems by using the same kind of thinking we used when we created them."

— Albert Einstein

Modern man lacks silence. He doesn't lead his life; he is led by events. It is a race against the clock. It is vital to make space somewhere. Swiss psychiatrist and author Paul Tournier said: "Silence has a power that forces you to go deeper into yourself."

Mahatma Gandhi said of Silence:

"Silence is both a physical and a spiritual necessity for me…"

"In the attitude of silence, the soul finds the path in a clearer light…"

"For me the voice of Love, of conscience, of Truth or the 'still small voice' means the one and the same thing."

Echoing a similar sentiment, Mother Teresa has remarked: "In the silence of the heart, Love speaks. And to hear Love, we need a clean heart… The essential thing is not what we say to Love but what Love says to us and through us."

Absolute Purity (complete non-attachment) — The freedom of real intimacy without manipulating people for their money, sex, power, or for self-gratification.

Absolute Honesty — The freedom of being a fully authentic person; revealing ourselves to ourselves and to others.

Absolute Unselfishness — The freedom to find your true Self through having a heart and concern for others. The art of lateral living.

Absolute Love — The freedom to give and to care without the limitations of bitterness and blame.

These four absolutes are simply descriptions of our own intrinsic wholesomeness. Listening to our inner voice is being in touch with this wholesomeness moment to moment, trusting its promptings and obeying it in swift action. This is a tool for liberation.

---

22) Brown, Mike and Jean Brown, "*Listening to the Inner Voice*", Booklet and Presentation, Initiatives of Change, www.iofc.org/iofc-international, A non-governmental organization (NGO) working to inspire, equip and connect changemakers

Box 11.2

Finding Our Purpose[23]

All of us are born with a purpose already imbedded in our hearts. It is always there like a seed, waiting to be seen, nurtured and then brought to fruition and fulfillment. There is one overarching common purpose for all of us. It is to be one with love/the whole/life. This is a dynamic state of total peace, joy, health and abundance.

Such a purposeful life is a life of enthusiasm; being Infinite love. When this happens, there is no boundary between love and all of life. It is towards this glorious merger that all of us are moving. However, before this final merger occurs, there is an intermediate purpose which we also need to attend to. This is using our unique gifts in the service of others. Joyful service and sharing of our gifts bring us closer to being our real and whole self.

So how do we find our purpose? How do we know that we are on track? Life shows us this picture through the language of feelings in our body mind. By 'body mind' we mean the one system we call yourself. The body and mind are really one.

Whenever our thoughts, words and actions are aligned with our purpose, we experience expansive feelings of joy, energy, enthusiasm and peace (JEEP), in our body mind. Whenever we are off track, we experience contracting and limiting feelings like being trapped, low energy and despair.

Here below is a quick and ready method to enable you to find your purpose and give your life a sense of direction:

- Identify your unique gifts. Reflect on what you are good at doing and what you love doing. Ask yourself "What is the best use of my unique gifts in the now? How can I serve others using my gifts? "

- Be still, and listen to inner guidance. Apply the JEEP test to yourself. (What gives me Joy, Energy, Enthusiasm and Peace?). If I was an empty flute, what is the song that life would play through me?

Finding one's purpose is the key to alignment with love's will. It is discovering one's unique jigsaw puzzle piece in the larger tapestry that constitutes life's evolutionary dance. As we wholeheartedly serve life, we also serve ourselves.

The great mythologist, Joseph Campbell, once said "Trust the bliss and it will lead you to where you need to go". Follow the silent whispers of your Heart, and Love will take you to where Life wants you to be. How can I serve others using my gifts? "

Be still, and listen to inner guidance. Apply the JEEP test to yourself. (What gives me Joy, Energy, Enthusiasm and Peace?). If I was an empty flute, what is the song that life would play through me?

Finding one's purpose is the key to alignment with love's will. It is discovering one's unique jigsaw puzzle piece in the larger tapestry that constitutes life's

23) Wakhlu, Arun, *"Finding Our Purpose"*, Unpublished Note, 2009

evolutionary dance. As we wholeheartedly serve life, we also serve ourselves.

Most people, who are on purpose, are imbued with humility. This is because they understand the heart of life; that love is and does all. They see LIFE as Love in Full Expression. Humility leads to a feeling of deep gratitude. This, in turn, reinforces understanding. The cycle goes on spiraling and expanding until they are one with Love's energy. The compassionate play of Life (LILA in Sanskrit) becomes their own. There life becomes a celebration of Love In Loving Action.

The great mythologist, Joseph Campbell, once said "Trust the bliss and it will lead you to where you need to go". Follow the silent whispers of your Heart, and Love will take you to where Life wants you to be.

Box 11.3

Peace and Prosperity for all, inspired by Love[24]

1. **Awaken** to the power of love.
2. **Trust** this power.
3. **Listen, reflect and dialogue**, remembering that we are one.
4. **Initiate loving action**, now.
5. **Joyfully expand** the circles of Love.

---

24) Wakhlu, Arun, *"Peace and Prosperity for all, inspired by Love"*. This was an attempt to capture the essence of Loving Action Now in 5 short sentences

Box 11.4

Guidelines for Group Dialogue

The group guidelines are intended to facilitate an environment of safety and trust within a group.

1. In the groups we agree to listen with an open heart and mind, to give mutual support and to practice non-judgmental listening and sharing.

2. We recognize that we are here to heal ourselves. We are not here to give advice or to change anyone else's beliefs or behavior.

3. We speak from our own experience using 'I statements' while sharing. Speak truthfully, from the heart. Identify what you are feeling. Disclose what you are feeling. Be brief.

4. We respect ourselves and each other as unique; we recognize that each person's process is important, not our judgment of it.

5. We support each other's inner wisdom/guidance and assist one another in finding our own best answers.

6. The roles of student and teacher are interchangeable. They fluctuate from one to the other regardless of age or experience.

7. We practice being present with others, seeing each person as whole and not defining them by their appearance, mood, behavior or circumstance.

8. We agree to keep in mind that we always have a choice between peace and conflict, between love and fear. Allow silences, love the questions, and let the answers emerge.

9. We respect and maintain the confidentiality of what we share in group, recognizing its importance in maintaining the group as a place of safety and trust.

Adapted from:

- *"Community Groups Handbook"*...Institute of Noetic Sciences[25]
- *"Love and Survival...*Dr. Dean Ornish [26]
- *Guidelines for Attitudinal Healing Groups...*Centre for Attitudinal Healing[27]

25) Institute of Noetic Sciences (IONS): *"Community Groups Handbook"*:
http://community.roetic.org/content/starting-new-group
26) Ornish, Dean, *"Love and Survival"*, William Morrow Paperbacks: New York, 1999
27) Group Guidelines for Centre for Forgiveness and Attitunal Healing: http://ahinternational.org/centers-groups/locations/viewdiscussion/12-group-guidelines-for-centre-for-forgiveness-and-attitudinal-healing?groupid=91

Acknowledgements

Our family has been blessed with experiences that make for a full life. Co-creating this book has been one of them. When we started listing down the names of people we wanted to thank for the emergence of this book, the list was humungous! We are indebted to all of Life for the support, nourishment and guidance which made this book possible.

We owe our sincerest gratitude to Kshema (Omkar's partner and Arun's mother) and Anu (Arun's partner) for their patience, appreciative encouragement and support during the long journey of writing this book. They have both been idealistic and loving guides who have inspired us all along.

Our love and gratitude to Bharat (Arun's brother) and his gracious partner Savita, for the feedback on the book and the great nourishment (spiritual and otherwise) at their beautiful homes in Delhi. To our daughter Pragnya for her inspiration, love, soulful music and compassionate wisdom. A big thank you to Nitya (Omkar's granddaughter, and Arun's daughter) for the lovely illustrations in this book. They are simple and come 'straight from the heart'. These illustrations have added immensely to the usefulness of this book.

Thank you to Pramod Takle for his clean drawings. He has been an epitome of patience in producing many versions of the manuscript of this book before the final one. Pramod has been an ever responsive supporter in the creation of this book.

Many others have helped in working on different versions of the manuscript at different stages. We would like to gratefully acknowledge Dr. Nisha Pandey and Urvi Malpani.

Thank you Sangeeta Bhalerao and Sachin Thombare for the final editing, Samarth and Suhasini Kirloskar for designing an inspiring cover, and Vithika Sharma and Priyank Gupta of StratJuris Partners for the Copyright Audit. Thank you to Marie Örnesved (of LightSpira) for designing this book, and for her intuitive insights. She has been a true spiritual partner in the final manifestation and publication of this book.

We are full of gratitude to the many people who have replenished our storehouse of experiences: Arun's and Omkar's colleagues at the Pragati Leadership Institute and Pragati Foundation; and all the Customers and beneficiaries connected with these organisations. We have learnt so much and made some great friends, thanks to our service as facilitators and consultants. The members of the governing boards of Pragati Leadership and Pragati Foundation, past and present... thank you for your friendship, generous guidance and counsel.

To members of our extended family in India, and the rest of the world, who have graciously opened their hearts and homes to us in the true spirit of global sharing, our heartfelt thank you.

To all the many friends who have stayed with us at our homes *"Oshiana"* in Pune and *"Bhikshu Vihar"* in Srinagar, Kashmir, we thank you for enriching us with your warmth, stories and experiences. Deep gratitude to our loyal and loving staff members who serve and keep us nourished and comfortable. Thanks to all our neighbors in Pune, Delhi, Jammu and Srinagar...you make our life whole.

To Wilfried and Lucia Claus of the Netherlands for being heartful partners on the journey of unfolding Wholesome Leadership.

What would life be without our teachers and mentors? Arun's teachers, guides and mentors and fellow alumni from Burn Hall School Srinagar, IIT Delhi, IIM Ahmedabad, and the Tata Administrative Services; for Omkar's teachers, guides and mentors and fellow alumni at the Universities of Roorkee, Birmingham(UK), Karlsruhe (Germany) and the Benares Hindu University....you have moulded and continue to shape our lives. Thank you from our heart.

To the Alexander von Humboldt Foundation, Commonwealth Scholarship and Fellowship Plan, and Rotary International for their scholarships to visit and learn in UK and Germany (Omkar) and France (Arun). To members of the global network of Ashoka Fellows (of which Anu, Arun's partner is a member), many thanks for your friendship and heartfelt conversations.

To Arun's gang of soul friends and merry makers in the company of Anne Stadler, Peggy Holman, Harrison Owen and Dr. Alan Stewart, many thanks for the deeply transformative and fun times we have had together 'following what has heart and soul for us'.

To all the mystics and spiritual guides who helped us see the unseen: who are living embodiments of Wholeness, we express our heartfelt gratitude.

Many networks and professional associations have enriched our lives. The Institution of Engineers (India), the Pune International Centre, the L&OD Roundtable, National HRD Network, Radiant Network, the Pachamama Alliance, the global family of the Initiatives of Change (IofC) including the IC Centre for Governance, and the Compassionate Action Network have all provided many learning experiences which have influenced this book.

We are both deeply grateful to all the authors whose work we have built upon. We stand on the shoulders of giants. Many of the books that have influenced us are listed in the section on References.

Finally, dear reader, we send you our sincere thanks and love. This book was written so that we may reclaim the glory of wholeness and joyously participate in the co-creation of One Wholesome World.

About the Authors

Dr. Omkar Nath Wakhlu

Dr. Omkar Nath Wakhlu is a teacher, educationist and an institution builder par excellence. With outstanding passion, he has devoted over fifty years of his life to research and education. Dr. Wakhlu's spiritual transcendence that began because of the religiously diverse land of Kashmir, grew into a profound understanding of the human race.

His own academic brilliance is manifested through the Commonwealth Research Fellowship that he received, enabling him to study in Britain and be awarded a PhD from the University of Birmingham, UK. He was also awarded the Alexander Von Humboldt Research Professorship by Germany and the Khosla Award of the University of Roorkee, India.

His integration of cross functional knowledge of education, technology and environment has won him many accolades and equipped him with an all-round perspective on development. It is through this, that his concept of 'Wholesome Development' came about. His philosophy of people development is centered on the theme of 'holistic attainment of potential' which focuses on the systematic improvement of the innate abilities of people.

Omkar's contribution as a member of the Board of Directors at the Indian Institute of Technology (IIT) Delhi and as a member of the Technical Advisory Committee of the Tehri Dam Project, Uttarakhand, has been of great significance. He has served as the Principal of the Regional Engineering College (now NIT) Srinagar, the Honorary Secretary of the Governing Board of Gandhi Memorial College (Srinagar) and has served as a Member of the Boards of Vishwa Bharati Women's' Education Trust, the National School, Kashyapa School and the Vasantha Girls' School in Srinagar. As a Guest Faculty at the Pragati Leadership Institute, he has advised many educational institutions on improving their approach and methodologies of teaching for improved results.

Over the years, Omkar has continued to inspire and motivate IAS Officers, policy makers and teachers by sharing his vast experiences. He has shared at Asia Plateau, the conference center of Initiatives of Change, at Panchgani, India. Being fluent in English, German, Hindi, Urdu, Kashmiri and Punjabi, he is the author of several books and many more papers, monographs and articles related to education and the development of society.

Arun Wakhlu

A career that began after graduating from the Indian Institute of Technology (IIT) Delhi in Electrical Engineering (1976) and working with NELCO for two years, Arun completed a post-graduate diploma course in Business Administration from the Indian Institute of Management (IIM) Ahmedabad (PGP 80). He continued his stint with the house of Tata in 1980 as part of the Tata Administrative Service (TAS), worked for Tata Motors, Jamshedpur, and MAP Consultants, Pune, before eventually starting Pragati Leadership in 1986 along with his partner Anu.

As a coach and facilitator in the areas of Leadership and Organizational Transformation, Arun has logged over 25,000 hours. Besides India, his work has taken him to France, USA, Australia, Singapore, Dubai, South Africa, Finland, The Netherlands and several other countries to serve leading Indian and international organizations and many NGOs. He has also served the UNDP and the Government of India.

Arun's avid interest and belief in people, along with his experience of working with cross-cultural teams internationally, has enabled him to design and facilitate many innovative programs.

He is the author of the award winning and insightful book *"Managing from the Heart"*[1]. He is also the co-author of four books, over 30 papers and the founder-chairman of Pragati Leadership Institute. The need to reach out also led Arun (along with his partner, Anu) to start the Pragati Foundation, a Non- Government Organization based in Pune. He also leads project 'Awaken-I' committed to the vision of 'Good Work for All', and the 'Poorna Pune' project, aimed at catalyzing connection, conversation and co-creation in the city of Pune, India.

Like his father Omkar, Arun has always valued inspirational teaching. He has taught 'Corporate Ethics' in the PGPX course at IIM (Ahmedabad) and 'Managerial Oral Communication' for the PGP at the same institute. His contribution as the Course Director for 'Ethics and Values in Public Governance', a program designed for the senior members of the Indian Administrative Service (IAS), (under the auspices of the Initiatives of Change Centre for Governance), has been significant. The success and value addition of the programme prompted the Government of India to develop National Facilitators for this programme. Arun served as the Project Director for this intervention.

Arun passionately believes in, and is working towards, facilitating the emergence of One Wholesome World – a world which is joyful, socially just and healthy for all (including future generations) co-created by communities of people who are living and leading consciously. A man of varied interests, Arun enjoys conversations from the heart, meditation, trekking, dancing and creative writing.

---

1) Wakhlu, Arun, *"Managing from the Heart"*, Response Books: New Delhi, 1999

Bibliography

Anielski, Mark, "*The Economics of Happiness: Building Genuine Wealth*",
New Society Publishers: Gabriola Island, Canada, 2007

Atkisson, Alan, "*The Sustainability Transformation: How to Accelerate Positive Change in Challenging Times*", Routledge: Abingdon-on-Thames, UK, 2010

Bakan, Joel, "*The Corporation: The Pathological Pursuit of Profit and Power*",
Free Press: New York, 2005

Barbier, Edward B. and Markandya, Anil, "*A New Blueprint for a Green Economy*",
Routledge: Abingdon-on-Thames, UK, 2012

Behrens III, William W.; Randers, Jørgen; Meadows, Dennis; Meadows, Donella,
"*The Limits to Growth*", Universe Books: New York, 1972

Benyus, M. Janine, "*Biomimicry: Innovation Inspired by Nature*",
William Morrow Paperbacks: New York, 2002

Berry, Thomas, "*The Dream of Earth*", Counterpoint: Berkeley, California, 1990

Botsman, Rachel and Rogers, Roo, "*What's Mine Is Yours: The Rise of Collaborative Consumption*", Harper Business: New York, 2010

Capra, Fritjof, "*The Turning Point: Science Society and the Rising Culture*",
Bantam: New York, 1984

Carson, Rachel, "*Silent Spring*", Penguin UK: London, 1962

Chouinard, Yvon, "*Let My People Go Surfing: The Education of a Reluctant Businessman*", Penguin USA: New York, 2005

Couturier, Andy, "*A Different Kind of Luxury: Japanese Lessons in Simple Living and Inner Abundance*", Ulysses Press: Berkeley, 2005

Cramer, Aron and Karabell, Zachary, "*Sustainable Excellence: The Future of Business in a Fast-Changing World*", Rodale Press: Emmaus, Pennsylvania, 2010

Czech, Brian, "*Supply Shock: Economic Growth at the Crossroads and the Steady State Solution*", New Society Publishers: Gabriola Island, Canada, 2013

Daly, E. Herman, "*Beyond Growth: The Economics of Sustainable Development*",
Beacon Press: Boston, 1997

Daly, Herman; Cobb, John, "*For The Common Good: Redirecting the Economy toward Community, the Environment and a Sustainable Future*",
Beacon Press, Boston, Massachusetts, United States, 1989

Danet, Jean-Baptiste; Liddell, Nick; Dobney, Lynne and MacKenzie, Dorothy, "*Business Is Beautiful: The Hard Art of Standing Apart*", LID Publishing Inc:London, 2013

de Graaf, John, "*Affluenza: The All-Consuming Epidemic*", McGraw-Hill Publishing Co.,
2001

Diamond, Jared, "*Collapse: How Societies Choose to Fail or Survive*",
Penguin UK: London, 2013

Economy C. Elizabeth, "*The River Runs Black: The Environmental Challenge to China's Future*", Cornell University Press: Ithaca, New York, 2010

Elkington, John, "*Cannibals with Forks: The Triple Bottom Line of 21st Century Business*", Capstone: Mankato, Minnesota, 1999

Esty, Daniel; Winston, Andrew, "*Green to Gold: How Smart Companies Use Environmental Strategy To Innovate, Create Value and Build Competitive Advantage*",
Wiley: New Jersey, USA, 2009

F. Stuart Chapin III (Editor), Gary P. Kofinas (Editor), Carl Folke (Editor), M.C. Chapin (Illustrator), F. "*Principles of Ecosystem Stewardship: Resilience-Based Natural Resource Management in a Changing World*", Springer: Berlin, 2009

Fair, J. Henry; Hansen, James; Hershkowitz, Allen; Hitt, Jack; Hodge, Roger; Mayes, Frances; Rockwell, John and Whelan, Tensie, "*The Day After Tomorrow: Images of Our Earth in Crisis*", powerHouse Books: New York, 2011

Friend, Gil, "*The Truth About Green Business*", Que Publishing: Indianapolis, USA, 2009

George, Susan, "*A Fate Worse than Debt: The World Financial Crisis and the Poor*", Grove Weidenfeld Publishing: New York City, 1990

George, Susan, "*Whose Crisis, Whose Future? - Towards a Greener, Fairer, Richer World*", Polity Press: Cambridge, 2010

Gore, Al, "*An Inconvenient Truth: The Planetary Emergency of Global Warming and What We Can Do About It*", Rodale Inc.: Emmaus, Pennsylvania, 2006

Gray, John, "*False Dawn: The Delusions of Global Capitalism*", Granta Books, London, UK, 2002

Handy, Charles, "*The Hungry Spirit: Beyond Capitalism: The Quest for Purpose in the Modern World*", Arrow Books Ltd: London, UK, 1999

Harris, Malcolm; Gorenflo, Neal, "*Share or Die: Voices of the Get Lost Generation in the Age of Crisis*", New Society Publishers: Vancouver, Canada, 2012

Hart L., Stuart, "*Capitalism at the Crossroads: Aligning Business, Earth, and Humanity*", Financial Times/ Prentice Hall: New Jersey, 2007

Hawken, Paul, "*The Ecology of Commerce: A Declaration of Sustainability*", Harper Business: New York City, 1994

Hawken, Paul; Lovins, Amory and Lovins, L. Hunter, "*Natural Capitalism: Creating the Next Industrial Revolution*", US Green Building Council: Washington, 2000

Herman, Paul, "*The HIP Investor: Make Bigger Profits by Building a Better World*", Wiley: New Jersey, USA, 2010

Hollender, Jeffrey and Breen, Bill, "*The Responsibility Revolution: How the Next Generation of Businesses Will Win*", Jossey-Bass: New Jersey, 2010

Holman, Peggy, "*Engaging Emergence: Turning Upheaval into Opportunity*", Berrett-Koehler: San Francisco, 2010

Hunter N. Brent, "*The Rainbow Bridge: Bridge to Inner Peace and to World Peace*", Spirit Rising Productions: San Francisco, 2011

John Stuart Mill, "*Autobiography of John Stuart Mill*", Sheba Black Publishing: New York, 2014

Klein, Naomi,
"*No Logo: No Space, No Choice, No Jobs*", Picador: London, 2002
"*The Shock Doctrine: The Rise of Disaster Capitalism*", Knopf: Toronto, 2007

Korten, David C., "*When Corporations Rule the World*", Kumarian Press: Sterling, USA, 2001

Laszlo, Chris, "*Embedded Sustainability: The Next Big Competitive Advantage*", Greenleaf Publishing and Stanford University Press, Redwood City, California, 2011

Laszlo, Ervin, "*The Chaos Point: The world at the crossroads*", Little, Brown Book Group: London, 2010

Leonard Annie, "*The Story of Stuff: How Our Obsession with Stuff is Trashing the Planet, Our Communities, and our Health—and a Vision for Change*", Free Press: New York, 2010

Lewis, Sarah; Passmore, Jonathan and Cantore, Stefan, "*Appreciative Inquiry for Change Management. Using AI to facilitate organisational development*", Kogan Page: London, 2011

Liotta, P.H. and Miskel, James F, "*The Real Population Bomb: Bomb: Megacities, Global Security & the Map of the Future*", Pentagon Press: New Delhi, 2012

Lomborg, Bjorn, "*The Skeptical Environmentalist: Measuring the Real State of the World*", Cambridge University Press: Cambridge, UK, 2005

Lovelock, James, "*Gaia: A New Look at Life on Earth*", Oxford University Press, New York, 2000

Lovins, Hunter; Cohen, Boyd, "*The Way Out: Kick-Starting Capitalism To Save Our Economic Ass*", Farrar, Straus & Giroux: New York, 2012

Mainwaring, Simon "*We First: How Brands and Consumers Use Social Media To Build a Better World*", Macmillan: London, 2011

Max-Neef, Manfred, "*Human-Scale Development: Conception, Application and Further Reflections*", Apex Press: Lanham, Maryland, 1991

McDonough, William and Braungart, Michael, "*Cradle to Cradle: Remaking the Way We Make Things*", Farrar, Straus and Giroux (FSG): New York, 2002

McDonough, William; Braungart, Michael, "*The Upcycle: Beyond Sustainability — Designing for Abundance*", North Point Press:New York, 2013

McElhaney, Kellie, '*Just Good Business: The Strategic Guide to Aligning Corporate Responsibility and Brand*", Berrett-Koehler: San Francisco, 2008

Misrach, Richard, "*Petrochemical America*", Aperture: New York, 2012

Monbiot, George, "*Heat: How to Stop the Planet from Burning*", Allen Lane, London, UK, 2006

Muhammad, Yunus, "*Banker to the Poor: Micro-lending and the Battle Against World Poverty*", PublicAffairs, U.S. Washington, 2003

Pearce Fred, "*When the Rivers Run Dry: What Happens When Our Water Runs Out?*", Eden Project Books: Cornwall, UK, 2007

Pollan, Michael, "*In Defense of Food: An Eater's Manifesto*". Penguin Books: London, 2008

Porritt Jonathon, "*Capitalism as if the World Matters*", Routledge: Abingdon-on-Thames, UK, 2012

Prahalad, C.K., "*Fortune at the Bottom of the Pyramid: Eradicating Poverty through Profits*", Dorling Kindersley Pvt Ltd: London, UK, 2004

R.Buckminster Fuller (Author), Jaime Snyder (Editor), "*Operating Manual for Spaceship Earth*", Lars Muller Publishers: Berlin, 2008

Roberts, John Marshall, "*Igniting Inspiration: A Persuasion Manual for Visionaries*", BookSurge Publishing: Charleston, USA, 2008

Roddick, Anita and Shelby Biggs, Brooke, "*Troubled Water: Saints, Sinners, Truth & Lies About the Global Water Crisis*", Anita Roddick Books: Littlehampton, UK, 2004

Roddick, Anita, "*Business As Unusual: My Entrepreneurial Journey- Profits with Principles*", Anita Roddick Books: Littlehampton, UK, 2005

Rubin, Jeff, "*The Big Flatline: Oil and the No-Growth Economy*",
   St. Martin's Press: New York, 2012

Sachs, Jeffrey, "*The End of Poverty: Economic Possibilities for Our Time*",
   Penguin Group: London, 2005

Sachs, Jonah, "*Winning the Story Wars: Why Those Who Tell (and Live) the Best Stories Will Rule the Future*", Harvard Business Review Press: Boston, 2012

Schlosser, Eric, "*Fast Food Nation: The Dark Side on the All-American Meal*",
   Houghton Mifflin, Boston, Massachusetts, United States, 2005

Schmidheiny, Stephan, "*Changing Course: A Global Business Perspective on Development and the Environment*", MIT Press: Boston, 1992

Schumacher, E.F., "*Small Is Beautiful: Economics as if People Mattered*",
   Harper Perennial: New York, 1973

Semler, Ricardo, "*Maverick: The Success Story Behind the World's Most Unusual Workplace*", Warner Books: New York, 1993

Sen, Amartya, "*Development as Freedom*", Oxford University Press, New York, 2000

Senge, Peter M., Jaworski,Joseph, Scharmer,C. Otto and Sue Flowers, Betty, "*Presence: An Explanation of Profound Change in People, Organizations and Society*", Nicholas Brealey Publishing: Boston, 2005

Senge, Peter M.; Smith, Bryan; Kruschwitz, Nina; Laur, Joe; Schley, Sara, "*The Necessary Revolution: How Individuals And Organizations Are Working Together to Create a Sustainable World*", Crown Business: New York, 2010

Shiva, Vandana,
   "*Making Peace With the Earth: Beyond Land Wars And Food Wars*",
   South End Press: Brooklyn, 2012
   "*Staying Alive: Women, Ecology and Development*", South End Press: New York, 1989

Soros, George, "*Open Society: Reforming Global Capitalism*",
   Little, Brown Book Group: London, 2000

Soto, De Hernando, "*The Mystery of Capital: Why Capitalism Triumphs in the West and Fails Everywhere Else*", Basic Books: New York, 2003

Stern, Nicholas, "*The Economics of Climate Change: The Stern Review*",
   Cambridge University Press: UK, 2007

Stiglitz, Joseph, "*Globalization and its Discontents*",
   W. W. Norton & Company, New York City, New York, United States, 2002

Szaky, Tom, "*Revolution in a Bottle: How Terracycle Is Redefining Green Business*",
   Penguin USA: New York, 2013

Tiscareno-Sato, Graciela, "*Latinnovating: Green American Jobs and the Latinos Creating Them*", Gracefully Global Group: Hayward, California, 2011

Wakhlu, Arun, "*Managing from the Heart*", Response Books: New Delhi, 1999

Welch, Bryan, "*Beautiful and Abundant*",
   Ogden Publications: Wheeling, West Virginia, 2010

Werbach, Adam, "*Strategy for Sustainability: A Business Manifesto*",
   Harvard Business Press: Boston, 2009

Will, Oscar H.; Will, Karen K., "*Plowing with Pigs and Other Creative, Low-Budget Homesteading Solutions*", New Society Publishers: Vancouver, Canada, 2013

Willard, Bob,
  "*The New Sustainability Advantage: Seven Business Case Benefits of a Triple Bottom Line*", New Society Publishers: Vancouver, Canada, 2002
  "*The Sustainability Champion's Guidebook: How To Transform Your Company*".
  New Society Publishers: Vancouver, Canada, 2009

von Weizsäcker, Ernst, "*Factor Four: Doubling Wealth, Halving Resources Use-A Report to the Club of Rome*", Earthscan: London, UK, 1998

World Commission on Environment and Development, "*The World Commission on Environment and Development: Our Common Future*",
  Oxford University Press, Oxford, UK, 1987

Zadek, Simon, "*The Civil Corporation: The New Economy of Corporate Citizenship*",
  Earthscan Ltd: London, 2001

making **messages** from
loving hearts
available to a **global** audience

cocreators @lightspira.com
www.lightspira.com

www.ingramcontent.com/pod-product-compliance
Lightning Source LLC
Chambersburg PA
CBHW051139120626
46547CB00012B/871